Food and the Internet

Violetta Krawczyk-Wasilewska/
Patricia Lysaght (eds.)

Food and the Internet

Proceedings of the 20th International Ethnological Food
Research Conference, Department of Folklore and
Ethnology, Institute of Ethnology and Cultural
Anthropology, University of Łódź, Poland,
3.–6. September 2014

Bibliographic Information published by the Deutsche Nationalbibliothek
The Deutsche Nationalbibliothek lists this publication in the Deutsche Nationalbibliografie; detailed bibliographic data is available in the internet at http://dnb.d-nb.de.

Library of Congress Cataloging-in-Publication Data
International Commission for Ethnological Food Research. Conference (20th : 2014 : Uniwersytet Łódźki)
Food and the Internet : proceedings of the 20th International Ethnological Food Research Conference, Department of Folklore and Ethnology, Institute of Ethnology and Cultural Anthropology, University of Łódź, Poland, 3.-6. September 2014 / Violetta Krawczyk-Wasilewska, Patricia Lysaght (eds.).
       pages cm
    ISBN 978-3-631-65314-2 — ISBN 978-3-653-04474-4 (e-book) 1. Food—Computer network resources—Congresses. 2. Food habits—Congresses. I. Krawczyk-Wasilewska, Violetta, editor of compilation. II. Lysaght, Patricia, editor of compilation. III. Title.
    GT2860.I67 2014
    025.06'641--dc23
                        2015003867

This publication has been sponsored by the University of Łódź

Cover illustration: Courtesy of Perach Ben Chaim

ISBN 978-3-631-65314-2 (Print)
E-ISBN 978-3-653-04474-4 (E-Book)
DOI 10.3726/978-3-653-04474-4

© Peter Lang GmbH
Internationaler Verlag der Wissenschaften
Frankfurt am Main 2015
All rights reserved.
Peter Lang Edition is an Imprint of Peter Lang GmbH.

Peter Lang – Frankfurt am Main · Bern · Bruxelles · New York · Oxford · Warszawa · Wien

This publication has been peer reviewed.

www.peterlang.com

Contents

Foreword

This volume presents a selection of the papers delivered during the 20th SIEF Conference of the International Ethnological Food Research Group. This jubilee meeting was titled *Food and The Internet*, and ran from 3 to 6 September 2014, in Łódź, Poland.

The meeting commemorated the 6th International Ethnological Food Research Conference held in Poland in 1985, as well as the 50th anniversary of *Société Internationale d'Ethnologie et de Folklore*. The conference was chaired by Professor Dr. Violetta Krawczyk-Wasilewska – a member of SIEF since its inaugural congress in Paris in 1971 – on behalf of the host institution, the Department of Ethnology and Folklore, Institute of Ethnology and Cultural Anthropology, University of Łódź.

The aim of the conference was to discuss the phenomenon of food culture in the age of globalisation and the spread of computer technology. The digital revolution has opened up a new cultural sphere and new modes and styles of communication from person to person and between people and institutions. Nowadays, post-modern and web-entangled humans use the Internet to overcome the boundaries of their local and inherited traditions. One result of this is that contemporary food culture, in many western and westernised countries, is influenced by trans-cultural food knowledge, global marketing and advertising, new behavioral patterns, eating habits, and ways with food. The benefits of this brave new digital world are still unavailable to most of the world's population, but coverage is increasing rapidly.

The Łódź meeting provided an opportunity for discussion of the global character and influence of the Internet on the state of national, regional, and local culinary cultures. Thousands of food-related websites show that the Internet is a global cookbook and a home to food bloggers and networks, and our Internet habits reveal a lot about our food preferences in daily menus. There is also an enormous number of sites devoted to, for example, the aesthetics of food display; guides to drinks, wines and table manners; food tourism and restaurant reviews; healthy diets and food movements; the technicalities of food production, preservation, and consumption; and to self-sufficiency. Last, but not least, thanks to the ongoing digitalisation of library and archive holdings, the Internet is a source and a scientific tool that enables us to study food culture, not only synchronically, but also diachronically.

The conference was attended by 50 delegates from various disciplinary backgrounds, plus 10 observers, as well as representatives of the mass media. The participants came from four continents (Asia, Europe, North America, and South America), representing Brazil, Canada, Denmark, Germany, Greece, Finland, Hungary, Ireland, Japan, Latvia, The Netherlands, Northern Ireland, Norway, Scotland, Slovenia, Spain, the United States of America, as well as Poland. The delegates were accommodated in the Conference Centre of Łódź University, where the conference sessions were held. Vibrant discussions were accompanied by shared on-site meals, as well as workshops, a bus sightseeing tour, culinary trips to sustainable farming sites, and a gala evening provided for the conference participants. In this way, the guests were able to experience Polish traditional culinary culture combined with modern gastronomy.

The Conference began on the morning of 3 September with a welcoming speech by the Conference Chair, Professor Dr. Violetta Krawczyk-Wasilewska, and an opening address by the University of Łódź Pro-Rector in Charge of Research, Professor Dr. Antoni Różalski. The opening lecture ("SIEF ethnological food research group: past, present and future") by the President of the SIEF Ethnological Food Research Group, Professor Dr. Patricia Lysaght (Ireland) followed, together with the keynote lecture ("Rice as a foodstuff and a medication in ancient and Byzantine medical literature") delivered by Professor Maciej Kokoszko (University of Łódź, Poland).

The conference was organized in six sessions, as follows: 1. The Internet as local, national and global cook book and culinary research tool; 2. Food, marketing, and the Internet; 3. The Internet and food values: ethics, aesthetics, environment, health and lifestyle; 4. Food, identity, gender and the Internet; 5. Food blogging as a new Internet genre; 6. Food: past and present in the light of Internet sources. A total of 30 papers and communications, enriched and supported by multimedia tools, were presented over a period of four days. The variety of theoretical and applied approaches evident in the conference lectures, showed the importance and added value of the conference theme and discourse.

Reflecting on such perspectives, our volume showcases 25 conference research reports from today's online fieldwork laboratory. We hope that these insights will contribute to a fuller and deeper understanding of the new role of the Internet in the life of post-modern *Homo irretitus*, as well as in the meaningful development of world food cultures.

Łódź and Dublin, October 2014

Violetta Krawczyk-Wasilewska and Patricia Lysaght

Opening Lecture

Patricia Lysaght

SIEF International Ethnological Food Research Group: Genesis, Aims and Progress[1]

It was in 1970 that the first symposium on ethnological food research, which would influence and shape regional ethnological food studies in the succeeding decades, took place in Lund, Sweden, from the 21st to the 25th of August of that year.[2] Organised by Nils-Arvid Bringéus, Professor of Nordic and Comparative Folklife Studies, the Institute of Ethnology, University of Lund, the theme of the symposium was "Ethnological Food Research – Development, Methods and Future Tasks". An important aim of the meeting was to gain an overview of the state of ethnological food research in different parts of Europe and the USA at that time. Reports on the situation in their respective countries, solicited by the organisers, and provided by delegates from many of these areas prior to the symposium, were distributed in advance to the participants. This enabled them to get a picture of the general position of ethnological food research internationally at that time and to plan co-operation in and development of this branch of food studies for the years ahead (Valeri 1971, pp. 185). This approach is set out in a joint introductory paper entitled "Ethnologische Nahrungsforschung in Europa. Stand, Probleme, Aufgaben" ("Ethnological Food Research in Europe. Position, Problems, Tasks") by Nils-Arvid Bringéus (Lund) and Günter Wiegelmann (1928–2008) (Münster, Germany), in a subsequent symposium volume, *Ethnological Food Research in Europe and USA*, edited by them (Bringéus / Wiegelmann 1971, pp. 6–13).[3] Twenty-two other papers in that volume dealt with the position of research on food habits in the following countries and regions of Europe – Austria, the Baltic States, Britain, Bulgaria, Czechoslovakia, Denmark, the Faroe Islands, Finland,

---

1   Following discussions at its 10th conference held in Freising, Germany, in 1994, the International Ethnological Food Research Group has worked in association with SIEF (*Société Internationale d'Ethnologie et de Folklore*). It also styled itself the International Commission for Ethnological Food Research at that time. It is now referred to as "Food Research", one of SIEF's current "Working Groups". See "Food Research", retrieved 18.8.2014, from www.siefhome.org/wg/fr/index.shtml.
2   In this paper it is possible to deal only in outline with the genesis, aims and progress of the international ethnological food research group. See also Bringéus 2000 for an analysis of the ethnological food conferences from 1970–1998.
3   For a review of the volume see Jørgensen 1973.

France, Germany, Greece, Hungary, Ireland, Luxembourg, Norway, Poland (two papers), Sweden, Switzerland (two papers), the USSR, and Yugoslavia – while another paper focused on the position of food studies in the USA.[4] A further twenty-two thematic papers presented at the symposium – and grouped under the following headings – "Problems and Methods"; "Sources and their Treatment"; "Hunger and Plenty"; "Kitchen Utensils and Food Habits"; "Food Complex Studies"; "Distribution and Change" and "Individual Food Elements" – were published in *Ethnologia Scandinavica* 1971 (Bringéus 1971; See also Fig.1).

Fig. 1: *Cover of Ethnological Scandinavica 1971. "Jacob slaughters a kid from which Rebekah prepares a dish for Isaac, Genesis 27. Painting from around 1430-40 in the old church at Risinge, Östergötland. Photo: Soren Hallgren."*

Ethnologia Scandinavica

A JOURNAL FOR NORDIC ETHNOLOGY 1971

---

4   A report on the International Committee for the Anthropology of Food and Food Habits, of which Margaret L. Arnott, Philadelphia (also a member of the ethnological food research conference) was President, set up during the 8th Congress of Anthropological and Ethnological Sciences which took place in Tokyo / Kyoto in September 1968, was provided by Dr. Igor de Garine, France, at the conference, and it also appeared in the conference volume (Bringéus / Wiegelmann 1971, pp. 211-213). See also Bringéus 2000, pp. 19-20 in this regard.

The scientific programme of the first symposium on ethnological food research was broadened and complemented by study visits and excursions to food-related sites in the Swedish countryside, and by a range of gustatory experiences as delegates sampled a variety of Swedish regional food specialities (Valeri 1971, p. 186). This "field" aspect remains an integral part of the international ethnological food research conferences to the present day.

In their joint article dealing with the position, problems and tasks facing ethnological food research in Europe, mentioned above, Bringéus and Wiegelmann stated:

"Als erster Arbeitsschwerpunkt der nächsten Jahre kommt vor allem infrage, einen Überblick über die regionalen Unterschiede der alten ländlichen Kost in Europa zu arbeiten. Ein derartiger Überblick böte sowohl eine Grundlage für historische Studien wie für Analysen zum modernen Wandel" (Bringéus / Wiegelmann 1975, p. 9).

[A matter of crucial importance over the coming years is to work towards getting an overview of regional differences in the old rural diet of Europe. Such an overview would offer not only a basis for historical studies but also for analyses of change in modern times.]

The theme of the second ethnological food research symposium – "Dominierende Züge in regionalen Speisesystemen im 20. Jahrhundert" / "Dominant Traits in Regional Food Systems in the 20th Century"[5] – which was held in Helsinki, Finland,[6] three years later (13–18 August 1973), partly reflected the above statement. Organised by a committee consisting of Professor Dr. Toivo Vuorela (Helsinki) (1909–1982), Professor Dr. Ilmar Talve (Turku) (1919–2007), Hilkka Vilppula, Doz. Dr. Bo Lönnqvist, Päivikki Kokkonen and Hilkka Uusivirta, under the chairmanship of Professor Dr. Niilo Valonen (Helsinki) (1913–1983), forty-three delegates attended the meeting (Valonen / Lehtonen 1975, p. 5) and the subsequent symposium publication *Ethnologische Nahrungsforschung / Ethnological Food Research* (Valonen / Lehtonen 1975) contained twenty-seven papers.[7] This

---

5   For a report on the conference see Genrup 1974, pp. 138-142.

6   According to Valeri (1971, p. 186), a second symposium for international ethnological food research, with the preliminary theme, "Famine Food and Poor Man's Fare", was planned to take place in Poland, but this obviously did not happen since the second meeting was held in Helsinki, Finland, in 1973.

7   Included in the conference volume are papers by middle and eastern European scholars – Wassil Marinow (Bulgaria), Vacys Nilius (Lithuania) Zofia Szromba-Rysowa (Poland) Ofelia Văduva (Romania), and Romulus Vulcănescu (Romania) – who did not actually attend the conference. The possibilities for scholars from these regions of Europe to participate in the ethnological food research conferences have varied over

volume pointed the way forward for the future thematic, theoretical and meth-
odological emphases of food studies for a considerable time.[8] A number of participants in these initial symposia in Lund and Helsinki, respectively – especially
Nils-Arvis Bringéus, Eszter Kisbán (Hungary), Konrad Köstlin (Austria), Grith
Lerche (Denmark), Renée Valeri (Sweden) and Johanna Maria van Winter (The
Netherlands), continue to be active members of the international ethnological
food research group. Also contributing to the above-mentioned symposia was the
German social and economic historian, Hans Jürgen Teuteberg, who subsequently
formed The International Commission for Research into European Food History
(ICEFH) in Münster, Germany, in 1989.[9]

Delegates from the Welsh Folk Museum,[10] Trevor M. Owen, Curator, and
S. Minwell Tibbott, also participated in the 1973 meeting. This is of interest as the
third conference was held four years later (22–27 August 1977) in Cardiff, where it
was hosted by the Welsh Folk Museum. According to the editors, the proceedings
resulting from the conference were entitled *Food in Perspective* (1981), because
"the 33 contributions from many different countries each throw a different light
on the study of food and the relevance of such study to social history" (Fenton /
Owen 1981, p. v). While German and English were the languages of the previous
symposia volumes, *Food in Perspective* was, according to the editors, an English
language publication for "the English-speaking world, since the subject and the
various methods of approach that are demonstrated here have been familiar in
several other countries for some time" (ibid.).[11]

These three international meetings put the international ethnological food
research group, led by Professor Nils-Arvid Bringéus,[12] on a solid footing, and

---

the years. Papers by Nils-Arvid Bringéus (Sweden) and Bo Lönnqvist (Finland) who
also did not attend the conference were published in the volume. (See "Teilnehmer –
Participants" in Valonen / Lehtonen 1975, p. 6.)

8   See Valeri 1976 for a review of the volume.

9   Professor em. Dr. Hans Jürgen Teuteberg was President of ICREFH from 1989 to
    1994. See "The International Commission for Research into European Food History...
    information about ICREFH, its colloquia and publications", retrieved 1.6.2014, from
    http://www.vub.ac.be/SGES/ICREFH.html.

10 Now St. Fagans National History Museum, Cardiff, Wales.

11 Thereafter, the conference publications were mainly in English; for an exception see
    note 18.

12 Professor Bringéus was also President of SIEF (1982–1987) having been elected at the
    Suzdal SIEF conference of 1982. See "Previous Presidents of SIEF", retrieved 1.6.2014
    from www.siefhome.org/about/president/previous.shtml. See also, Bringéus 1982,
    pp. 149-150; Bringéus 2000, p. 21.

helped to stimulate further national and international research and co-operation in the area of ethnological food studies, which is still ongoing today.

The fourth conference, arranged by Dr. Maria Kundegraber (1924–2014) and Dr. Anni Gamerith (1906–1990),[13] and held in, Styria, Austria (24–30 August 1980), after a three-year interval, examined food from a communicational perspective. By taking as its theme "Nahrung als Kommunikation" ("Food as Communication"), the conference recognised that food is not just a means of survival but that it is also a key element of social, cultural, political, and personal discourse. While the proceedings of this conference were not published, a substantial review of the meeting appeared in Österreichische Zeitschrift für Volkskunde 1980, pp. 252-263 (= Schindler 1980).

Concepts and processes such as innovation, adaptation, and change in food and eating habits from the Middle Ages onwards, engaging scholars, such as, for example, Günter Wiegelmann (e.g. Wiegelmann 1967, 1974, 2006), became the themes of the fifth and sixth ethnological food research conferences, respectively. The fifth conference (16–20 October 1983) arranged by Dr. Eszter Kisbán, Institute of Ethnology of the Hungarian Academy of Sciences, and held at Mátrafüred, in the Mátra Mountain area of Hungary,[14] had as its theme "Sequences and Shifts in the History of Popular Diet". It thus had a strong historical focus with periodisation in food habits being a key concept. The proceedings of this meeting appeared in the volume entitled *Food in Change. Eating Habits from the Middle Ages to the Present Day* (Fenton / Kisbán 1986). Two of the papers in this work – by Eszter Kisbán ("Food Habits in Change: the Example of Europe") (ibid. pp. 2-10), and by Hans J. Teuteberg ("Periods and Turning-Points in the History of European Diet: A Preliminary Outline of Problems and Methods") (ibid. pp. 11-23), respectively – sought to discern, and to reach general conclusions about, the causes and effects of the major periods of change in European food habits. Further papers looked

---

13 Anni Gamerith was a well-known European ethnologist. At the First International Symposium for Ethnological Food Research, Lund 1970, she put forward her theory that there was "an interdependence between food, cooking utensils, and cooking processes ... and the fireplace", in her paper "Feuerstättenbedingte Kochtechniken und Speisen". She distinguished two basic cooking technologies – the open hearth and the cooking oven, the former giving rise to *Herdkost* ("hearth food") and the latter to *Ofenkost* ("cooking-oven food") (Hörandner 2003, pp. 96-97; Gamerith 1971, pp. 78-85).

14 According to Schindler 1980, p. 263, the 5th International Ethnological Food Research Conference was due to take place in Münster, Germany, in 1983. Instead, as is evident, it took place in Hungary.

at changes in such habits in a number of individual countries, or areas, and two
papers dealt with medieval fasting regimes.

The sixth conference (8–13 October 1985), organised by Dr. Anna Kowalska-Lewicka (1920–2009), Institute of Archaeology and Ethnology, Polish Academy of Sciences, Kraków, was held in Karniowice, Poland, the theme of which
was "Innovations in Food Habits".[15] While the proceedings of this conference
were not published, reviews of the meeting appeared in *Ethnologia Scandinavica*
1986, pp. 161-163 (= Borda 1986) and *Etnografia Polska* 31(1), 1987, pp. 213-215
(= Szromba-Rysowa 1987).

Seventeen years after the first symposium in Lund, the ethnological food research conference went north again to Scandinavia where the seventh congress
(10–14 June 1987) was held in Søgndal, in south-western Norway. It was organised
by Professor Andreas Ropeid (1916–1996), Norsk Etnologisk Gransking (NEG),
University of Oslo, and Astri Riddervold, Oslo, a food ethnologist and an independent scholar. The conference theme was "The Storage and Preservation of
Food". Central to the discussions on that occasion was how people in different
parts of the world, at different time-periods, managed ecological and economic
conditions in order to prepare food in such a manner that, when stored, it would
not undergo decomposition and become a health hazard. Such knowledge of preservation procedures was of vital importance for the management of household
food supplies and meals. In the course of the conference, the topic of the storage
and preservation of food was examined from technical, cultural and historical
perspectives, an approach evident also in the subsequent volume of proceedings
entitled *Food Conservation. Ethnological Studies*, which was published one year
later (Riddervold / Ropeid 1988).

The representational role of food was dealt with at the eighth conference (18–23
June 1989), held in Philadelphia, USA, the theme of which was "Food as Symbol". The conference was co-organised by William Woys Weaver, food historian
and writer, and Dr. James Turk of the Balch Institute for Ethnic Studies, which
also acted as institutional host. A key question dealt with by the conference participants was why food is so often charged with powerful symbolism. While the
proceedings of this conference – the only one held in the USA to date – remain
unpublished, a report on the meeting appeared in *Ethnologia Scandinavica* 1990,
pp. 144-146 (= Genrup 1990).

---

15 Dr. Anders Salomonsson (1946–2004), Institute of Ethnology, Lund University, succeeded Professor Nils-Arvid Bringéus as President of the International Commission
for Ethnological Food Research at the Karniowice, Poland, conference in 1985 (Borda
1986, p. 163; Bringéus 2000, p. 21).

In the two succeeding conferences, specific foods featured as conference topics. The theme of the ninth conference (17–22 June 1992), which was held in Ireland, was "Bainne agus Táirgí Bainne / Milk and Milk Products" in recognition of the historical and contemporary importance of milk and its products in the Irish diet and economy. It was hosted by the Department of Irish Folklore, University College Dublin, and was organised by Dr. Patricia Lysaght of that Department. After its formal opening in University College Dublin, the conference, in view of its topic, moved southwestwards to Kilfinnane, Co. Limerick, a rural village located in the rich dairying area known as the Golden Vale.[16] Here, the formal indoor lectures were complemented by field excursions – including visits to commercial and private cheese-making enterprises, and to Dromcolliher in the west of the county where the first dairy co-operative in Ireland was founded in 1889[17] – which emphasised the importance of milk and milk products in the local, regional, and indeed, in the national economy of Ireland also. Thereafter the conference moved to the Burren area in northwest Co. Clare, in the west of Ireland, where the final sessions were held. As an extensive *karst* region with an oceanic climate, and unique winter grazing systems or reverse transhumance, the Burren is an area, about which it has been said, that there "the cowman and not the ploughman is king" (Parr / Moran / Dunford / Ó Conchúir 2009, p. 145). Thus, the conference delegates had an opportunity to experience a number of different kinds of landscapes, stock-raising methods, and milk-production systems in Ireland. Overall, the conference presentations and the conference publication which followed, entitled *Milk and Milk Products from Medieval to Modern Times* (Lysaght 1994), examined the role of milk and its products in the food structures and meal systems of diverse cultures in many parts of the world, including the role of women in dairying culture and the folklore associated with that economic activity.

The theme of the tenth conference (6–10 June 1994), which was held in Freising, Germany, was "Kulturprägung durch Nahrung: Die Kartoffel" / "Culture Formation through Food: The Potato". Since food and eating are phenomena which

---

16 Known in the Irish language as *Machaire Méith na Mumhan* / "The Rich Vale of Munster", the Golden Vale consists of rich, rolling pastureland in the southwest of Ireland. See "Golden Vale – Ask about Ireland", retrieved 9.9.2014, from *www.askaboutireland. ie/narrative-notes/golden-vale/*.

17 For more information on the Dromcolliher / Dromcollogher co-operative, see "Plunkett Heritage Centre – National Dairy Co-operative Museum", Dromcolliher / Dromcollogher, Co. Limerick, retrieved on 9.9. 2014, from http://www.discoverireland.ie/ Arts-Culture-Heritage/plunkett-heritage-centre-national-dairy-co-operative-museum/45216.

both underpin and express culture, the potato was seen as an excellent illustration of this reciprocal cultural relationship and thus worthy of discussion on an international interdisciplinary level. Arranged by Professor Dr. Sigrid Weggemann (Freising) and Dr. Gertrud Benker (München), in co-operation with the Technische Universität München, Freising-Weihenstephan, and the Arbeitsgemeinschaft Ernährungsverhalten (AGEV), the proceedings of this conference, bearing the same title, were published in part, three years later (Weggemann / Benker 1997).[18]

In 1996, the eleventh ethnological food research conference travelled south to Cyprus, an island lying strategically in the eastern Mediterranean Sea, and host to an array of culinary influences which reached the island as a result of invasion, conquest and colonisation over the centuries, and intensive tourism in the course of the twentieth century. The conference (8–14 June 1996) which was organised by Nicholas Andilios with Intercollege, Nicosia, as institutional partner, held its formal opening session in the capital Nicosia, then moved to Agros village in the Troodos Mountains in the centre of the Island, and held its final sessions in Drousia village in the Paphos district of western Cyprus. Working with the theme "The Impact of Migration, Immigration and Tourism on Ethnic Traditional Food", the conference itself and the subsequent publication, *Food and the Traveller. Migration, Immigration, Tourism and Ethnic Food* (Lysaght 1998), explored the impact of the movement of people and foodstuffs on traditional foods and food habits historically and in contemporary times, in many parts of Europe and the New World.

After visiting the Mediterranean region, the conference went north to Sweden where the twelfth meeting (8–14 June 1998) was arranged by Dr. Kurt Genrup and hosted by Umeå University, Sweden, in co-operation with the Gastronomic Academy of Norrland, Åbo Akademi University, and the Frostviken community in Jämtland, north-western Sweden, where the second part of the conference was held. "Making the Most of Nature" was an appropriate conference theme in view of the acclaimed natural food resources of Norrland. The resulting conference volume, *Food from Nature. Attitudes, Strategies and Culinary Practices* (Lysaght 2000), dealt with the historical and contemporary dynamics of wild foods in the diet and food habits of environmentally and climatically different regions of the world.

The first of two visits by the ethnological food research conference to the Adriatic region occurred in 2000, when Dr. Maja Godina Golija, Institute of Slovenian Ethnology, Scientific Research Centre of the Slovenian Academy of Sciences, in co-operation with Inja Smerdel, Director of the Slovenian Ethnographical Mu-

---

18 These part proceedings were published in German only.

seum, Ljubljana, organised the thirteenth international conference (5–11 June 2000) on the theme, "Food and Celebration: From Fasting to Feasting" / "Hrana in Praznovanje: Od Posta do Preobilja", with sessions taking place in Ljubljana, Preddvor (with its Alpine climate), and Piran in Slovenian Istria. Both the conference itself, and the publication of the same title which followed (Lysaght 2002), dealt with the role of festive foods in different celebratory circumstances, in contrast to the use and meaning of fasting foods, in diverse regions and cultures of the world. The impact of industrialisation on food culture was also analysed in a number of papers at that conference.

The industrialisation of food and its impact on everyday life and mentality, past and present, was taken as the theme of the next conference – the fourteenth conference (30 September–6 October 2002) of the international ethnological food research group, arranged by Professor Dr. Christine Burckhardt-Seebass, and held at Basel University and at the Alimentarium / Food Museum, Vevey, Switzerland, under the directorship of Dr. Martin R. Schärer. Working with the title, "Changing Tastes. Food Culture and the Process of Industrialization", the conference itself, and the subsequent conference publication, developed this important topic along a number of lines, with papers focusing on, for example, changes in taste arising from the introduction of new products, from product differentiation and homogenisation, from the development of new combinations and consistencies by the food industry, and from the influence of makers and mediators of new tastes, such as cooks, cookery books and cookery schools, scientists, technical processes and devices. The role of retro movements, re-inventions, fashion, and industrialisation, and the impact of the interaction of forces of tradition and modernisation, in innovation processes, were also dealt with. The part played by marketing in influencing taste preferences, product selection, and culinary practices as part of, and arising from, the industrialisation process, was also discussed during the conference. This, together with the above-mentioned aspects, featured in the succeeding conference volume entitled *Changing Tastes. Food Culture and the Processes of Industrialization* (Lysaght / Burchardt-Seebass 2004).

The second meeting of the international ethnological food research group in the Adriatic region took place from the 27th of September to the 3rd of October 2004, when Dr. Ass. Professor Nives Rittig-Beljak of the Institute of Ethnology and Folklore Research, and Mirjana Randić of the Ethnographic Museum, Zagreb, organised the fifteenth conference in Dubrovnik on the Croatian coast, on the theme, "Mediterranean Food and Its Influences Abroad". A lively debate ensued at the congress as to whether a "Mediterranean Region", or "Mediterranean Food" or indeed, a "Mediterranean Diet", actually existed or exists, and various theoretical responses to these issues, and others, discernible in the conference discussions, were also reflected in the volume of conference proceedings, *Mediterranean Food. Concepts and Trends*, published two years later (Lysaght / Rittig-Beljak 2006).

The sixteenth conference of the international ethnological food research group, the theme of which was "Sanitas Per Aquas (Spa). Foodways and Lifestyles in the Search for Health and Beauty", took place in two locations and in two countries from the 25th of September to the 6th of October 2006. It was hosted initially by the Institute for Historical Sciences and European Ethnology, Innsbruck University, Austria, and then by Touriseum / The South Tyrolean Museum of Tourism, Meran(o), Italy, under the directorship of Dr. Paul Rösch. Arranged by Mag. Oliver Haid, Innsbruck, and Dr. Rösch, Meran(o), the conference debated the part played by tourism in the development of regional cuisines, and role afforded to dietary attitudes, lifestyle choices, and recourse to healing-related activities of different kinds – including health tourism, visits to spas and the taking of the waters – in the search for health, wellness, and beauty. Thus, key aspects of food, health and well-being as reflected in historical and contemporary discourses were discussed and analysed during the conference and in the resulting publication, *Sanitas per Aquas. Spas, Lifestyles and Foodways* (Lysaght 2008).

After visiting Austria and Italy in the south of Europe, the conference moved north again and the next three meetings were held in Norway, Finland and Sweden, respectively.

The seventeenth conference (15–19 September 2008) was hosted by Norsk Folkemuseum / Norwegian Museum of Cultural History, Oslo, in co-operation with Norsk Landbruksmuseum (Norwegian Museum of Agriculture), the theme of which was "Cultural Crossroads. Food and Meals at Cultural Crossroads". It was organised by a committee led by Professor Ann Helene Bolstad Skjelbred, together with senior scholars from the Norwegian Museum of Cultural History, the University of Bergen, the Norwegian Museum of Agriculture, and the staff of Norwegian Ethnological Research. The conference itself, as well as the subsequent publication entitled *Food and Meals at Cultural Crossroads* (Lysaght / Skjelbred 2010), explored the complex diversity of multicultural societies, the cultural dialogues which emerge when fundamental cultural elements, such as those concerned with food and meals, cross boundaries, meet at cultural crossroads, and try to negotiate their future paths across space and time. The representational and interpretational roles of museums in relation to foodways in multicultural societies were also discussed.

An aspect of food culture which is also of special interest to ethnologists is the transformation of food into dishes since regional and national perspectives are then often to the fore. Thus the eighteenth conference (18–21 August 2010), hosted and arranged by Professor Dr. Anna-Maria Åstrom and staff, Department of Ethnology, Åbo Academi University, Finland, took as its theme, "Time for Food. Everyday Food and Changing Meal Habits", with the aim of examining the topic from regional, national, transnational, ethnic, ethical, ecological and organic standpoints. As was evident from the conference publication, *Time for Food. Everyday Food and Changing Meal Habits in a Global Perspective* (Lysaght 2012; Fig. 2), the focus was thus on the principled management of food-production and global food-trade mechanisms, on ethical food marketing and consumption, and on the food choices and habits involved in the daily organisation of food intake in domestic, public and institutional settings. The manner in which global trends influence or even re-invent the notion of traditional food was also examined.

Fig. 5: Time for Food. Everyday Food and Changing Meal Habits in a Global Perspective (2012). (With permission of Åbo Akademi University Press.)

Time for Food

Everyday Food and Changing Meal
Habits in a Global Perspective

Patricia Lysaght (ed.)

In 2012, the nineteenth international ethnological food research conference was held in Lund University, Sweden (15–18 August 2012), the place where the first international symposium for ethnological food research had been held forty-four years previously. Arranged by Associate Professor Håkan Jonsson and Anna Burstedt of the Department of Arts and Cultural Sciences, Lund University, the conference theme, "The Return of Traditional Food", and the subsequent publication bearing the same title (Lysaght 2013), led to a discussion of the return to prominence of traditional food in various gastronomical settings and under certain conditions and creative impulses. A strong focus on the New Nordic Kitchen and on *terroir* was evident throughout the conference, as was discussion of the impact which specific EU protection schemes may have on how regional products are perceived, promoted, and marketed. The effects on traditional foodways of the commercialisation of revitalised food traditions in different parts of the world, and the complex role which traditional foodways play in the immigrant process, were also examined.

In 2014, after an interval of almost thirty years, the international ethnological food research group returned to Poland, where the twentieth conference (3–6 September 2014) was organised by Professor Dr. Violetta Krawczyk-Wasilewska, and hosted by the Department of Ethnology and Folklore, Institute of Ethnology and Cultural Anthropology, University of Łódź, the theme of which was "Food and the Internet".[19] The aim of the twentieth conference was to discuss the impact of the global reach of the Internet on national and regional culinary cultures. The present volume, *Food and the Internet*, based on the results of that conference, demonstrates the multi-faceted influence on food culture of the global transfer of knowledge by means of the Internet, and its influence on daily cultural interaction, including matters of nutrition, in many parts of the world.

Conclusion

From its inception in 1970, the international ethnological food research group has been committed to the development of ideas, themes, and co-operation among scholars and disciplines for the furtherance of food studies on an international scale. Of the twenty international conferences which have been organised by the group so far, nineteen, as we have seen, have taken place in European countries,[20]

---

19 This aspect of food cultural studies was dealt with by Bernhard Tschofen in a paper delivered at the Slovenian conference in 2000 and published in its proceedings (Tschofen 2000).

20 An alphabetical listing of the European countries involved is as follows: Austria, Austria / Italy, Croatia, Cyprus, Finland (x2), Germany, Hungary, Ireland, Norway (x2), Poland (x2), Slovenia, Sweden (x3), Switzerland, and Wales.

and one was held in the USA. Over the years, the conference topics have reflected, to a certain extent at least, focal themes in ethnology. The volumes of conference proceedings published so far, have addressed a range of existing and emerging questions relevant to food research in ethnology and neighbouring disciplines. These publications have contributed to the development of programmes in food culture at third level institutions, and dynamic collaborations between different disciplines are emerging in this context. The growing interest in food studies among graduate students and early-career academics has been evident at recent conferences (e.g. Lysaght 2010; Lysaght / Skjelbred 2012; Lysaght 2013), and a number of papers presented by this cohort at the recent conference in Łódź (2014) appear in this volume.

The ongoing discourses about food, especially on social media, affect the dietary choices of many people, in different parts of the world, on a daily basis. In recognition of this phenomenon, the Łódź conference explored the effects of the digital age on food culture. It examined the influence of the Internet – as a provider of a seemingly limitless flow of information and discourse about food sources, production, distribution, and consumption – on attitudes towards food, in the context of ecological, environmental, ethical, health, and everyday lifestyle issues, at local, regional, and global levels.

List of References

Printed

Borda, Beatriz: "The Sixth International Ethnological Food Research Conference, October 8–13, 1985, Cracow, Poland". *Ethnologia Scandinavica* 1986, pp. 161-163.

Bringéus, Nils-Arvid: "Ethnological Food Conferences 1970-1988: Ideas and Routes for European Collaboration". In: Lysaght, Patricia (ed.): *Food from Nature. Attitudes, Strategies and Culinary Practices.* (Acta Academiae Regiae Gustavi Adolphi LXXI.) The Royal Gustavus Adolphus Academy for Swedish Folk Culture: Uppsala 2000, pp. 19-29.

Bringéus, Nils-Arvid: "The Second Congress of the International Society for European Ethnology and Folklore (SIEF) in Suzdal, USSR, September 30–October 6, 1982". *Ethnologia Scandinavica* 1982, pp. 149-150.

Bringéus, Nils-Arvid (ed.): ["First International Symposium for Ethnological Food Research, Lund 1970"], *Ethnologia Scandinavica* 1971, pp. 6-184.

Bringéus, Nils-Arvid / Wiegelmann, Günter (eds.): *Ethnological Food Research in Europe and USA. Reports from The First International Symposium for Ethnological*

Food Research, Lund, August 1970. Otto Schwartz & Co.: Göttingen 1971. (= *Ethnologia Europaea* 5, 1971, pp. 1-213).

Dembińska, Maria: "Dziesięciolecie międzynarodowych spotkań naukowych poświęconych etnologicznym i historycznym badaniom nad pożywieniem" (Tenth Anniversary of the International Scientific Meetings on Ethnological and Historical Food Research). *Kwartalnik Historii KulturyMaterialnej* 29(4), 1981, pp. 557 -561.

Fenton, Alexander / Owen, Trefor M. (eds.): *Food in Perspective.* John Donald Publishers: Edinburgh 1981.

Fenton, Alexander / Kisbán, Eszter (eds.): *Food in Change. Eating Habits from the Middle Ages to the Present Day.* John Donald Publishers: Edinburgh 1986.

Gamerith, Anni: "Feuerstättenbedingte Kochtechniken und Speisen". *Ethnologia Scandinavica* 1971, pp. 78-85.

Genrup, Kurt: "Eighth International Ethnological Food Research Conference in Philadelphia". *Ethnologia Scandinavica* 1990, pp. 144-146.

Genrup, Kurt: "The Second International Symposium for Ethnological Food Research in Helsinki, August, 1973". *Ethnologia Scandinavica* 1974, pp. 138-142.

Hörandner, Edith: "Gamerith, Anni". In: Katz, Solomon H. / Weaver, William Woys (eds.): *Encyclopedia of Food and Culture.* Vol. 2. Thomson Gale: New York et al. 2003, pp. 96-97.

Jørgensen, Birte Stig: Review of: Bringéus, Nils-Arvid / Wiegelmann, Günter (eds.): *Ethnological Food Research in Europe and the USA. Reports from The First International Symposium for Ethnological Food Research, Lund, August 1970.* Göttingen 1971, 213 pp. *Ethnologia Scandinavica* 1973, pp. 157-159.

Lysaght, Patricia (ed.): *The Return of Traditional Food.* Lund Studies in Arts and Cultural Sciences 1: Lund 2013.

Lysaght, Patricia (ed.): *Time for Food. Everyday Food and Changing Meal Habits.* Åbo Akademi University Press: Åbo 2012.

Lysaght, Patricia (ed.) / with Skjelbred, Ann Helene: *Food and Meals at Cultural Crossroads.* Novus Press: Oslo 2010.

Lysaght, Patricia (ed.): *Sanitas Per Aquas. Spas, Lifestyles and Foodways.* Studien Verlag: Innsbruck 2008.

Lysaght, Patricia (ed.) / with Rittig-Beljak, Nives: *Mediterranean Food. Concepts and Trends.* Biblioteka Etnografija: Zagreb 2006.

Lysaght, Patricia (ed.) / with Burckhardt-Seebass, Christine (eds.) *Changing Tastes. Food Culture and the Processes of Industrialization.* Schweizerische Gesellschaft für Volkskunde: Basel / The Department of Irish Folklore: Dublin 2004.

Lysaght, Patricia (ed.): *Food and Celebration. From Fasting to Feasting.* Založba ZRC/ ZRC Publishing, ZRC SAZU: Ljubljana / The Department of Irish Folklore: Dublin 2002.

Lysaght, Patricia (ed.): *Food from Nature. Attitudes, Strategies and Culinary Practices.* (Acta Academiae Regiae Gustavi Adolphi LXXI.) The Royal Gustavus Adolphus Academy for Swedish Folk Culture: Uppsala 2000.

Lysaght, Patricia (ed.): *Food and the Traveller. Migration, Immigration, Tourism and Ethnic Food.* Intercollege Press /The Department of Irish Folklore: Nicosia and Dublin 1998.

Lysaght, Patricia (ed.): *Milk and Milk Products from Medieval to Modern Times.* Cannongate Academic: Edinburgh / The Department of Irish Folklore: Dublin / The European Ethnological Research Centre: Edinburgh 1994.

Parr, S. / Moran, J. / Dunford, B. / Ó Conchúir, R.: "Grasslands of the Burren, Western Ireland". In Veen, P. / Jefferson, R.G. / de Smidt, J. / van der Straaten, J. (eds.): *Grasslands in Europe of High Nature Value.* KNNV Publishing: Zeist, The Netherlands 2009, pp. 144-151.

Riddervold, Astri / Ropeid, Andreas (eds.): *Food Conservation. Ethnological Studies.* Prospect Books: London 1988.

Schlinder, Margot: "Bericht über die 4. Internationale Konferenz für Ethnologische Nahrungsforschung. Österreichische Zeitschrift für Volkskunde 34, 1980, pp. 252-263.

Szromba-Rysowa, Zofia: "Innowacje w zwyczajach żywieniowych.VI Międzynarodowa Konferencja poświęcona etnologicznym badaniom nad pożywieniem, Karniowice pod Krakowem, 9-12.X.1985 r". *Etnografia Polska* 31(1), 1987 (Kronika), pp. 213-215.

Tschofen, Bernhard: "Celebrated Origins: Local Food and Global Knowledge. Comments on the Possibilities of Food Studies in the Age of the World-Wide Web". In: Lysaght, Patricia (ed.): *Food and Celebration. From Fasting to Feasting.* Založba ZRC / ZRC Publishing / The Department of Irish Folklore: Ljubljana and Dublin 2002, pp. 101-112.

Valeri, Renée: Review of: Valonen, Nilo / Lehtonen, Juhani U. E. (eds.): *Ethnologische Nahrungsforschung. Ethnological Food Research.* Vorträge des zweiten Internationalen Symposiums für ethnologische Nahrungsforschung. Reports from The Second International Symposium for Ethnological Food Research Sonderdruck aus / offprint from Kansatieteellinen Arkisto 26. Hotel and Restaurant Museum / Hotel und Restaurant Museum: Helsinki 1975, 340 pp. *Ethnologia Scandinavica* 1976, pp. 213-217.

Valeri, Renée: "The First International Symposium for Ethnological Food Research". *Ethnologia Scandinavica* 1971, pp. 185-187.

Valonen, Nilo / Lehtonen, Juhani U. E. (eds.): *Ethnologische Nahrungsforschung. Ethnological Food Research.* Vorträge des zweiten Internationalen Symposiums für ethnologische Nahrungsforschung. Reports from The Second International Symposium for Ethnological Food Research. Helsinki, August 1973. Sonderdruck aus / offprint from Kansatieteellinen Arkisto 26). Hotel and Restaurant Museum/Hotel und Restaurant Museum: Helsinki 1975.

Weggemann, Sigrid / Benker, Gertrud (eds.): *Kulturprägung durch Nahrung: Die Kartoffel.* Edition Infotainment Verlags GmbH: München 1997.

Wiegelmann, Günter. *Alltags- und Festspeisen. Wandel und Gegenwärtige Stellung.* N. G. Elwert: Marburg 1967.

Wiegelmann, Günter. *Alltags- und Festspeisen in Mitteleuropa. Innovation, Strukturen und Regionen vom später Mittelalter bis zum 20. Jahrhundert.* Waxmann: Münster 2006.

Wiegelmann, Günter: "Innovation in Food and Meals". *Folklife* 12, 1974, pp. 20-30.

Internet

"Food Research", retrieved 1.6.2014, from www.siefhome.org/wg/fr/index.shtml.

"Golden Vale – Ask about Ireland", retrieved 9.9.2014, from *www.askaboutireland. ie/narrative-notes/golden-vale/.*

"The International Commission for Research into European Food History… information about ICREFH, its colloquia and publications", retrieved 1.6.2014, from http://www.vub.ac.be/SGES/ICREFH.html.

"Plunkett Heritage Centre – National Dairy Co-operative Museum", Dromcolliher / Dromcollogher, Co. Limerick, retrieved on 9 September 2014, from http://www.discoverireland.ie/Arts-Culture-Heritage/plunkett-heritage-centre-national-dairy-co-operative-museum/45216.

"Previous Presidents of SIEF", retrieved 1.6.2014, from www.siefhome.org/about/ president/previous.shtml.

"SIEF Working Groups", retrieved 18.8.2014, from http://www.siefhome.org/ wg.shtml.

PART I:
The Internet as Local, National and Global Cookbook and Culinary Research Tool

Violetta Krawczyk-Wasilewska

A Global Food Tale in the Age of the Internet

Post-modern humans use the Internet to overcome the boundaries of their physical and social environment as well as the constraints of their "tribal" and inherited traditions. In the light of Internet sources, the global food culture phenomenon reveals a post-modern culinary outlook. During the last two decades transcultural food and nutritional knowledge, transnational behavioural patterns, and global marketing have influenced food culture. It has also been affected by global eating habits and by a cuisine influenced by fast food and slow food trends, particularly by organic and non-genetically modified healthy foods, as well as by so-called local and traditional farm market products. The author's research is based on an overview study of Internet websites linked to food. Innumerable food-related sites show that the Internet is a global cookbook, a tourism food guide, a food bloggers' and networks' home, as well as a domain for stories about well-known chefs. All of these factors serve to create the background for global and transcultural post-modern food tales.

But let us start our tale *ab ovo*. From the physiological point of view, humans need to eat food to stay alive. Food is a basic need in Abraham Maslow's well-known pyramidal hierarchy of human needs (Maslow 1943, pp. 370-396) (Fig.1).

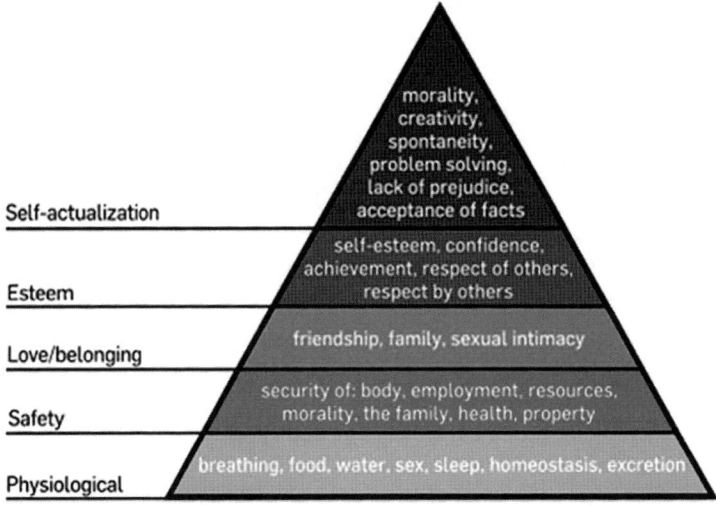

From the cultural point of view, food is also a universal notion (Counihan / van Esterik 1997), even though many cultures have their own particular food preferences and taboos (Harris 1974; 1986; Harris / Ross 1987; Jones 2008). Let us recall the French structuralist Lévi-Strauss's culinary triangle [*raw* – *cooked* – *rotten*] (Levi-Strauss 1964; Leach 1994, pp. 30-34). His scheme was based on two opposite polarities: *nature–culture* and *elaborated–unelaborated*. Within the scheme, there were three main types of cooking: boiling, roasting, and smoking. Lévi-Strauss looked at how methods of cooking in a society form a language that can reveal universal truths about societies. Nowadays, of course, his scheme seems a little outdated, because traditional cooking has been replaced, in many parts of the world, by the industrial preparation of factory-farmed food cooked in microwave ovens or by using other technologies. Nevertheless food was the great civiliser, the kitchen - the studio of the first art. Recent innovations cannot change the fact that tales of food exist in all narrating societies. The tales socialise their audiences as food consumers, distributors, and producers. The ways in which a society has always talked about food are reflected in the language of old proverbs, beliefs, and tales, as well as in literary and art reminiscences.

From the historical point of view, many literary, scientific, and popular studies present dietary choices that are related to a given local culture's cuisine. The first European written cooking recipes and culinary reports date from classical antiquity. Over three centuries before the Common Era, Archestratus of Gela, whom some call the father of gastronomy, wrote a humorous didactic poem or rather an early cookbook in Greek, entitled *Hedypatheia* ("Life of Luxury"). At about the same time, Plato's dialogue *The Feast* gave an account of his culinary culture. In the second century BCE, Cato wrote *De agri cultura* as well as *De re coquinaria*, and in the first century BCE, Apicius wrote *Libri decem* (Wilkins / Harvey, Dobson 1995). A few centuries later, in the second century of the Common Era, Galen of Pergamon published a recipe for barley soup in his *Powers of Foods* (Grant 2008), which is accessible to modern cooks thanks to the related websites.

In the fine arts (e.g. the Pietro Lorenzetti scenes), as well as in literature, culinary references during the Middle Ages are not hard to find (Weiss Adamson 2002; Dembińska / Weaver 1999; Woolgar 2006), also thanks to Internet sources. For example, the first written Polish sentence was concerned with food preparation and went as follows: "...*day ut ia pobrusa a ti poziwai* ..." ("... I will grind [the corn] in the quern and you will rest) or ("Let me grind [I will curl the quern] while you rest [or sit back and look on]"). This sentence was said by a Czech settler called Boguchwal to his Polish wife and appeared in *Księga henrykowska* ("Book of Henryków") written in Latin in 1270 C.E. (www.en.wikipedia.org/wiki/ Book_of_Henryków, retrieved 10.6.2014). Also, a Polish didactic poem on table manners (the Polish text is accessible on the Internet) was written by Przecław Słota in the early fifteenth century.

Słota's poem and other culinary references corresponded to European Renaissance (Fitzpatrick 2010) interest in food and feasts as popular motifs in writing and paintings. Let us recall *The Last Supper*, a fifteenth century mural painting by Leonardo da Vinci, as well as paintings by Pieter Breughel, Frans Snyders, Vincenzo Campi, Pieter Aertsen and others – all of which can be viewed on the Internet.

Between the sixteenth and eighteenth centuries, thanks to the spread of Gutenberg's printing discovery, the first cookbooks appeared, mainly in France (La Varenne 2001). Since 1825, when the epicure Anthelme Brillat-Savarin published his famous *Physiology of Taste* (Brillat-Savarin 1825, 1838; eBooks@Adelaide), and in parallel with the development of social sciences, culinary culture has become the subject of many serious ethnographic-type studies.

In the second half of the twentieth century, many historians (some influenced by the French historical Annales School) contrasted the relationship between food, culture and nutrition with the socio-economic history of various societies. They also compared the role of food in constructing what were called the collective identities (Ferniot / Le Goff 1986; Couffignal 1970; Girard 1977; Chang 1977; Caplan 1997; Falk 1991) of ethnic or national character. Since then, public awareness of nutritional issues, gastronomic activities such as displaying an interest in ethnic cuisine, custom-made kitchens and specialised cookery equipment, as well as in the cultural saliency of food in general, have increased alongside the development of a more scientifically-grounded form of nutritional knowledge.

In the last twenty years, topics in the area of culinary culture have become ever more popular in American and European scholarship (Counihan / van Esterik 1997; Katz / Weaver 2003). The resulting research has revealed that food plays a symbolic part in the modernisation process (Margolin / Sauzet 1982; Fenton / Kisbán 1986; Lysaght / Burckhardt-Seebass 2004). Thanks to the digital revolution, and the increased pace of information exchange and communication at a global level, food culture has been influenced by transcultural food knowledge, global marketing, new lifestyles and eating habits, and by new ways of preparing and consuming food. A wide range of food companies now promotes world cuisine online, as well as fast and slow food, organic and genetically unaltered food, and much more. On the one hand, an increase in the production of ready-made food based on standardised global defaults regarding consumption and taste can be observed, while on the other, tradition has become an important factor in the production and consumption of food today, especially in areas such as the revitalisation of forgotten regional products and culinary heritage. Sites on the Internet represent both trends. In the virtual global village, an avid *homo culinarius* meets and communicates with two main culinary tribes – cooks and gourmands – also known as connoisseurs or just foodies. Both groups narrate their own stories under the umbrella perspectives of an anthropology (Classen 1993; Hoves / Classen 2013; Korsmeyer 2005) and a psychology (Shepherd 2011) of the senses.

Thousands of food-related sites show that the Internet hosts a global cookbook for modern civilisation. Online authors reveal a lot about popular – and unpopular – food preferences in daily and ritual (ceremonial or religious) menus. There is also an enormous number of sites regarding table manners (illustrated by film presentations, e.g. on YouTube), the aesthetics of food display, the art of decoration and the serving of meals (e.g. www.Instagram.com), drink and wine guides, viticulture programmes and oenology tours, food tourism, restaurant reviews and rankings, food festivals, fairs and competitions, healthy and anti-obesity diets, raw foodism, the issues of sustainable consumption and self-sufficiency, the new technicalities of food production and preservation, as well as the newest scientific approaches to home cuisine (Myrhvold / Young / Bilet 2011; www.modernistcuisine.com, retrieved 10.6.2014).[1]

In addition, Internet and television cookery shows give rise to the media promotion of chefs who are treated by their audiences as global pop culture celebrities. Here, the popularity of Nigella Lawson, Gordon Ramsay, or "The Naked Chef" Jamie Oliver, and the newest discovery – Brazil's Helena Rizzo, the World's Best Female Chef 2014 (www.theworld50best.com/awards/best-female-chef, retrieved 20.6.2014), can be mentioned, as well as the numerous chefs who are popular at a national level. All of these chefs follow the example of Julia Child, an American chef, author, and television personality from the 1960s to the late 1990s, who was the subject of a recent, well-known film, *Julie and Julia* (2009).[2] Celebrity-chef careers reproduce the same general scheme (plot type) as Julia Child's. As well as being regarded as cuisine and pop culture celebrities, philosophers of food, interesting personalities, and showbiz professionals, these people behave, at the same time, as modern cooking shamans who believe that they are spreading the magical art of cooking to a global audience assisted by their own personal narratives.

The combination of television cookery shows, tabloid or magazine coverage, and celebrity chef websites, as well as the contribution of food critics and leading

---

1   Nathan Myrhvold is regarded as one of the most visionary technology and business leaders of recent years.

2   In the movie directed by Nora Ephron, Amy Adams starred as Julie Powell and Meryl Streep as Julia Child.

culinary writers (e.g. Steingarten 1996) serve to illustrate the cultural convergence of the postmodern mass media tale (Jenkins 2008).

This convergence creates a background to what is called *transmedia storytelling* (also known as transmedia narrative or multiplatform storytelling), which is the technique of narrating a single story, or experiencing the story across multiple platforms and franchise-type formats using digital technologies. Transmedia intertextuality works to place food consumers in the powerful position of participants in transmedia storytelling while disavowing any commercial manipulation by food producers and others. The convergence media theoretician, Henry Jenkins, underscores the point that co-ordinated use of storytelling across platforms can make characters (together, it might be added, with associated cookery concepts and the wit and wisdom of the performance) more compelling (Jenkins 2008). The result is a story that unfolds across multiple media outlets and platforms, and in which some of the end users take an active role in the process of reinforcing (by expanding and elaborating) and distributing (by forwarding and recommending) the memetic units (the chapters or episodes) of the ongoing story.

Cooking is a fashionable modern hobby that tends to contrast with fast food outlets servicing hurried diners, and with restaurant or catering gastronomical services for richer consumers. Some enthusiasts even shoot photos while cooking anything that looks appetising and immediately post their pictures online in order to share their latest creations. This is a visual affirmation of pride in their cookery skills, which they may or may not augment with an informative text.

Participatory culture is also represented by food bloggers. These bloggers are creative authors of food stories and pictures, and their individual websites collect fans or audiences, sometimes to be counted in thousands, which make them attractive as marketing and advertising platforms. Blogging is an electronic form of self-presentation that involves narrative reporting on a more or less regular basis. Food bloggers tend to be original, but they often follow each other intentionally or accidentally, repeating types and motifs from the cooking stories of others. The most influential is the story told by the American food blogger, Julie Powell, who in 2002 began to write a blog chronicling her attempt to cook all of the hundreds of recipes in Julia Child's huge book entitled *Mastering the Art of French Cooking* (Child / Beck / Bertholle 1961, 1970). The blog quickly achieved great popularity and it resulted in Powell's book, *Julie and Julia*, which was published in 2005 (Powell 2005), and which was then followed in 2009 by the movie mentioned earlier.

The popularity of food blogging in the frame of Food Network franchised sites and food-networking communities reveals a new behavioural pattern. Food forum participants and network users exchange and publicise their knowledge, opinions, and criticisms. This knowledge can be rooted, not only in science and books, but also in the home and in local tradition, as well as in personal experience. Some of the activity on these sites gives rise to modern food superstitions, quoted as *relata refero* stories, known to folklorists as "friend of a friend" personal narratives. These friends of culinary folklore love to talk about what types of food or ingredients are healthy and good for people, or unhealthy and toxic, or whatever.

The Internet has also become the home of food philosophies and dietary movements, such as worldwide vegetarian and vegan communities in contrast to anti-dietary movements, as well as of the growing alternative agro-food networks connecting farms, producers, shops, and consumers.

Local food as a concept and as a reality is redolent with meaning for many people, and it has the potential to detach them from conventional food networks and to attach them to alternative food sites. The meanings which they may attribute to local food can be classified under five headings: functional, ecological, aesthetic, ethical, and political (Brunori 2007). In this context, it is of interest to note the publication of research on alternative western food networks and their struggle to defend their ethical and aesthetic values against the standardising pressures of the corporate mainstream, with its "placeless and nameless" global supply networks, in recent years (Goodman / Dupuis / Goodman 2011).

As the era of "cheap food" draws to a close, the future of alternative food economies and the knowledge and cultural politics of the Fair Trade movement, are bound up with the move from transparent to virtual livelihoods, as noticed in the above-mentioned research.

Summing up what has been said (as well as what has been left unsaid), food has been narrated on the Internet using multiple media systems, including text, image, and sound recording, for different narrative purposes, including production, marketing and advertising reasons, the art of table decoration, social history, academic research, and cultural promotion. At the same time, food has served as the central part of a wider culinary culture in modern societies, where artifacts related to food embody workmanship, tastes, lifestyles, and so on. We should also add a semiotic aspect, because food has always been both a system of production and a system of signs ("You are what you eat" [Brillat-Savarine 1825, 1838, eBooks@Adelaide; Feuerbach 1863/4]). The arts and crafts of cookery have always involved different people whose purposes have often been divergent, and which have ranged from everyday cooking to highly refined gastronomy. At the same time, we have witnessed a surge in the promotion of food events and fairs, cookbooks, TV shows, magazines, advertisements, scientific essays and interviews, blogs, tales and writings, all of which has been concerned with the narrative representation of food. Media professionals, communication and marketing specialists, academic researchers and medical doctors, professional cooks and household kitchen hobbyists, have developed discourses, used similar language, and have tried to work together by comparing and sharing products and methods, in order to contribute their approaches to postmodern culinary culture. These tales inform the global food imagination.

In the field of food anthropology, which has also developed as the anthropology of gastronomy and the anthropology of the senses, a need is felt to consolidate an interdisciplinary reflection on themes, methodologies, and different or mixed forms of narration that constitute today's *corpus* of food cuisine (cooking) knowledge, culture, and imagery. There are three different types of narrative reflexivity that might be of interest in this context – the first type of discourse is created by people who produce and sell food and meals, the second type concerns stories about food and celebrities as well as about food events and shows, and the third type of story is told by scholars who study food as a cultural, social, and economic phenomenon and who try to understand the role of food narratives in the contemporary world.

The above text was written, not with the aim of exploring fully this entire topic, but with the hope of sharing opinions, images, practices, methodologies, and comments which arise in the context of the global food tale.

List of References

Printed

Brillat-Savarin, A.: *Physiologie du goût, ou Méditations de gastronomie transcendante ; ouvrage théorique, historique et à bordre du jour, dédié aux Gastronomes parisiens, par un Professeur, membre de plusieurs sociétés littéraires et savantes.* Le texte est re-publié aux éditions Charpentier en 1838. Original edition. Sautelet, A.:1825, 2 vols, [eBooks@Adelaide].

Brunori, G.: "Local Food and Alternative Food Networks: A Communication Perspective", *Anthropology of Food* [web journal], S2, March 2007.

Caplan, Pat: *Food, Health and Identity*. Routledge: London 1997.

Chang, Kwang C. (ed.): *Food in Chinese Culture. Anthropological and Historical Perspectives*. Yale University Press: New York 1977.

Child, Julia / Beck, Simone / Bertholle, Louisette: *Mastering the Art of French Cooking*. Random House / A. Knopf: New York 1961 (vol. 1), 1970 (vol. 2).

Classen, Constance: *Worlds of Sense:Exploring the Senses in History and Across Cultures*. Routledge: New York 1993.

Couffignal, Huguette A.: *La cuisine des Pauvres*. Robert Morel: Paris 1970.

Counihan, Carole / van Esterik, Penny (eds.): *Food and Culture. A Reader*. Routledge: New York 1997.

Dębińska, Maria /Weaver, William Woys: *Food and Drink in Medieval Poland: Rediscovering a Cuisine of the Past*. Translated by Magdalena Thomas, revised and adapted by William Woys Weaver. University of Pennsylvania Press: Philadelphia 1999.

Falk, Pasi: "Homo Culinarius: Towards an Historical Anthropology of Taste". *Social Science Information – sur les sciences sociales* 30(4) 1991, pp. 757-790.

Fenton, Alexander / Kisbán, Eszter (eds.): *Food in Change. Eating Habits from the Middle Ages to the Present Day*. John Donald Publishers: Edinburgh 1986.

Ferniot, Jean /Le Goff, Jacques (eds.): *La cuisine et la table*. Seuil: Paris 1986.

Feuerbach, Ludwig A.: "Concerning Spiritualism and Materialism". [Essay] 1863/4. (www.phrases.org.uk/meanings/you are what you eat.html, retrieved 23.6.2014.)

Fitzpatrick, Joan (ed.): *Renaissance Food from Rabelais to Shakespeare. Culinary Readings and Culinary Histories*. Ashgate: Surrey, UK 2010.

Girard, Alain: "Le triomphe de la cuisinière bourgeoise, Livres culinaires, cuisine et société aux XVIIe et XVIIIe siècles". *Revue d'histoire moderne et contemporaine* 24, 1977/10. PUF: Paris, pp. 497-523. See www.gallica.bnf.fr/ark:12148, retrieved 30.6.2014.

Goodman, David / Dupuis, Melanie E. / Goodman, Michael K: *Alternative Food Networks: Knowledge, Practice, and Politics* (Routledge Studies of Gastronomy, Food and Drink). Routledge: London 2011.

Grant, Mark: *Roman Cookery: Ancient Recipes for Modern Kitchens*, Serif: London 2008.

Harris, Marvin: *Cows, Pigs, Wars and Witches: The Riddles of Culture*. Random House: New York 1974.

Harris, Marvin: *Good to Eat: Riddles of Food and Culture*. Simon and Schuster: New York 1986.

Harris, Marvin / Ross, Eric B. (eds.): *Food and Evolution: Toward a Theory of Human Food Habits*. Temple University Press: Philadelphia 1987.

Hoves, David / Classen, Constance: *Ways of Sensing: Understanding the Senses in Society*. Routledge: London 2013.

Jenkins, Henry: *Convergence Culture: Where Old and New Media Collide*. New York University Press: New York 2008. Revised edition.

Jones, Martin: *Feast. Why Humans Share Food*. Oxford University Press: Oxford 2008.

Julie and Julia, 2009. Movie directed by Nora Ephron and starring Amy Adams (as Julie Powell) and Meryl Streep (as Julia Child).

Katz, Salomon H., Weaver, William Woys (eds.): *Encyclopedia of Food and Culture*. 3 vols. Charles Scribner's Sons: New York et al. 2003.

Korsmeyer, Carolyn (ed.): *The Taste Culture Reader: Experiencing Food and Drink (Sensory Formations)*. Bloombsbury Academic: London 2005.

La Varenne, Pierre Francois: *The French Cook*. 1651. New edition: Equinox Publishing: Sheffield 2001.

Leach, Edmund: "Oysters, Smoked Salmon and Stilton Cheese". In: Leach, Edmund: *Lévi-Strauss*. Fontana: London 1994. 4th edition, revised by James Laidlaw.

Lévi-Strauss, Claude: *Les mythologique. I. Le cru et le cuit*. Plon: Paris 1964.

Lysaght, Patricia (ed.) / with Burckhardt-Seebass, Christine: *Changing Tastes. Food Culture and the Processes of Industrialization*. Verlag der Scweizerischen Gessellschaft der Volkskunde: Basel, Switzerland / The Department of Irish Folklore: Dublin 2004.

Margolin, Jean-Claude / Sauzet, Robert (eds.): *Pratiques et discours alimentaires a la Renaissance*. G.-P. Maisonneuve et Larose: Paris 1982.

Maslow, Abraham: "A Theory of Human Motivation". *Psychological Review* 50(4) 1943, pp. 370-396.

Myrhvold, N. / Young, Chris / Bilet, Maxime: *Modernist Cuisine. The Art and Science of* Cooking: Taschen: Köln 2011. 5 vols. See: www.modernistcuisine. com, retrieved 10.6.2014.

Powell, Julie: *Julie and Julia: 365 Days, 524 Recipes, 1 Tiny Apartment Kitchen*: Little, Brown & Co.: New York 2005.

Shepherd, Gordon M.: *Neurogastronomy: How the Brain Creates Flavor and Why It Matters*. Columbia University Press: New York 2011.

Steingarten, Jeffrey: *The Man Who Ate Everything*. Vintage: London 1996.

Steingarten, Jeffrey: "Transmedia Storytelling". *MIT Technology Review*, 15.1.2003. See: www.technologyreview.com/news/401760/transmedia-storytelling/, retrieved 30.6.2014.

Weiss Adamson, Melitta (ed.): *Regional Cuisines of Medieval Europe: A Book of Essays*. Routledge: New York 2002.

Wilkins, John / Harvey, David / Dobson, Mike: *Food in Antiquity*. Exeter: Exeter University Press 1995.

Woolgar, Chris: *Food in Medieval England: Diet and Nutrition*. Oxford: Oxford University

Internet

www.en.wikipedia.org/wiki/Book_of_Henryków, retrieved 10.6.2014.

www.gallica.bnf.fr/ark:12148, retrieved 30.6.2014.

www.phrases.org.uk/meanings/you are what you eat.html, retrieved 23.6.2014.

www.modernistcuisine.com, retrieved 10.6.2014.

www.technologyreview.com/news/401760/transmedia-storytelling/, retrieved 30.6.2014

www.theworld50best.com/awards/best-female-chef, retrieved 20.6.2014.

Silke Bartsch, Christine Brombach and Gertrud Winkler

The Role of Internet Recipes in Cooking

Cooking recipes are a part of culinary knowledge (Ehlert 2008; Barlösius 2011). Internet recipes are a kind of collective summary of recipes. Today, the abundance of Internet recipes, often with accompanying commentaries, makes it unnecessary to collect them on an individual basis. There seems to be a new way of dealing with traditional and culinary knowledge, such as that in the form of cooking recipes, in western societies.

The Situation in Germany and Switzerland

Cooking is a topic that is much in evidence in the media – in TV Shows and food blogs,[1] for example. Many cookbooks are available on the market and an abundance of recipes are ready for downloading from the Internet. Almost everybody, especially young people, has experience of using the Internet and other media forms. In general terms, Internet utilisation consists of (1) communication by using social media, emails and so on; (2) online and offline games; and (3) searching for information, and also for entertainment in the form of music and videos (MPFS 2013; BMFSFJ 2013).

Information about cooking recipes is easily accessible on the Internet. In addition to the recipes themselves, peer-to-peer advice on, and reviews of, the recipes in question are also to be found. On the web, cooking recipes are available on web portals with online databases of recipes, on social media and food blogs, and in video-sharing websites. Often the web presentations of recipes are linked. Food apps and a specialised camera function for food photos are more and more common. Typical recipe websites in German[2] are "Chefkoch. de" (www. chefkoch.de, retrieved 20.8.2014) (with 250,000 recipes), "lecker. de"(www. lecker.de, retrieved 20.8.2014) (with 50,000 recipes) or "kochbar.de" (www. kochbar.de, retrieved 20.8.2014) (with 421,403 recipes). But there are

---

1   Blogs are websites updated on a regular basis, which are sorted in reverse chronological order, and have feedback instruments. Kofahl and Adda mentioned 200 million food blogs worldwide in the year 2010 (Kofahl / Adda 2010, p. 11).
2   The situation on 20.8.2014.

also simple database collections such as a wiki,[3] e. g. "rezeptewiki.org" ((www.rezeptewiki.org.de, (with 10,414 recipes). Recipes are also popular on social media. Facebook (https://de-de.facebook.com/Rezeptideen, retrieved 20.8.2014), for example, started to include information on cooking in 2010 and nowadays it has cooking groups involving students and families, among other interested parties (https://de-de.facebook.com/StudentenRezepte, retrieved 20.8.2014). In addition there are video-sharing websites such as YouTube, where private videos on cooking practice can be found. Mobile Internet utilisation is also increasing in popularity and this is accompanied by a new trend, the so-called "foodie movement", which means that pictures of food are being presented to friends via email or social media.

Studies have been carried out about cooking knowledge, and about cookbooks and recipes as part of culinary wisdom, and there is a growing volume of literature available in that regard (e.g. Ehlert 2008; Barlösius 2011). Studies and literature about the general use made of the Internet (e.g. MPFS 2013; BMFSFJ 2013) and, increasingly, about (Food) Blogs (e.g. Kofahl / Adda 2011; Kuti 2014), also exist. To date, however, there is no literature available on the use of Internet recipes in cooking practice. To fill this gap, a project entitled "Internet Recipes in Cooking Practice", in which the University of Education Karlsruhe, the University of Applied Science Albstadt-Sigmaringen (Germany), and the University of Applied Science Zurich (Switzerland) co-operated, was commenced in October 2013. This paper looks at some of the first results of that undertaking.

Aim and Central Questions of the Project

The aim of the project was to study the way in which people, especially the young generation, deal with Internet recipes. Therefore, the following questions were asked:

1. Do adults use web cooking recipes for cooking or / and baking?
2. How do they use the web cooking recipes?
3. Does the handling of web cooking recipes change culinary discourse and, if so, in what way?

---

3   Wiki is a content management system as a web application, which permits people to add additional information, modify it, or delete the content in collaboration with other web users (*en.wikipedia.org/wiki/Wiki*, retrieved 20.8.2014).

Methods

For the purposes of our research, we commenced with a standardised questionnaire containing six questions on the topic of Internet recipes, in May 2014. This was a component of an online survey consisting of thirty-one questions and formed part of a project about food rating and cooking practice in two countries – Switzerland and Germany. We used mailing lists of five universities (students and staff) – three in Germany (Jena, Albstadt-Sigmaringen and Karlsruhe), and two in Switzerland (Zürich and Bern) – and we sent an online questionnaire to participants.[4] Due to its design as an explorative study no representative data was sought or obtained.

Online Survey

1587 persons in total (441 male, 1134 female, 12 "no answer") participated in the online survey. 1118 students (70.4% of total participants) filled in the questionnaire. Overall, we found no significant differences in participation between men and women, student or non-student.

Fig. 1: Online Survey (N = 1571).[5,6]

Age groups (N = 1571)	Numbers	Per cent
Young Adults (up to 30 years)	1037	66%
Middle-aged Adults (31 - 59 years)	499	32%
Seniors (60 and older)	35	2%

Results and Interpretation

Part 1: Do Adults Use Web Cooking Recipes for Cooking or / and Baking?

Most of the participants knew about Internet collections of cooking recipes and many used them for cooking purposes (Fig. 2).

---

4   Online survey tool "2 ask" (2ask.ch).
5   N = 1571, data are adjusted. 16 participants are not included in the table (Fig. 1), because they gave no valid answer (= N.S., "Not Specified").
6   Data are adjusted, therefore the total numbers could be different in each question.

Fig. 2: Knowing about and using an online database of cooking recipes.[7]

Do you know about Internet collections of recipes? (N = 1587)			Do you cook / bake using Internet recipes? (N = 1587)		
	numbers	per cent		numbers	per cent
Yes	1185	74.7%	Yes	1093	68.9%
No	389	24.5%	No	103	6.5%
N. S.	13	0.8%	N. S.	391	24.6%

From the above date it is evident that nearly three quarters of the persons who responded to the questionnaire knew about Internet recipes and about 69% stated that they use them. On the other hand, only 6.5% indicted that they do not use Internet recipes, and nearly a quarter did not answer the question at all (Fig. 2). It is probable that those who gave no answer to the question tend not to cook or bake on a general basis.

Personal Collections of Cooking Recipes are also Popular

On being asked directly if they had their own personal collection of cooking recipes, 72.3% of the questionnaire respondents answered that they had.[8] They were also asked for the sources of the recipes. The ranking of the sources of the respondents own recipe collections shows that mothers, the Internet, friends, and journals / magazines are in the top positions in this regard. Grandmothers, cookbooks, family, cooking shows, etc., are also common sources, but less important than the four top nominations above (Fig. 3).

---

7   N.S., "Not Specified", means that a valid answer is missing, e. g. "I do not know", or no (valid) answers provided.

8   In numbers, there are 1147 respondents who said that they have such a personal recipe collection, 434 participants who said that they have none, and 6 who gave no answer. That is different to the answers to the next question (Fig. 3): only 326 respondents said that they have not a personal recipe collection.

Fig. 3: Sources of personal recipe collections. Multiple answers were possible (N = 1587).

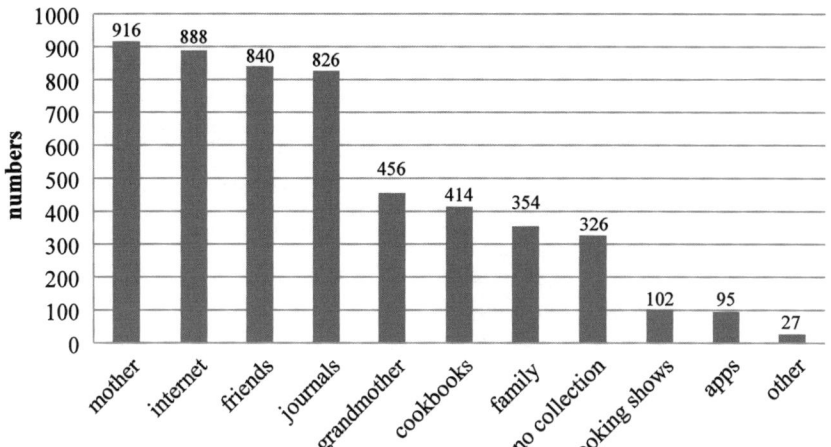

From the above data it is clear that the family – mothers, grandmothers, and other family members – is the most important source, being substantially more significant than the Internet, when compiling a personal collection of recipes.

Predominant Use of Family and Personal Cooking Recipes

The results of an extra question put to respondents act to reinforce the role of family recipes in cooking practice. When using cooking recipes, it is mainly family and personal recipes (around 40%) that are used, while cookbooks (29%), and Internet recipes (25%) also figure. 6% indicated (by using "other") that they have sourced recipes elsewhere. The persons who ticked the box "other" were allowed to write down their answers. The multiple answers they gave – such as that they got the recipes from food packages, etc. – were of equal value and importance for them.

Fig. 4: *Types of recipe sources used (N = 1558).*[9]

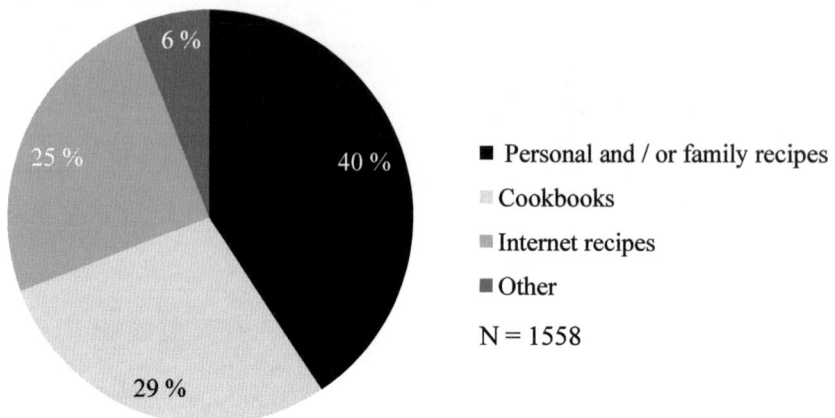

■ Personal and / or family recipes

▨ Cookbooks

▩ Internet recipes

■ Other

N = 1558

The ranking of recipes used for cooking and / or baking, shows that family recipes (one's own collection and / or those of the wider family) predominate in this context, followed by cookbooks and Internet recipes (Fig. 4).

Part 1 can be summed up as follows: Internet recipes do not replace family recipes in terms of popularity as sources, but they are as important as cookbooks in this regard.

Part 2: How are Web Cooking Recipes Used?

If people use Internet cooking recipes it is of interest to know how they deal with them. Around a quarter of all interviewed persons responded that they *never* print the recipes, and about one-third did so rarely or just sometimes. Around 30% did not answer the question (Fig. 5) – it is probable that those who did not answer do not cook or bake using web recipes (cf. Fig. 2).

Fig. 5: *Printing Internet recipes (N = 1587).*

How often do you print Internet recipes for cooking / baking? (N = 1587)		
	numbers	Per cent
Never	375	23.6
Seldom / sometimes	509	32.1
Often	209	13.2
Not specified	494	31.1

---

9   N = 1558, data are adjusted. Not included in the diagram (Fig. 4): "I do not cook" (25 participants), and 4 answers did not specify what sources were used.

Another question put to respondents aimed at finding out what people did with the recipes after using them. Multiple answers to this question were possible. The results are shown in Fig. 6. Nearly 50% (739 persons out of 1587) stored and saved the (files of) recipes. Around 28% (438 persons) said that they deleted the recipe files after using them while 158 of all interviewed persons (around 10%) distributed them to others. After using Internet recipes for cooking or baking, only a few participants stated that they subsequently commented on the recipes on the web. Almost all of the interviewed persons *never* commented on the web concerning recipes and / or became "followers" on social media in this regard.

Fig. 6: Dealing with Internet recipes. Multiple answers were possible (N = 1587).

What do you do with the recipe after baking / cooking?

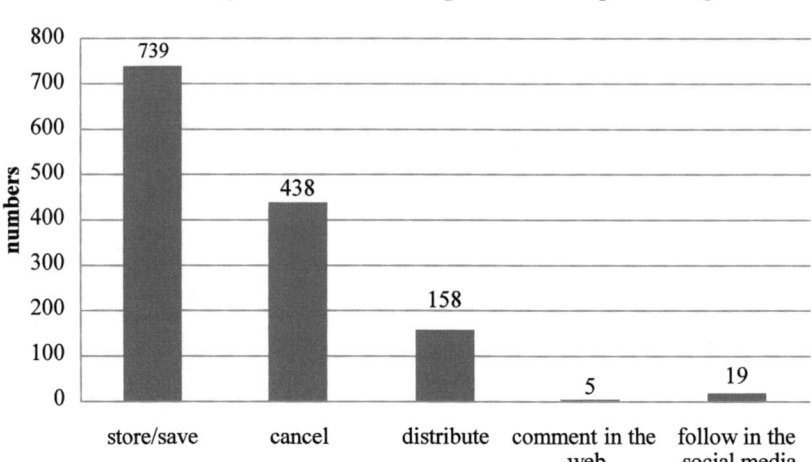

To sum up Part 2: The results show that the handling of web cooking recipes is different to the manner in which written cooking recipes are dealt with. One indication of this is that web cooking recipes are seldom printed and that they are less often stored than written ones. It is notable that while 10% of respondents distribute Internet recipes to others, only around 1% of them upload recipes onto the websites (Fig. 6). This means that there will be a major exchange of recipes between parties *without* each of them putting recipes on the Internet.

Part 3: Does the Handling of Web Cooking Recipes Change Culinary Discourse, and If so, in What Way?

After cooking or baking using Internet recipes, only a very few respondent stated that they subsequently commented on them on the web (Figs. 6, 7). Most people *never* posted a comment on the recipes on the web. Only 1% of respondents, who answered this question, said that they upload recipes on the Internet (Fig. 8). It is also remarkable that around 31% of all participants did not answer both questions (Figs. 7, 8). Perhaps the "not specified" answers belonged to who do not cook.

In short, many people get recipes from the Internet but only a few of them play an active part by engaging with feedback instruments or by uploading content in the sense of web 2.0. On the one hand, this is not amazing, because data concerning the use of the Internet by the young German generation comes to the same conclusion: only a small proportion of them are active web 2.0 users (MPFS 2013; BMFSFJ 2013; Bartsch / Schaal 2014). On the other hand, it is a notable situation because cooking recipes contain simple and fashionable content.[10]

Fig. 7: Comment on Internet recipes, after cooking / baking, on the web (N = 1093).[11]

Do you comment on the Web about the Internet recipes after cooking / baking? (N = 1093)		
	numbers	Per cent
Always	4	0.4
Sometimes	50	4.6
Never	1039	95.1

Fig. 8: Uploading recipes on the web (N = 1092).[12]

Do you upload recipes on the Web? (N = 1092)		
	numbers	Per cent
Yes	16	1.0
No	1076	98.5

---

10 Cf. "Internet4Classrooms: Web 2.0 Tool", retrieved 20.8.2014, from *www.internet4classrooms.com/web2.htm.*

11 N = 1093, data are adjusted. Not included are 494 not specified answers (Fig. 7).

12 N = 1092, data are adjusted. Not included are 495 not specified answers (Fig. 8).

If only a small number of the users upload content and gives comments on recipes, the question is: from where / whom do the recipes come? And what does this means for culinary discourses?

In view of the possibilities afforded by web 2.0 it has been thought that its content is strongly influence by peers, but our results and data appear to contradict this hypothesis. It is evident that peer influence does not replace the authority of cookbook writers. It is also clear that, apart from engaging in web searches and communicating via social media, only a small number of Internet recipe users are active web users. It is possible, however, that peers have an indirect influence on the content and the recipe selection. Websites often offer the same features in addition to the recipes. Photos, often (web-shared) videos, links to social media, registration for a newsletter, a toolbar for searching, the possibility for response-like comments, advertisements and so on, are specific. Our research points, in particular, to word clouds with the most popular search words, which serve to rank lists of favourite cooking recipes and features like "recipes for today", which could easily influence the websites users. And marketing research looks at the choices of the consumers. It is likely that consumers and the market interact indirectly via instruments like this. A typical website with cooking recipes is "Chefkoch.de" (www. chefkoch.de/, retrieved 20.8.2014.) in Germany. Food blogs are similar in function. On the other hand, advertisements and product placements are common on web portals and influence consumer choices. In order to be able to discuss this matter further it is necessary to analyse the different types of cooking recipe websites that are available today (cf. Báti 2014).

Amalgamation of Cookbooks and Websites

Cookbooks are part of culinary discourse systems (Ehlert 2008, p. 248; cf. Barlösisus 2011). There are three main types of culinary books – educational books, collections of recipes, and the edutainment [education and entertainment] of cooking – which have different functions. A function could be the constitution, implementation, conservation or change of an eating system (ibid.). Today, cookbook authors are often cooks, as is the case with Jamie Oliver, for example. The authors usually have a pedagogic intention in mind, like Jamie Oliver's slogan, "Good food for everyday", or they offer "edutainment by cooking" (cf. Ehlert 2008, p. 258).

This seems to be different from the situation in relation to Internet recipe collections, because Internet recipes have another context. Recipes can be located quite simply by using a search engine such as Google, and they can used without getting more information, if the searcher so wishes. Recipes can be found on online databases (wikis), and are presented in different ways as part of social media, video-sharing websites on the web, and so on. The content is generally not edited as is the case with a cookbook, which will usually have a preamble, goal, and a formal arrangement of chapters. Unlike cookbooks, the origin of recipes on a website differs a great deal and sometimes the searcher or user does not know where they come from. It would be worthwhile to explore the way cooking recipes are presented on the Internet and to systematise the results.

Cookbooks are part of culinary discourses – and they are linked more and more to websites. Websites often exist in addition to cookbooks. They complement each another, which also means that the contents of cookbooks and websites with Internet recipes tend to amalgamate with each other. Traditionally, the authors of cookbooks were trendsetters, like Paul Bocuse for French Cuisine (Ehlert 2008, p. 249f.). Nowadays, cookbook writers also have a presence on the web. The websites of cookbook authors are similar to other websites such as chefkoch.de, but a pedagogic intention is also evident in them as in the case of printed cookbooks. For example, on the website of Jamie Oliver, regional and seasonal, as well as well-being cooking etc., are the keywords – just as in his cookbooks.

Summary and Conclusion

Cooking is a topic much in the media nowadays. Internet recipes do not replace family recipes in terms of popularity of use, but they are similar in status to other sources of recipes, such as cookbooks and so on. There are indications that written and web cooking recipes are handled differently by those who use them. There are many consumers of Internet recipes but only a few contributors to culinary discourse.

We assume that the change in the way in which traditional and culinary knowledge is handled, is more than just a change from one media (cookbook) to another (Internet) (cf. Baecker 2007; Kofahl / Adda 2011). But in order to discuss this matter adequately more research is necessary.

List of References

Printed

Baecker, Dirk: *Studien zur nächsten Gesellschaft*. Suhrkamp: Frankfurt a. M. 2007.

Barlösius, Eva: *Soziologie des Essens: Eine sozial- und kulturwissenschaftliche Einführung in die Ernährungsforschung*. 2. überarbeitete Auflage. Juventa: Weinheim 2011.

Bartsch, Silke / Schaal, Steffen: "Mit digitalen Medien auf der Spur von regionalen Lebensmitteln – ein Pilotprojekt zum mobilen, ortsgebundene Lernen". *Haushalt in Bildung und Forschung* 3 (2) 2014, 36-47.

BMFSFJ (Bundesministerium für Familie, Senioren, Frauen und Jugend (Hrsg.). "14. Kinder- und Jugendbericht". Berlin 2013.

Ehlert, Trude: "Kochbücher von Gastronomen und Köchen als Indikatoren kultureller Entwicklungen". In Wierlacher, Alois / Bendix, Regina (eds.) *Kulinaristik. Forschung – Lehre – Praxis*. LIT: Münster 2008, pp. 247- 262.

Kofahl, Daniel / Adda, Ferdaouss: "Ernährungskommunikation im Internet. Ein explorativer Blick auf Food-Blogs anhand der Themenfelder Natürlichkeit und Innovation". IAKE. *Mitteilungen* 18, 2011, pp. 11-19.

Kuti, Klára: "Verzehren oder Zerreden. Alltagswissen in den virtuellen Tischgesellschaften der Gastroblogsphäre". In: Csáky, Moritz / Lack, Georg-Christian (eds.). *Kulinaristik und Kultur. Speisen als kulturelle Codes in Zentraleuropa*. Böhlau Verlag: Köln, Weimar, Wien 2014, pp. 51-68.

MPFS (Medienpädagogischer Forschungsverbund Südwest) (ed.): JIM-Studie 2013. Jugend, Information, (Multi-) Media. Basisstudie zum Medienumgang 12- bis 19-Jähriger in Deutschland. Stuttgart: 2013.

Internet

www. en.wikipedia.org/wiki/Wiki, retrieved 20.8.2014.

"Internet4Classrooms: Web 2.0 Tool", retrieved 20.8.2014, from www.internet4classrooms.com/web2.htm.

https://de-de.facebook.com/StudentenRezepte, retrieved 20.8.2014.

https://de-de.facebook.com/StudentenRezepte, retrieved 20.8.2014.

www. kochbar.de/, retrieved 20.8.2014.

www. lecker.de/, retrieved 20.8.2014.

www. rezeptewiki.org.de/, retrieved 20.8.2014.

www.2ask.ch/.

Aristea Baschali and Antonia-Leda Matalas

The Comeback of Homemade Foods and the Role of the Web. The Case of Non-Alcoholic Fermented Beverages

Introduction

A growing interest in the preparation and consumption of homemade foods is currently to be observed especially among people living in urban centres. Homemade foods have a special role in the construction of family identities (Moisio / Arnould / Price 2004), mainly through their importance in contemporary consumption and their opposition to the market's attempts to commodify the homemade food category. Furthermore, citizens regard these foods as being of superior quality to industrially-produced ones, and as offering additional benefits in the areas of nutrition, health and economics (Reuters 2011; Hispanic Business.com 2013). In contrast to industrially-processed foods, homemade foods are more often based on all natural ingredients, better cooking methods are involved (American Heart Association 2014[a]), and unhealthy ingredient substitutions are usually avoided (American Heart Association 2014[b]). Nowadays, with the economy in recession, people prefer homemade food, because, from an economic perspective, it offers better all-round value than fast food or pre-cooked meals (*New York Times* 2011).

Eating homemade food also provides health benefits. It enables appropriate portion sizes to be maintained and makes it possible for people to avoid the urge to indulge in oversized restaurant meals. Recent research has found that families who eat more fast-food meals than home-cooked ones, are less likely to eat healthy fruit and vegetables, and also that there is, as a result, an overall increase in the consumption of salty snacks and soda (Boutelle et al. 2007, pp. 16-23). Eating homemade food thus helps people, especially children and teenagers, to adopt healthy eating habits.

A great variety of fermented solid and liquid foods can be produced naturally arising from the fermentation of raw foodstuffs by indigenous microorganisms, or by adding microorganisms (starter cultures) to them to achieve fermentation (Tamang / Kailasapathy 2010). The preparation and consumption of fermented beverages has a long tradition in many parts of the world. Because there is an almost endless variety of fermentable substrates available, the range of beverages traditionally produced as a result of fermentation is remarkably wide. In western societies, beverages such as beers and wines, which are made with alcohol-producing yeasts, are the dominant ones. But fermentation need not result in the production of a beverage with an alcoholic content. The preparation of sour or acidic non-alcoholic beverages may be a characteristic of religious groups, among whom the consumption of beverages produced through an alcohol-producing fermentation process, is forbidden. To date, these non-alcoholic fermented beverages have received rather little attention, from either consumers or scientists.

The Web has emerged as a social and cultural phenomenon with a very substantial impact on communication (Beck et al. 2014, p. 28), as it enables people to publish their thoughts and to participate in a global dialogue. The information on the Internet is exchanged in real time and in a way that has been impossible for most people to achieve until relatively recent times. Networks allow tens of thousands of specific groups of people to perform a series of social, professional and educational activities in places in which they work or live, or in other locations. A recent addition to online media relates to healthy eating and healthy food choices, and several websites, blogs and forums now focus on these themes (Valente 2010).

The objective of the content analysis study carried out by the authors, and dealt with in this paper, was to evaluate information on traditional non-alcoholic fermented beverages available on the Web, since there has been a lack of studies exploring issues of this kind to date. Thus, an in-depth examination of information on websites, blogs and forums about this topic, to which users may be exposed, was conducted. We applied an extensive first- and second-generation sampling methodology and a well-developed and detailed coding manual, to the data when carrying out our study. As a result, a valid depiction of what visitors to webpages concerning homemade, non-alcoholic fermented beverages, may encounter in digital space, was produced.

Methods

Study sample

In order to obtain a valid and representative sample for a systematic content analysis, we first established a population of sites, blogs and forums in the English language, using Yahoo and Google search engines, dealing with our topic. Five terms were included in our search, as follows: "homemade", "non-alcoholic", "fermented", "beverages", "fermentation" The first 5 pages of search results for each term, from each search engine, were used to generate a list of relevant websites, blogs and forums ("first" generation). After this, viable links offered on these sites were included in the sample ("second generation"). This resulted in a total sample of 86 pertinent unique URL addresses being identified for the purposes of systematic content analysis. All websites, blogs and forums characterised by having their primary focus on, or the promotion of, homemade, non-alcoholic fermented beverages, were included at this level of our search. We included only websites, blogs and forums in the English language, which focused on homemade, non-alcoholic fermented beverages, as well as on relevant information, topics, discussion, and features in that context. Medical journals, video links, directories, repeated sites, sites with restricted access, and sites containing web layouts only, were excluded. A total of 52 active websites, blogs and forums, met the first level of criteria for our analysis. We then selected from this list the top 20 websites, blogs and forums with the highest PageRank of Google PageRank (Google PR), which is one of the methods used to determine a page's relevance or importance (second level of inclusion criteria) for a given topic.

The selected websites and blogs were visited by the authors of this paper on a regular basis during a 6-month period, and their content, with regard to types of homemade, non-alcoholic fermented beverages, preparation methods, cultural aspects, ways of promoting these beverages, and messages regarding their health effects, was recorded and evaluated. Almost all of the websites, blogs and forums which we examined were available in the public domain, and only 20% (n=4) required approval from a maintainer for exclusive entry to certain pages. In these cases, however, we collected data only from the publicly available portions of these media.

Variables and features of websites, blogs and forums

Before coding the sample of twenty websites, blogs and forums, we reviewed the existing literature on our topic, and proposed variables for our analysis. Variables were pilot tested on a random sample of 10 sites. This testing was conducted in order to streamline the number of variables considered and we removed many variables from consideration because they were not providing new information.

In the interest of standardising techniques across sites with varying amounts of content, approximately 10 minutes were spent searching for each variable on any site, blog or forum. For each of them, we coded 15 variables. Most variables were objective and easy to code; however, the constructs for the features of each variable were more subjective because of the act that we combined information from the existing literature on the topic and from a pilot study on a random sample of 10 sites.

Statistical Analysis

Our analysis was straightforward and primarily descriptive and all the variables were categorical. In this study, quantitative research methods (frequencies) were used in order to investigate the profile of the sites, blogs and forums available on the Web, which contained information on non-alcoholic fermented beverages. We used SPSS13.0 software for Windows (SPSS Inc, Chicago, IL) in conducting the analysis.

Results

In the following section, we first present information on the various features of the twenty websites, blogs and forums reviewed. Then we present the comments that visitors made regarding the non-alcoholic fermented beverages and which appeared on these websites, blogs or forums.

Site, blog and forum logistics

From the selected study sample (n=20), half (n=10, 50%) were websites, 45% (n=9) were blogs, and 5% (n=1) were forums, with a mean grade of PageRank equal to 4. The majority of them (n=19, 95%) had open-access information, and only 5% (n=1) required registration or subscription. Most of the sites, blogs and forums (n=12, 60%) held "free" Web addresses and were hosted through another site; 40% (n=8) had purchased URLs.

Of the sites, blogs and forums visited, 20% (n=4) focused on home fermentation, 45% (n=9) had a substantial amount of Food and Drink or Cooking content, 15% (n=3) had nutritional content, 15% (n=3) endorsed focus being placed on concerns addressed to the general public, 5% (n=1) centred on tourism, while none of them involved health-care topics (Figure 2). Only 5% (n=1) of the study sample promoted their content (information) in a written form; the majority (n=19, 95%) combined the written form with images, photos and videos. Approximately all of them (n=18, 90%) were lacking in cited scientific literature.

Most of the study sample was interactive (n=19, 95%), rather than being static or just meant to be read only, that is, a community could form in which users could post comments or communicate via an online forum or message board with named or anonymous posts. Regarding the manner of communicating, most of the sites/forums (n=14, 70%) required no registration or subscription as a condition of use, and only 30% (n=6) required registration or subscription.

Approximately 45% (n=9) of the study sample appeared to be maintained by individuals, and 55% (n=11) by a group. Contact listing for site maintainers was provided on sixteen (16) of them; ten (10) offered e-mail contact, five (5) offered telephone contact; five (5) offered postal contact via a mailing address, twelve (12) used an automatic system for filling in a conduct form, and, finally, four (4) offered other tools such as discussion forums, live chats, and so on.

Three quarters (n=15, 75%) of the study sample had a search engine and only 5% (n=5) did not offer one. Furthermore, most of them (n=17, 85%) shared information on search engines (19% on Google, 30% on Facebook, 26% on Twitter, and 25% on others such as Pinterest, YouTube and Pin it).

Only a minority of the sites, blogs and forums (n=3, 15%) were offering fermented beverages, or the main ingredients for the fermentation process, for sale. Most of them (n=18, 90%) contained advertisements for different products, and only 10% (n=2) were non-commercial in character.

Visitors' comments

Arising from our research, we found that 79 posts in these twenty sites, blogs and forums, were related to various traditional homemade, non-alcoholic fermented beverages, originating from different parts of the world. To monitor and track visitors' concerns about these beverages, we gathered information from the comments or responses which were contained in most of these 79 posts, and which were written by visitors to these webpages.

Regarding health, consumers asked a lot of questions about this matter, or made statements about the perceived health benefits of certain beverages, particularly regarding positive digestive effects resulting from their consumption. The remark that consuming *beet kvass* has a beneficial effect on liver function is an example of such a comment. Another visitor stated that *water kefir* is good for people who are allergic to milk protein. Many of the comments were in fact questions, particularly regarding digestive issues, and statements involved the provision of information about the amount *milk kefir* considered suitable for beginners and children. The following is an example of a statement regarding the beneficial effects of a fermented beverage: "Acidophilus milk cured my daughter's constipation and discomfort problems".

Issues involving the organoleptic properties of the beverages were found on most of the posts. These included questions or details about the taste, flavour and texture of the beverages (for example, "Is *milk kefir* sweeter than milk?" or *"Beet kvass* tastes kind of effervescent and minerally"). Many visitors proposed recipes for the achievement of different flavours or made suggestion about how natural flavouring could be gained. Others raised questions about the texture of the final product that they had already prepared – for example, "The beet kvass I made was bubbly".

Practically all of the comments showed that people were concerned about using the correct method of preparation and preservation of these beverages. The questions raised were mainly about the time frame of the fermentation process, the ingredients which should be used, alternative choices of ingredients that were available, and recipes for special groups of people or for various other reasons. The preservation section involved mainly questions about (or information provided on) storage information – for instance: "Can it be frozen and then thawed and used?", and the period of safe consumption – for example, "Best consumed before...?".

Because these fermented beverages are characterised as being non-alcoholic in content, many of the viewers wished to clarify whether or not they contained even a small quantity of alcohol, and if they could be safely used by pregnant women and children, and by patients suffering from conditions such as liver cirrhosis. An example of such a query was: "What is the alcoholic content of the *ginger beer*?" Also, for the same reasons, some visitors raised questions about the caffeine content of certain beverages – for example, "How much caffeine does Kombucha contain?"

Visitors to the websites, blogs or forums, from different countries, wrote about their own personal experiences of preparing or consuming a non-alcoholic fermented beverage – for example, "*Kvass* has got a very long tradition in Eastern Europe and I would like to share my family's delicious recipe." They also posed questions about recipes available on websites, blogs or forums – for example, "Can I use honey instead of sugar?"

A large proportion of the comments contained data (required, or provided by the visitors) about health, nutrition, and consumer information. An example of the kind of health information requested was, "Does the acidity of *kefir* harm our teeth?" The nutritional information provided in the comments dealt with the way in which some ingredients used in the fermentation process could alter the nutrient content of the final product. Consumer information was concentrated on the buying of cultures and starters and / or on the sharing of culture "babies" for free.

Consumers also had concerns about home economics, especially about food waste and the cost of the final product. Most of the viewers raised questions about the re-use of the perishable ingredients involved – for example, "Can you do anything with the beets in the jar after the *kvass* has been made? Can they be eaten or only added to the compost?" Furthermore, they wished to be informed about the total cost of these homemade fermented beverages, or the corresponding prices of commercial, non-alcoholic fermented beverages.

Another important issue raised in the website comments revolved around the seeking of information about safety and hygiene. Examples of questions posed in this context were: "Are there negative effects from *ginger* if it is consumed during pregnancy?" and "A white substance floating on the top of the liquid, is it safe? Is it mold or milk solid? Is it safe to drink?" Concerns regarding recommendations for special groups involved questions about the suitability of the beverages for weight losers and athletes, and about sugar content, performance enhancement and lactose intolerance issues.

A great deal of discussion took place about different versions of recipes, about substituting them for other foods, and about other uses for these beverages. An example of a query about whether a beverage could be substituted for another food was, "Can it be [used as] a substitute for raw milk in order to make a baby formula?"; and an example of a suggestion for other uses of a particular beverage was, "*Beet kvass* can be used not only as a beverage but also as a salad dressing". A large proportion of the viewers wished to be informed about healthier versions of recipes – with low fat, low sugar and low salt content – than those already available.

Our research found that many consumers wished to give their opinions about beverages bought from certain web stores. In addition, they gave references to, or made suggestions about, certain sites which contained information about these beverages, or which were selling these products or their ingredients. Finally, they often recommended different brands of, or gave different names and recipes for, a particular beverage that was consumed in different countries or regions. Some of them also offered information about special brands, stating, for example, "This brand is very refreshing".

Discussion and Conclusions

Webpages, blogs and forums concerning homemade, non-alcoholic fermented beverages, often serve as sites where users can voice their opinions about these beverages, or post traditional recipes for them, and they are thus an interactive resource making a range of information and features available to anyone with an Internet connection. From the analysis of the profile of the webpages, blogs and forums which we carried out, we concluded that half of them were websites and that most of them were easy to access and understand, with very few requiring membership, and that the writing standard of half of them was low – less than High School grade level.

Almost half of the webpages, blogs and forums included information on home fermentation processes, and videos depicting preparation methods were found on almost every webpage. The giving of suggestions about where to find the ingredients for these home-fermented beverages, and how to prepare them, was very common. Furthermore, the majority of the sites, blogs and forums shared information about search engines or about other social networking websites – an understandable situation since social interaction is the most common reason why young people use the Internet. It is clear from our analysis that the population under study consists of dynamic communities with ever-changing, user-provided content.

Content analysis such as the one described in this paper provides systematic data on what is available and likely to be seen by users of homemade, non-alcoholic fermented beverages, webpages, blogs and forums. In addition, we have provided a methodology to evaluate information available on the Web about these beverages. Different methodologies must be employed to determine whether, and how, users are affected by exposure to such material and to such media.

Our study showed that a substantial variety of traditional beverages, such as the homemade non-alcoholic fermented variety, originating in different parts of the world, are included in the webpages that we studied. These results provide us with some insight into the variability, preparation methods, and the consumption rate of these beverages in the western world – where, as already stated, this group of fermented products has received little attention from the scientific community to date.

From the analysis of the comments of the visitors to the webpages, we concluded that the most common themes of concern to people were health issues, the methodology of preparation and preservation of the beverages, their organoleptic characteristics, and nutritional information. People had many questions about the impact of these beverages on certain organs of the human body, such as the liver, stomach and intestines, on food allergies and on special age groups (e.g. children, pregnant and lactating women, or on special groups such as weight losers, athletes, lactose intolerant people, and so on). The most common questions regarding special age groups concerned digestive issues, safety, and hygiene matters, portions for consumption, and the alcohol or caffeine content of the final product. Practically every message board included questions concerning the organoleptic characteristics of the final product and the preparation and preservation methods involved in producing it. Many of the viewers were beginners in home fermentation procedures, and they wished to be informed about their mistakes, or to learn in detail about every stage of the fermentation process. Personal experiences or opinions, mainly from viewers living in different counties or regions, who posted different names, recipes, or ingredients, for the same beverage, were of special value for our research, as these data enabled us to gain further insight into the character of the beverage in question.

A large proportion of the comments were concerned mainly with home economy and they included many questions about food wastage and the cost of the final product (both homemade and commercial). This was to be expected since almost half of the population under study had a home fermentation concern. In contrast to the home fermentation option, a great number of visitors to the websites offered information about certain web stores where these beverages could be purchased. They also recommended particular brands, and expressed their opinions about the special characteristics of these beverages, mainly concerning their organoleptic attributes.

Because technology is constantly developing and progressing, these webpages, blogs and forums will also evolve and change. It is already evident that sites now use more video and social networking approaches than formerly, and we can hypothesise that this interactivity will in fact increase as time goes on. To better understand how messages with the potential for good or harm are communicated through such media venues, researchers must continue to investigate both the messages and their impact on individuals exposed to them.

Limitations

The present study has certain limitations which should be taken into account when interpreting the data. First, it should be kept in mind that websites are a dynamic, and sometimes, a short-lived, phenomenon. A return to the sampled sites might reveal new data. Although we visited these sites on a regular basis during a six-month period, some data may have been missed. Thus a more systematic monitoring of the sites in question may have been warranted.

Furthermore, the many different names which were used for the same beverage, depending on the country or even the region in which it originated, or was consumed, raised difficulties in distinguishing the different types of homemade, non-alcoholic fermented beverages on all occasions. Thus, in these cases, and also when the preparation method of the beverages in question was not included in the information gathered, we tried, where possible, to integrate them into existing beverage types.

It should also be noted that approximately all of the websites, blogs and forums lacked cited scientific literature. Furthermore, as food blogs do not always provide sound information on nutritional issues, the public should be aware of the limitations of popular food blogs in this regard, and dieticians could assist in modifying blog recipes for individuals in order to improve their nutritional profiles (Schneider / McGovern / Lynch / Brown 2013).

A final limitation concerns the subjectivity involved in an analysis such as ours. We did not have the services of multiple researchers to consider the data objectively and the selection of the variables, their features, and the content analysis of the sites, may thus be biased. Although we believe that many of the sites examined were more commercial than informative in character, site maintainers or users might disagree with this evaluation.

List of References

Printed

Beck, François, et al.: "Use of the Internet as a Health Information Resource Among French Young Adults: Results From a Nationally Representative Survey". *Journal of Medical Internet Research* 16(5), 2014, p. 28.

Boutelle, K. N. et al.: "Fast Food for Family Meals: Relationship with Parent and Adolescent Food Intake, Home Food Availability and Weight Status". *Public Health Nutrition* 10(1), 2007, pp. 16-23.

Moisio, Risto / Arnould, Eric J. / Price, Linda L.:"Between Mothers and Markets: Constructing Family Identity through Homemade Food". *Journal of Consumer Culture* 361(4), 2004, pp. 385-405.

New York Times 2011

Schneider, E.P. / McGovern, E.E. /Lynch, C. L. / Brown, L.S.: "Do Food Blogs Serve as a Source of Nutritionally Balanced Recipes? An Analysis of 6 Popular Foodblogs" *Journal of Nutrition Education and Behavior* 45(6), 2013, pp. 696-700.

Tamang, Jyoti / Kailasapathy, Kasipathy: *Fermented Foods and Beverages of the World.* 1st. ed. CRC Press: New York 2010.

Valente, Thomas W.: *Social Networks and Health. Models, Methods, and Applications.* Oxford University Press: Oxford 2010.

Internet

"American Heart Association 2014", retrieved 19.7.2014 from http://www.heart.org/HEARTORG/GettingHealthy/NutritionCenter/HealthyCooking/Healthier-Preparation-Methods-for-Cooking_UCM_301484_Article.jsp.

"American Heart Association: Smart Substitutions for Healthy Cooking 2014", retrieved 19.7.2014 from http://www.heart.org/HEARTORG/GettingHealthy/NutritionCenter/HealthyCooking/Smart-Substitutions_UCM_302052_Article.jsp.

http://www.heart.org/HEARTORG/GettingHealthy/NutritionCenter/HealthyCooking/Smart-Substitutions_UCM_302052_Article.jsp.

CheckPageRank.net, 2014, retrieved on 20.7.2014, from http://checkpagerank.net/

Hispanic Business.com, 2013, retrieved 10.7.2014, from http://www.hispanicbusiness.com/2013/1/23/food_trends_2013_homemade_fermentation.htm

Reuters 2011, retrieved 10.7.2014, from http://www.reuters.com/article/2011/01/26/idUS218878+26-Jan-2011+PRN20110126. http://www.nytimes.com/2011/09/25/opinion/sunday/is-junk-food-really-heaper.html?pagewanted=all

Maja Godina Golija

When Old Meets New. The Demonstration of Traditional Slovene Dishes and Locally Produced Food on the Internet

Introduction

Living with the Internet and communicating in cyberspace have become every-day praxis and our new reality. Even very intimate fields of culture, such as food, love, sexuality and family life, have become important parts of the new media and means of communication, often under a veil of anonymity. As virtual worlds develop on the Internet and become more integrated into people's daily lives, it is necessary to examine issues concerning how these online representations through the electronic medium affect people's social life and personal identities (Palmgren 2009, p. 20). Whenever identity is mediated in this way, it is also remediated because a particular medium is always understood in relation to other media both past and present (Waskul 2003, p. 3). Today, we view ourselves and our culture in and through media representations. We are not fully constructed by the media, since we also employ and work with these media as vehicles for defining personal and cultural identities. New media offer new opportunities for self-definition, and also for the presentation of culture (Bolter / Grusin 1998, p. 231). Food culture is an important aspect of the various kinds of cultural representations to be found on the Internet. It is sometimes portrayed as being a part of heritage, but in other instances it is presented in the context of fashion, creativity and modernity. Food is, like other fields of the material world, an object, which is experienced and filled with various cultural and social meanings, in relation to the social and economic status of a person, his or her ethnic or religious affiliations, gender, age group, and so on.

In previous centuries, food was regarded as a realm related to the intimate world of an individual and his family, but with the spread of television and other electronic media – especially computers and the expansion of the Web – food gradually became incorporated into the public sphere of life. What was previously available to individuals only through collections of recipes and cooking instructions to be found in manuscripts or in rare printed cookery books, has recently become accessible to the masses. In the course of last ten years, food culture has become an important part of the world's largest arena for dialogue – the Internet –

where people can chat about food preparation techniques, the best ingredients to use, recipes, kitchen utensils, and the art of serving food. They can discuss and connect with other people, often disguising their names and professions while creating different discussion forums related to food culture. The consequences of this are that food has become an important area of interest, not only for professional cooks, but also for many others, allowing them to establish social networks, which are not based on geographical proximity but on a communal interest about how to prepare and serve certain dishes, and also about how to use the best and healthiest ingredients.

Traditional Slovene Dishes and their Presentation on the Internet

Traditional Slovene dishes are an important part of national and regional heritage, and, as such, they have not only economic but also political and social significance. Indicative of this is the increasing interest being shown by the Slovene tourist industry in certain traditional Slovene dishes and local food products. These have become a significant factor in the touristic development of certain areas of Slovenia, for instance, *mohant* cheese in the Triglav National Park area, and pumpkinseed oil in Prekmurje (Godina Golija 2012, p. 92).

In recent years, the Internet has begun to play an important role in the presentation of traditional Slovene dishes and local farm produce. Traditional Slovene dishes and food products are depicted on the official website of the Slovene Tourist Association, and on the websites of various tourism associations and tourism service-providers, such as hotels, restaurants, pubs, agritourism farms, tourist destinations, and regions. Such dishes are described as an important element of tourism promotion in Slovenia. The section titled "What to See & Do" of the official Slovene tourist and information portal named "I Feel Slovenia" (http://www. slovenia.info/?Ing=l, retrieved 3.6.2014), which is created and maintained by the Public Agency of the Republic of Slovenia for the Promotion of Entrepreneurship, Innovation, Development, Investment and Tourism (SPIRIT), and the Ministry of Economic Development and Technology of the Republic of Slovenia, includes a heading about Slovene food and wine. It introduces some traditional Slovene dishes as well as local products, wine from different geographical regions, and food products which have Protected Designation of Origin (PDO) status within the European Union. Among the latter are prosciutto from the Karst, cured pork stomach meat from Zgornjesavinjska Dolina, cheeses from Bovec and Tolmin, pumpkinseed oil from Štajerska and Prekmurje, *gibanica* (layered cake) from Prekmurje, žlikrofi (dumplings) from Idrija, *pogača* (leavened flat bread) from

Bela Krajina, ham from Prekmurje, and *tünka* (preserved meat in minced lard) from Prlekija. The feature mentions the methods of protection afforded to individual products, and readers also learn something about the typical culinary regions of Slovenia.

In addition to the major regional differences evident between the cuisines of the Pannonian Plain, the Mediterranean area, the Alpine region, and also parts of the Balkans, all of which are present in the territory of Slovenia, the ethnologist, Janez Bogataj, has spoken of twenty-four different gastronomic regions in Slovenia, which differ from each other in the manner in which the majority of daily and festive dishes of Slovenia are prepared (Bogataj 2000, p. 7). Although geographically small and with a population of only two million people, Slovenia is a highly transitory territory in which various cultural and other influences meet and blend, something which gives it an extremely diversified gastronomy. While briefly describing one hundred and seventy typical dishes, Bogataj's section on "Dishes and Recipes" presents the most comprehensive list of Slovene traditional dishes so far available. Among the most numerous dishes are traditional soups, dishes made of cabbage, beans, and potatoes, štruklji (dumplings), and a variety of cakes, phyllo dough pies (*gibanica, pogača)*, and roll cakes (*potica*). The impression that one gets is that the author has tried to fascinate the reader by showing him / her the abundance and variety of dishes in Slovenia's diversified gastronomy rather than by giving details of their composition, interesting aspects, and their pleasant taste.

The section on traditional Slovene dishes includes the description of a project entitled *Gostilna Slovenija* ("Slovene Inns") and a selection of restaurants that are marked with the *Gostilna Slovenija* tag. These inns promote Slovene culinary features and serve typical local dishes made with homegrown ingredients. At least 80% of the dishes on their menu must be of Slovene origin and must include food products with PDO status. Furthermore, at least half of the foodstuffs used by chefs in the preparation of meals are required to have been produced in Slovenia, and at least 5% of these must result from organic production methods.

The "I Feel Slovenia" webpage also presents tourist events associated with Slovene cuisine. It is of interest to note that such events are organised in all regions of Slovene and not just in areas that are more popular in tourism terms than others and which also have a larger number of visitors. The fact that they also take place in locations that have fewer tourist attractions – for example, in the Zasavje and Kostelsko regions – confirms the hypothesis that the significance of local cuisine for the building of local identity within Slovenia and the European Union is increasing. Slovene delicacies can be sampled when visitors attend events such as competitions for the making of the best *bograč* stew, the preparation of roast potatoes, or the making of the most savoury *kranjska klobasa* (Carniolan sausage). There are also many events that celebrate various local foodstuffs – such as, the cherry, strawberry, chestnut, persimmon, honey or cheese festivals.

Traditional Slovene dishes are also presented on other websites, such as, the tourist websites of certain places and regions, the websites of tourist associations and of the associations of farming women, as well as the websites of Slovene agritourism farms, among others. Some dishes, particularly those that have been awarded EU PDO status, are also listed on the official website of the Ministry of Agriculture and Environment. The presentation of Slovene traditional foods on the website of the Association of Tourist Farms of Slovenia (http://www.turistic-nekmetije/, retrieved 3.6.2014), is particularly detailed. Although the principal aim of this website is to present Slovene agritourism farms to their potential visitors, the website also contains a wealth of information on the culinary features of Slovene regions. The section under the heading "Gastronomy" describes forty typical dishes from various parts of Slovenia, such as Prekmurje, Gorenjska, Kozjansko, Prlekija, Haloze, Štajerska, Dolenjska, and so on. Included in this section are some extremely old, almost-forgotten dishes, most of which are no longer prepared. Among those included are the following: *loške smojke* (stuffed turnips), *oprešak* (a cake with cracklings), *sirnica* (cottage cheese soup), *ubrnjenik* (buckwheat dumplings), and *mežerli* (ground lungs roasted in a pan). All of the dishes are described in great detail and are furnished with attractive photographs and recipes. Thus, they appeal not merely to people who wish to spend their holidays on agritourism farms, but also to those who are interested in traditional Slovene dishes. A careful perusal of the recipes shows that they have been adjusted in order to meet the tastes and needs of modern consumers and their attitude to food in general and also to meals. Certain recipes, therefore, include sugar, vanilla, cinnamon, and other spices that were not originally used in traditional Slovene cuisine. Another characteristic of these adjusted recipes is the reduced amount of fat included, since, in the past, fat played a very important role in the Slovene diet.

Gastronomy and culinary specialties are frequently included in the website presentations of Slovene municipalities, particularly in connection with farm produce or a dish with the EU Protected Appellation of Origin status. One such example is the famed cured pork stomach meat from Zgornjesavinjska Dolina, the so-called *Zgornjesavinjski želodec*. This excellent culinary specialty, and a renowned cured meat product from the hilly region along the Savinja River, is depicted in detail on the website of the Ljubno ob Savinji municipality where it originates. Due to its high quality and excellent preparation technique, this product has been awarded EU PDO status. Different locations in the municipality promote it as their unique specialty, and the municipality organises an annual competition in the tasting and evaluation of this delicacy (http://www.lju bno. si/?q=node/184/, retrieved 3.6. 2014).

Fig. 1; Cured pork stomach (Zgornjesavinjski želodec), 2008 (Author's collection).

In addition to descriptions and photographs of cultural and natural heritage which are specific to each region of Slovenia, the tourist websites of individual regions of the country also mention local cuisine and traditional regional dishes. These are usually everyday and festive dishes of the farming population once prepared in individual places. Tourists can order them in certain restaurants and when visiting agritourism farms. An example of such a website is "Slovenska Istra" (Slovene Istria), a tourist website that discusses the principal culinary features of Istria and its most important foodstuffs and wines forming the basis of local meals. Meals were based primarily on vegetables, polenta, olive oil, fish, and certain meat products such as prosciutto, for example. Typical features of the local cuisine were the baking of bread and also the baking of *pogača* under the so-called *pekva*, a domed clay lid, and the frying of sweet festive pastries, such as *kroštule* (http://www.slovenska-istra.si//index.php?lang=1&id=33/, retrieved 3.6.2014).

The website (http://www.goprekmurje.si/slo/kulinarika/, retrieved 3.6.2014), concerning the cultural and natural features of Prekmurje, the most easterly region of Slovenia, presents the Pannonian type of cuisine that is relatively less well known. Its filling dishes are usually prepared from wheat or buckwheat flour, pumpkin oil, cream, cottage cheese, and poppy. In addition to old, traditional dishes, the website text includes some new culinary creations that are based either on the local tradition of food preparation or on traditional ingredients – one such example being ice cream made from pumpkin oil and sprinkled with roasted pumpkin seeds.

Such presentations of traditional local cuisines are usually limited to the descriptions of everyday and festive dishes consumed by the farming population.

These dishes are habitually served in a traditional manner, namely in ceramic containers, metal kettles, bowls, or on wooden boards. These websites typically emphasise the rural character of local cuisines, which indicates that the population of a certain place or region is perceived as being largely rural. Thus, we learn little about social differentiation in these areas or about the traditional food culture of other population groups, such as the affluent city dwellers, workers, miners, artisans, and so on.

Traditional Slovene Dishes on Slovene Cultural Heritage Websites

The digitisation of ethnological material in Slovenia, such as drawings, manuscripts, photographs, and plans, is frequently connected with the implementation of projects from the field of cultural heritage, which are funded by the European Union or by the state of Slovenia (Križnar 2010, p.10). The material collected by various ethnological institutions is first digitised, then processed, and finally presented on different websites that result from studies carried out by different scientific disciplines. They are an integral part of the so-called cultural heritage of Slovenia project, which not only promotes new forms of material documentation, its collection and analysis, but also introduces innovative methods of data collection and processing, as well as new ways of perceiving and carefully considering it (Stuedahl 2009, p. 67). Projects such as these involve ethnologists from major Slovene ethnological institutions – from the Slovene Ethnographic Museum, the Institute for Slovenian Ethnology at the Research Centre of the Slovenian Academy of Sciences and Arts, the Department of Ethnology and Cultural Anthropology at the Faculty of Arts in Ljubljana, as well as some curator ethnologists from city and regional museums. The material on Slovene traditional dishes, their history, preparation, use, and safeguarding, is also an integral part of this digital cultural heritage of Slovenia project.

One of the oldest projects of this kind is DEDI – digital encyclopedia of heritage (http://www.dedi.si/info/, retrieved 3.6. 2014). In addition to cultural heritage, it also presents the natural heritage of Slovenia. It was designed by a number of researchers from various scientific disciplines, including ethnology. The beginnings of the encyclopedia go back to 2008 when researchers from the field of protection of cultural heritage started to co-operate with computer companies in order to create a digital encyclopedia. During the intervening years, the work continued to increase in size and the encyclopaedia presently features 460 units of heritage. The major part of the ethnological material which it incorporates deals with various ethnological characteristics of Slovenia, with only a smaller part dealing with traditional dishes.

Interest in websites related to the cultural heritage of Slovenia, including food culture, increased after the ratification by the Slovene parliament of the UNESCO Convention for the Safeguarding of Intangible Heritage in 2005. Responsibility for this endeavour fell initially to the Institute for Slovenian Ethnology at the Research Centre of the Slovenian Academy of Sciences and Arts, which dealt with it for three years; since 2011, this assignment has been undertaken by the Slovene Ethnographic Museum (Židov 2011, p. 283). One of the tasks to be performed by the Co-ordinator of the Body for the Safeguarding of Living Heritage is the registration, documentation, processing, and presentation of the phenomena of intangible heritage. The project, named the Register of Intangible Cultural Heritage, and supervised by the Ministry of Culture of the Republic of Slovenia, is presented on the Internet and includes the representation of dishes such as, *prleška gibanica* (layered cake made with cottage cheese, poppy seed and apples); *poprtnik* (Christmas fancy bread); *povitica* (rolled phyllo dough with filling), as well as typical food products such as *mohant* cheese and *kranjska klobasa* (Carniolan sausage). Some of these foods have been awarded the highest level of protection in the state of Slovenia and have been proclaimed a living masterpiece of national importance. Since these foodstuffs have been included in the Register, their Internet presentation is predominantly administrative in form and is thus largely lacking in appeal for potential visitors to the website.

Slovene traditional dishes also have a presence on some European cultural heritage websites. One such website is that of the Etnofolk project (http://www.etnofolk.eu/, retrieved 3.6. 2014), a Central European project that took place between 2011 and 2014 in ethnological institutes located in four countries in Central Europe – the Czech Republic, Hungary, Slovakia, and Slovenia. One of the partners in this project was the Institute for Slovenian Ethnology at the Research Centre of the Slovenian Academy of Sciences and Arts, which prepared a presentation on ethnological heritage in Slovenia. Although the initial aim of the project was to introduce the rich photographic material regarding local ethnological characteristics, in the possession of the four national institutions concerned, the website concept gradually evolved, changed drastically, and was greatly expanded. Its Internet pages now also contain data on ethnological heritage which is aimed at tourists, heritage experts, and entrepreneurs. The ethnologists that were involved in this project made a special effort to include those ethnological components of culture that would be of interest to the widest range of users. In addition, they also considered the potential educational role of this Internet portal, which could be used by primary and secondary school educators. The field of food culture on the Etnofolk website contains dozens of units representing traditional dishes and food products of the four countries involved in the Etnofolk project. Some of the most typical Slovene dishes and foods included in the project are the traditional ham from Prekmurje, pumpkinseed oil, *gibanica*, *Zgornjesavinjski želodec*, *kranjska klobasa*, *mohant* cheese, dumplings, and so on. A brief description of each food item is followed by a more comprehensive text concerning its ingredients, history, preparation, and the area in which it was – or still is – consumed. The text is supplemented with a literature list and furnished with rich visual material.

Conclusion

Traditional Slovene dishes are a part of cultural heritage that is now under the supervision of a number of ethnological and other institutions in Slovenia. In the past, however, these dishes played a prominent role in celebrations and were an important agent in the formation of national identities of smaller European nations, including Slovenia. In the nineteenth century, certain components of material culture, such as national costume, traditional dishes, and vernacular architecture, were regarded as being significant indicators of national affiliation and identity in multinational monarchies (Schippers 2002, p. 127). Learned individuals involved in different scientific disciplines, as well as amateur ethnographers, collected and studied them, and interpreted them as national symbols. Their work paved the way for the first museum collections, exhibits, and archives. Foods and dishes of that period, which were construed and interpreted as national foods, and which are now labelled as being traditional (Makarovič 1991, p. 127), are important for the creation of local identities and for the development of certain economic activities.

Modern phenomena such as globalisation, tourism, and migration, have brought about the birth of, or the resurgence of interest in, cultural heritage and tradition. Particularly pronounced in this connection is the interest shown in traditional dishes and local farm products. Traditional dishes are perceived as being important elements of cultural heritage and also as being part of an effort to consume healthier, more authentic, and, especially, organically-produced food (Godina Golija 2012, p. 100). This scenario is reflected in the official policy of the European Union, which promotes and funds projects for the development of European regions and for the safeguarding of local features and diversity. It is also reflected in the increasingly urgent realisation of the need to preserve and revitalise certain European regions in response to factors such as globalisation and creolisation (Köstlin 2010, p. 38). It is, therefore, possible to say that at present, traditional dishes are regarded as being part of the common past of people, of regions, and of national and local identities. Digital media play a significant role in these modern views of the interconnectedness of food and culture, in that they highlight the importance of social activity and collective awareness in this connection, As a result, it is possible to put forward the idea that the concepts of heritage and tradition are nowadays more open and more closely connected with the people, and with the actual living culture, than was the case in the past. Digital media help ethnologists to understand the complexity of cultural phenomena, the relationship between the past and the present, between different categories and objects, and between people, spaces, and narratives. Rather than being permanent and unchangeable, traditional dishes and their presentation, as well as perceptions of them and their evaluation, are evolving in the dynamic process of the present – also with the help, or indeed because of, digital media. This coincides with certain theoretical concepts that regard new technologies primarily as significant components of social and cultural activities (Stuedahl 2009, p. 76).

List of References

Printed

Bogataj, Janez: *Kuhinja Slovenije: mojstrovine nove kuharske umetnosti* ("Kitchen of Slovenia: New Masterpieces of Culinary Art"). Rokus: Ljubljana 2000.

Bolter, Jay David / Grusin, Richard: *Remediation. Understandig New Media*. MIT Press: Cambridge, MA 1998.

Godina Golija, Maja: "Contemporary Appropriations of Culinary Tradition in Slovenia." *Traditiones* 41(2), 2012, pp. 91-104.

Köstlin, Konrad: "A New Ascension of Regional Food". In: Lysaght, Patricia (ed.) / with Bolstad Skjelbred, Ann Helene: *Food and Meals at Cultural Crossroads*. Novus Press: Oslo 2010, pp. 36-46.

Križnar, Naško: "Nastajanje registra žive kulturne dediščine v Sloveniji" ("The Formation of a Registry of Living Cultural Heritage in Slovenia"). In: Križnar, Naško (ed.): *Živa kulturna dediščina*. Slovensko etnološko društvo 10: Ljubljana 2010.

Makarovič, Gorazd: "Prehrana v 19. stoletju na Slovenskem" ("Food Culture in the 19th Century in Slovenia"). *Slovenski etnograf* 33-34, 1991, pp. 127-205.

Palmgren, Ann-Charlotte: "Theoretical Approaches to the Self and Body in Relation to Blogs in a Swedish Context". *Ethnologia Scandinavica* 39, 2009, pp. 18-26.

Schippers, Thomas: "Od predmetov do simbolov. Spreminjajoče se perspektive proučevanju materialne kulture v Evropi" ("Objects of Memory. An Attempt at Defining the Concept and Research"). *Etnolog* 12, 2002, pp. 125-136.

Stuedahl, Dagny, "Digital Cultural Heritage Engagement". *Ethnologia Scandinavica* 39, 2009, pp. 67-82.

Waskul, Dennis D.: *Self-Games and Body-Play*. Peter Lang Publishing: New York 2003.

Židov, Nena: "Od Unescove konvencije o varovanju nesnovne kulturne dediščine do Registra žive kulturne dediščine na Slovenskem" ("Of the UNESCO Convention on the Safeguarding of the Intangible Cultural Heritage to the Registry of Living Cultural Heritage of Slovenia). *Etnolog* 21, 2011, pp. 281-290.

Internet

"Association of Tourist Farms of Slovenia": http://www.turisticnekmetije/, retrieved 3.6. 2014.

"Cured Pork Stomach" (*Zgornjesavinjski želodec*): http://www.lju bno. si/?q=node/184/, retrieved 3.6. 2014.

"DEDI digital Encyclopedia, Slovenia": http://www.dedi.si/info/, retrieved 3.6.2014.

"Etnofolk.eu. Folk Culture Heritage": http://www.etnofolk.eu/, retrieved 3.6. 2014.

"goPrekmurje.si": http://www.goprekmurje.si/slo/kulinarika/, retrieved 3. 6. 2014.

"I feel Slovenia": http://www.slovenia.info/?Ing=l, retrieved 3.6.2014.

"Slovenian Istria. Enjoy": http://www.slovenska-istra.si//index.php?lang=1&id=33/, retrieved 3.6.2014.

Aleksandra Krupa-Ławrynowicz

Mushrooms: Polish Traditions and Modern Practices. Online Examples

Between Botany and Cultural Anthropology

For many years, mushrooms have fascinated not only biologists and those who have discovered and appreciated their culinary qualities, but also cultural anthropologists and ethnologists who have recognised the significance of mushrooms in cultural systems, traditions and customs. Therefore, reflections on mushrooms are often located on the borderline between the natural sciences and the humanities, fitting into the broadly discussed nature–culture opposition. An interdisciplinary field concerned with studies of interactions between the natural and human worlds, between plants and people, is called *ethnobotany* (cf. Martin, 2004; Łuczaj 2013, pp. 9-15).

The multifaceted interest in mushrooms, which originated in the 1960s, gave rise to a narrower discipline in its own right – *ethnomycology*. Thanks to the work of Robert Gordon Wasson and his wife Valentina Pavlovna in the 1950s and 1960s, mushrooms became an object of thorough anthropological research (cf. Wasson / Wasson 1957; Wasson 1968). The results of their investigations, based on an immense amount of comparative material derived from many regions of the world, encouraged many scholars, including ethnologists, to take up research on this subject. Apart from the Wassons' studies, which aimed at determining the role of mushrooms in various ritual and mythological systems, a significant research direction resulted from the work of Claude Lévi-Strauss, which handled, among other matters, the issue of identifying the place occupied by mushrooms in various codes, including those concerning food (Lévi-Strauss 1966, pp. 45, 60, 151-152, 330). Ideas about mushrooms, and the cult of mushrooms, also became the point of departure for Vladimir Toporov in identifying their role in the semiotic systems of many cultural and historical traditions (cf. Toporov 1985).

In Polish ethnographic texts, mushrooms are mentioned by Kazimierz Moszyński, an outstanding Polish ethnographer (cf. Moszyński 1962). Józef Gajek, in his first surveys of 1948-1949 for the post-war *Polski Atlas Etnograficzny* ("Polish Ethnographic Atlas"), enquired about the use of edible and medicinal plants, including mushrooms, as part of his work (Kłodnicki / Drożdż 2008, pp. 109-124). However, the term "ethnobotany" did not appear in Polish ethnological scholarship until 1964 when it was used in her studies by the well-known scholar, Anna

Kowalska-Lewicka, and it then began to be more extensively employed in the 1980s by Adam Paluch and Zbigniew Libera, both of whom were engaged in research on Polish ethnomedicine.

Mushroom consumption and the perceived ambivalent nature of this fungus, have been linked to the mythical act of creation. The formation and reproduction processes of mushrooms, which are not a manifestation of natural fertility (fermentation), but rather regarded as being characteristic of plants and animals from the "other" world, determine their presence in all components of the death–fertility–life complex. This associates mushrooms with divine and devilish forces and with the lunar cycle. At the same time, the relation between mushrooms and the idea of fertility is noticeable in numerous traditions. It is clearly visible at the level of language, where it reveals itself, for instance, in nomenclature referring directly to male and female genitals, or at the level of plot structure in numerous mythological threads. A constituent feature of mushrooms is their perceived mediation capacity, which manifests itself in many magical and ritual actions in which they are involved.

Poland – The Country of Mycophiles

Ethnomycologists often point to the diverse attitudes to mushrooms that are to be found in different cultures. Mirosław Marczyk has noted that mushrooms are variously regarded as, for example, excrement, "the devil's bread", "the food of the gods", or "the divine body" (Marczyk 2003, p. 8). The different attitudes to mushrooms, to mushroom picking, and to their use in culinary and medicinal practices, have resulted in certain nations being recognised as so-called mycophobes (people who are terrified of eating mushrooms, particularly the wild varieties), while others are regarded as mycophiles (people who like to pick mushrooms and to prepare the sporocarps for eating). In a recent work, Krzysztof Grzywnowicz calls the Greeks, Indians, English, Americans, and the Scandinavians, mycophobes, while he considers the Slavs, Italians, the Swiss, Provençals, Catalans and the peoples of the Far East, to be mycophiles (Grzywnowicz 2002, pp. 12-13). Mycophiles have always considered mushrooms to be a dainty and important dietary supplement (especially at times of scarcity). Therefore, they have called them, for example, "forest meat" and the "beefsteak of the poor" (ibid. p. 13).

Poland is definitely a country of mycophiles. The picking and consumption of mushroom in Poland is mentioned in archival accounts and in old agricultural guidebooks. Mushrooms are present in everyday and holiday menus and in anecdotes and sayings. The only limitations on mushroom picking in Poland are concerned with protected areas and species. In every sanitary and epidemiological station, a properly trained person is employed who is responsible for deciding whether mushrooms he/she has been presented with for inspection, or consulted about, are safe to eat. In the age of the Internet, Poland is probably the only country that has created a map of current mushroom locations, which is updated by over a thousand people on an ongoing basis during the mushroom-picking season each year (see http://www.grzyby.pl/wystepowanie.htm, retrieved 30.7.2014). Many online portals and websites are dedicated to the subject matter of mushroom picking, mushroom recognition, and mushroom preparation.

www.nagrzyby.pl

The largest and oldest Polish online portal dedicated to mushrooms and mushroom pickers is www.nagrzyby.pl (retrieved 30.7.2014) and the accompanying discussion forum. It is a virtual space created for, and dedicated to, all those who treat mushroom picking as their passion rather than as an incidental pastime for autumn days. The information which can be found on the website includes a mushroom book, information about protected mushrooms, a map with marked mushroom locations, interesting facts about mushrooms, and mushroom-related riddles, recipes, methods of preparation prior to consumption, records of mushroom size, tips from experienced mushroom pickers, mushrooming accounts, and an enormously comprehensive photo gallery. The portal also publishes information about the Internet Mushroom Lovers Club – its regulations, invitations to go mushrooming together, and information about organised competitions and events (e.g. Mushroom Day, the Mushroom Festival, and the Great Mushrooming). A part of the online portal is dedicated to a discussion forum which has nearly 3,000 users and over 7,000 threads. The discussions deal, for example, with requests for assistance in order to identify mushrooms which a picker has found, providing information about helpful literature, as well as guidebooks and equipment for the mushroom picker.

Mushrooming

The online portal described above informs its users that mushrooming usually starts at the beginning of summer, after 29 June, that is after the feast day of Saints Peter and Paul, and that it ends in early November. The commencement date is certainly related to stories about the origin of mushrooms which are characteristic of Polish folk culture, and which, genre-wise, are normally classified by folklorists as tales.

One of the apocryphal tales tells about Jesus and St. Peter coming to a miller, who offered them bread. Jesus did not accept the gift while Peter took it. Later, when they were walking through a forest, Peter wanted to eat the bread in secret but whenever he put a piece to his mouth, Christ, who was walking in front of him, would turn around, and then the saint had to throw the bread away. When asked about what he was doing, he said he was planting mushrooms – which were said to have then started to grow (ATU 774L in Uther 2011; Stomma 1986, p. 220).

In Polish folk tradition, mushroom growth is also related to the first lightning strike and to the first spring storm. Lightning is connected with the destruction of devilish powers, demons, and the impure dead, and it also signifies fertility. The first storm is associated with the notion of the beginning of a new period, the opening of the sky for the first time in spring, and the closing of the old, departing period. Mushrooms have been stigmatised in Polish folk culture especially because of their extraordinariness, and they are regarded as being like something secretly stolen from another world. This "other world" is represented by the forest, which constituted a special space for old-time Polish villagers – an exceptional, unknown, dangerous and non-human area. A human who dared to enter the mysterious forest terrain in search of mushrooms, entered a strange space, and reproduced the mythical pattern of an expedition to the underworld, in order to get something that could not be found anywhere else.

Anna Zadrożyńska has noticed that many fairy tales focus on mushroom picking, and that numerous terrifying stories involve going mushrooming in a forest. Either the devil would appear and lead the mushroom picker astray or bring him or her to another world, never to return. Or apparitions would kidnap the unfortunate mushroom seeker and transform him or her into a completely different creature. The folk had very distinct, if occasionally also somewhat unusual, methods of fighting against such threats. One needed to make the Sign of the Cross on oneself, which everyone did just in case anyway. What is more, one was forbidden, under any circumstances, to go to the forest on a Sunday morning before Mass had been celebrated (Zadrożyńska 1985, p. 60).

Various folk ideas related to mushrooms and mushroom picking have survived in Poland to the present day. Here are two beliefs mentioned on the www. nagrzyby.pl portal, complemented by this author's additional cultural and ethnographical interpretations.

"It is said that it is best to pick mushrooms at dawn". The borderline nature of this time of the day is appropriate for the seeking of that which is also mediatory (i.e. the mushroom) in nature.

"A menstruating or pregnant woman should not go mushrooming". According to Polish folk belief, the openness of the menstruating woman to underworld influence and the initiatory nature of the pregnant woman's experiences should not overlap with the perceived similar properties of mushrooms, and of the time and place of picking them. Situations so intensely liminal in character, together with the exposed biological aspect of human existence, could end in tragedy, both for the woman herself and also for the unborn child (Zadrożyńska, p. 60).

The forum users exchange predictions, based on weather conditions, concerning the growth of mushrooms – for example, "When January is cool, there will be many mushrooms"; "When it rains on St. Peter Day, there will be many mushrooms"; "When the forest vapours in a mist, mushrooms will appear in three days".

According to traditional wisdom it is essential to be well prepared when going mushroom hunting in a forest. It is necessary to have knowledge of the forest environment, and also to have suitable equipment, the value of which is often unrelated to practicality but connected rather with sentiment. The objects that one carries, and the clothes that one wears only when going mushrooming, confirm the idea that an aura of magic or of mystery still accompanies the act of forest mushroom picking. The Internet forum users write, for example, about carrying an old knife, a wicker basket inherited from one's grandmother, comfortable wellingtons, and a sweater full of holes that has been worn and left unmended for years, when going mushrooming.

The accounts of mushrooming trips published on www.nagrzyby.pl have something in common with descriptions of expeditions to the unknown, when one suspends one's normal technical skills and becomes a hunter or an adventurer in search of something that is both ambivalent and precious. Here is one such description:

I was in a forest yesterday, 25 km from my town. I have a family there and there is a forest just behind the fence. We went for a walk to the forest where I had found beautiful boletuses in this birch and pine forest last year, but there was nothing there this time. I went to the forest three times this year and [still] nothing [no mushrooms] grew. I decided to go to another forest on the other side of the road, where I had once found many parasol mushrooms in a young pine forest. I went there with a friend; she was waiting, and I decided to push into that pine forest. I'm writing 'push into' because it was impossible to stand up straight there. I put something on to push through the dry and tight pine trees, and the heat was merciless. A white cap of a parasol mushroom loomed in the distance, so I closed my eyes and pushed through the grove almost on my knees. When I had crawled there, I saw more caps. I went on, scratching myself with more dry branches. There were ten odd of them there but they were in a bad condition. All were bone dry, some were broken and also dried up. I took a dozen or so photos in those devilish conditions and, since I had crawled there, I decided to also pick the dry parasol mushrooms, in order to grind them without drying and to use the powder for making dishes. And this is what I did. When I crawled out of the forest, I looked like a redskin Sioux after a battle with the Apache. My friend barely recognised me. And I was half-dead after going out of there but I had dried parasol mushrooms in my bag (http://nagrzyby.pl/relacje/krolowa-bolem-serca, retrieved 30.7.2014).

Roch Sulima emphasises that it is a characteristic of contemporary mushrooming culture in Poland that knowledge about mushrooms, including where they are to be found, is passed on in families from generation to generation, without any part being played by science in that transmission process. With regard to information about mushrooms, people tend to trust their grandmother, grandfather or uncle more than professional mushroom books. Mushrooms are one of the few remaining areas where intergenerational tradition is in the process of being revived (http://www.przeglad-tygodnik.pl/pl/artykul/grzyb-sprawa-polska, retrieved 30.7.2014).

The folk taxonomy divided mushrooms into the following categories: those regarded as being edible or conditionally edible, those considered to be inedible, those regarded as being of the male, female, spring, or autumn variety, and those thought to be inedible, or to be edible only when used for non-human purposes (Marczyk 2003, p. 75). Contemporary mushroom pickers and users of the above-mentioned online forum, have various ways of recognising and eliminating poisonous and unpalatable mushroom species. They trust, and rely on, acquired traditional knowledge and on their own experience of mushrooms. Among the criteria used to indicate mushrooms that are unfit for human consumption, are: taste (e.g. a spicy and bitter taste); colour (e.g. bright, becoming blue after breaking,); and smell (odour of excrements or potatoes). Mushroom experts and amateurs enthusiasts warn, however, against practices for determining whether or not a mushroom is safe to eat that were considered effective even in relatively recent times. These included the blanching the mushrooms several times and the straining away of the liquid regarded as harmful on each occasion, or the placing of reliance on the results of tests, such as, for example, the blackening of a silver spoon or an onion which had been placed in the boiling mushrooms, something which is believed to indicate that the mushrooms in questions were poisonous.

Culinary Practices

Mushrooms have always been a significant element of food, and not necessarily of just famine food, in Poland. They are prepared in various ways: by drying, pickling, boiling, frying, or roasting. The richness of aromas and the diversity of tastes associated with mushroom sporocarps, make them both a valuable flavour enhancer when added to various dishes, as well as an independent, and often a sophisticated, dish in their own right. Before they can be regarded as a delicacy, however, they need to be prepared in a special manner.

An accurate and extensive guidebook about the preparation stages of mushrooms can be found on the www.nagrzyby.pl portal and on the accompanying online forum. Mushroom pickers give the following advice online about mushroom picking (summary): Begin with checking to see if the mushroom is healthy. If you notice any holes or mildewed parts in it, throw it away. [If healthy], clean the stems and caps of the remains of dirt and sand. It is best to wipe mushrooms with a damp cloth or paper towel instead of rinsing them. Yet, sometimes they are so dirty that rinsing is necessary – it needs to be done quickly, though. When mushrooms are pre-cleaned, they can be segregated. Put big mushrooms with big ones and small mushrooms with small ones. Place the mushrooms to be dried or pickled separately from those intended for use for soup or sauce making. Mushrooms are best pre-dried in the sun, and then dried in a half-open oven which is only slightly heated. A special mushroom dryer can also be used. Keep dried mushrooms in sealed jars. For hanging in the kitchen, thread them on a string, but if this is done they can "catch damp", lose their aroma, and become a microbial habitat. It is worth making mushroom flour in a grinder or mortar from smaller or low-quality mushrooms just after drying, and using the flour for dishes.

In Polish folk culture, ritual dishes related to ceremonial practices often consisted of mushrooms. It was imagined that humans could offer them as gifts to creatures from beyond the human world, and also to the spirits of the dead members of their family or friends. An example of a sacrificial feast, when dishes made of mushrooms are still served, is the Christmas Eve supper. The menu for that supper, which is still part of contemporary Polish rituals, is not random, and mushrooms are its obligatory component. Poles who emigrated to countries where mushrooms are not part of the local cuisine have asked others to send mushrooms to them, arguing that Christmas loses its magic without them.

The above-discussed online portal usually includes an abundance of recipes for "Christmas mushrooms". The mushrooms are normally served in a variety of forms: as a mushroom soup, as a component of *borsch*, as an addition to sour cabbage served hot, as dumpling stuffing, and as one of the main ingredients of *łazanki* (noodles served with sour cabbage and mushrooms).

The website authors and the forum users share their own recipes, as well as those which they have found in cookery books and those received from their friends, with each other. The mixture of recipes, the conventionality of the style, the deconstruction of the tradition, the inspiration provided by diverse models and their free combination, result in the gathering together and the presentation of cuisines of individual regions and traditions on one large plate – always accompanied by mushrooms. For example, recipes for the following familiar dishes all include mushrooms: Provençal-style chicken with mushrooms (and tomatoes and white wine); hunter-style mushrooms (with pork fat, onions, dried plums, and juniper berries); scrambled eggs with chanterelles; pickled mushrooms for winter; Mexican soup with mushrooms (with pepper, beans and meat); pasta with mushrooms, pesto and tuna; and fried trout with mushrooms and broccoli.

Internet users ask questions, answer questions, and give advice about mushrooms by drawing on their own experience as mushroom pickers and users. Questions such as the following have appeared on the Internet and have been answered by other users: "Which mushrooms may not be combined with alcohol because this might result in unpleasant symptoms of poisoning?" "What ought to be done when a strange residue forms in a jar of pickled mushrooms?" "What does an odour produced when drying mushrooms mean?" "How long can dried mushrooms be stored? Should mushrooms be boiled before freezing?"

From a Mushroom to a Cultural Reflection

Mushrooms and the related picking, preparation, and consumption practices connected with them, fit into the Polish tastescape and into Polish culinary culture determined by the entirety of customs, prohibitions and orders concerned with the preparation and consumption of food.

A story about one of the components of an everyday and holiday menu can, therefore, become a basis for broader reflection on cultural practices. The presence of mushrooms in Polish cuisine conveys knowledge about Polish culinary heritage through which cultural distinctiveness is manifested. It also points to cultural syncretism, which draws from folk and Christian tradition, as well as from the processes of globalisation that entered Polish cuisine quite some time ago. This is because food involves communication – it reveals evidence of value systems, points to social stratifications, it has always been symbolic, religious and ritualistic in nature, it tells about complex nature–nurture relations, it reveals taboo areas and food aversions, and it constitutes a significant component of various discourses, including identity, ludic, ethical, and aesthetic ones.

List of References

Printed

Grzywnowicz, Krzysztof: *Grzyby i ludzie, czyli od etnomykologii do mykotechnologii* ("Mushrooms and People. From Ethnomycology to Mycotechnology"). Wydawnictwo UMCS: Lublin 2002.

Kłodnicki, Zygmunt / Drożdż, Anna: "Dzikie rośliny jadalne – materiały, mapy i opracowania tekstowe Pracowni Polskiego Atlasu Etnograficznego" ("Wild Edible Plants – Materials, Maps and Text Collection of the Polish Ethnographic Atlas"). In: Łuczaj, Łukasz (ed.): *Dzikie rośliny jadalne: zapomniany potencjał przyrody* ("Wild Edible Plants: The Forgotten Potential of Nature"): Krośnieńska Oficyna Wydawnicza: Krosno 2008.

Lévi-Strauss, Claude: *Mythologiques II: Du miel aux cendres.* Plon: Paris 1966.

Łuczaj, Łukasz: "Etnobotanika w Polsce u progu XXI wieku" ("Ethnobotany in Poland on the Threshold of the 21st Century"). *Wiadomości botaniczne* ("Botanical News") 57, 2013, pp. 9-15.

Marczyk, Mirosław: *Grzyby w kulturze ludowe* ("Mushrooms in Polish Folk Culture"). Wrocławskie Wydawnictwo Naukowe: Wrocław 2003.

Martin, Gary: *Ethnobotany: A Methods Manual.* Earthscan: Oxford 2004.

Moszyński, Kazimierz: *O sposobach badania kultury materialnej* Prasłowian ("Towards Research on Proto-Slavonic Material Culture"). Zakład Narodowy im. Ossolińskich: Wrocław 1962.

Stomma, Ludwik: *Antropologia wsi polskiej XIX wieku* ("The Cultural Anthropology of the 19th Century Polish Village).* Instytut Wydawniczy PAX: Warszawa 1986.

Toporov, Vladimir: *On the Semiotics of Mythological Conceptions about Mushrooms.* Mouton Publishers: Amsterdam, Berlin, New York 1985.

Uther, Hans-Jörg: *The Types of International Folktales. A Classification and Bibliography.* Part I: *Animal Tales, Tales of Magic, Religious Tales, and Realistic Tales, with an Introduction.* FF Communications 296. Finnish Academy of Science and Letters: Helsinki 2011.

Wasson, Robert G. / Wasson, Valentina: *Mushrooms, Russia and History,* vols. 1-2. Pharmacologica Phantastica: New York 1957.

Wasson, Robert G.: *Soma: Divine Mushroom of Immortality.* Harcourt Brace Jovanovich: New York 1968.

Zadrożyńska Anna: *Powtarzać czas początku* ("Beginnings' Repetition"). Wydawnictwo Spółdzielcze: Warszawa 1985.

Internet

http://www.grzyby.pl/wystepowanie.htm, retrieved 30.7. 2014.

www.nagrzyby.pl, retieved 30.7. 2014.

http://nagrzyby.pl/relacje/krolowa-bolem-serca, retrieved 30.7. 2014.

http://www.przeglad-tygodnik.pl/pl/artykul/grzyb-sprawa-polska, retrieved 30.7. 2014.

PART II:
Food, Marketing, and the Internet

Déirdre D'Auria and Patricia Lysaght

The Online Promotion of Irish Food as a Tourist Attraction

Introduction

Irish food and indigenous Irish produce have a considerable international reputation. This is evident from the protected status afforded to certain Irish foods
under European Union legislation, and especially from the demand that exists for
Irish food products in many parts of the world. As the most important indigenous
Irish industry, food and drink manufactured in Ireland serve not only to supply
the major portion of the domestic grocery and food-services sector, but also to
contribute significantly to Ireland's export profile, as such products are now sold
in about one hundred and twenty countries worldwide. Over eighty per cent of
Ireland's dairy and beef production, for example, is exported, and considerable
quantities of Irish lamb and pork are also sold overseas.[1] But the appeal of Irish
food products, against a production background of a lush, green environment,
is also used, among other attractions, to draw people to different parts of Ireland
and, in this way, to contribute to another important Irish industry – tourism. Thus
references to particular foods, eating establishments, and food-related activities
in Ireland, now feature regularly on a variety of Internet websites designed to
encourage people, at home and abroad, to visit different regions of the country.
These food-oriented advertisements are addressed sometimes to travellers with
a specific interest in food, but they are more often geared towards general tourists
who are looking for suggestions for activities in which they could take part while
on holiday in this country. This paper will explore how different websites currently
engage with the promotion of Irish food to tourists and what this exercise tells us
about attitudes to local and regional foods.

---

1   For key statistics and facts about Ireland's food industry in 2014, see: "Food and Drink
    Industry Ireland", retrieved 22.4.2014, from http://www.fdii.ie/Sectors/FDII/FDII.nsf/
    vPages/Food_Industry_in_Ireland~sector-profile?OpenDocument.

Irish Foods with European Union Protected Status – A Boost for Irish Tourism?

In recognition of their high quality and special status as authentic, regional produce, five Irish foods have gained Protected Geographical Status under European Union legislation through the PGI (Protected Geographical Indication) and the PDO (Protected Designation of Origin) regimes. These European forms of classification are designed to protect and to promote the names of high quality food products, allowing only those originating in the designated areas to use the name. This safeguards the reputation of the specific regional foods in question, helps producers to obtain a fair price for their authentic goods, and also guards against imitation products which may be of inferior quality or flavour. The five foods produced in Ireland which are protected in this way are: Clare Island Salmon (PGI) (1999), Timoleague Brown Pudding (PGI) (1999), Imokilly Regato cheese (PDO) (1999), Connemara Hill Lamb (PGI) (2007), and most recently, the Waterford Blaa (PGI) (2013).[2] The latter product is a soft, doughy, white, yeast bread roll, square or round in shape, with a crusty or soft top, traditionally dusted with flour before baking, and associated particularly with Waterford city on the south coast of Ireland.[3]

---

2 The geographical area to which the PGI Waterford Blaa designation (2013) actually applies is Waterford city and county, and a small area of neighbouring south Co. Kilkenny. See: "Department of Agriculture, Food and the Marine. Waterford Blaa Specification", retrieved 22.4.2014, from http://www.agriculture.gov.ie/media/migration/agri-foodindustry/geographicalindicationsprotectednames/ WaterfordBlaa311013.pdf. Indicative of the close identification of the blaa with Waterford is that Waterford people are sometimes nicknamed "blaas".

3 For Irish products with Protected Geographical Indication, see: "Department of Agriculture, Food and the Marine. Products with Protected Geographical Indications", retrieved 22.4.2014, from http://www.agriculture.gov.ie/gi/pdopgitsg-protectedfoodnames/products/, and Digby, Marie Claire, "Waterford Blaa Awarded Special Status by EU", *The Irish Times*, 19.11.2013, retrieved 23.4.2014, from http://www.irishtimes.com/life-and-style/food-and-drink/waterford-blaa-awarded-special-status-by-eu-1.1599966. In Northern Ireland, Comber Earlies, a potato crop, and Lough Neagh Eels, both have PGI status. See: "Potato Awarded Special EU Status". Belfast Telegraph.co.UK, 10 July 2014, retrieved from http://www.belfasttelegraph.co.uk/news/local-national/northern-ireland/potato-awarded-special-eu-status-28707657.html. See also: Melke, James: "Lough Neagh Eels the New Champagne", The Guardian.com, 6.9.2011, retrieved 8 July 2014, from http://www.theguardian.com/uk/2011/sep/08/lough-neagh-eels-are-new-champagne.

Dr. Oliver Moore, an Irish online food writer and blogger, suggests that this EU classificatory system for regional foods that have been granted protected status under EU legislation enjoys a certain element of recognition among consumers in Europe – perhaps more so than is currently the case with Irish consumers in relation to EU protected Irish products. He claims that "Whatever the exact value, in many parts of Europe, consumers look out for these markers as a quality sign."[4] It is likely, therefore, that Irish foods enjoying these EU classifications would be of interest to European food-oriented tourists visiting Ireland. Bord Bia [Food Board] Vantage, the online resource centre for small food businesses in Ireland, supports this view, and lists "regional development and tourism" as an indirect advantage of the PGI / PDO systems,[5] suggesting that tourists with an interest in regional foods might consider the availability of food products with these classifications as a reason to pay a visit a particular area – thus enhancing the sales value of the area and its products.[6]

Recent online research, to gauge the visibility of these EU-protected Irish foods, indicates that they are not currently specifically advertised on general tourist websites as a possible means of attracting tourists to Ireland, or to the particular areas of the country with which they are associated. However, information on these foods can be easily accessed online by any interested researcher. On conducting an online search using, for example, specific terms such as "protected

---

4   For a critique of Ireland's apparent approach to seeking PDO and PGI status for foods from Ireand, see: Moore, Oliver, "Making Ireland's Unique Foods Stand Out in the Market Place", Georgina Campbell's Ireland, retrieved 2.4.2014, from http://www.ireland-guide.com/article/making-irelands-unique-foods-stand-out-in-the-market-place.9521.html.

5   For projected benefits for various stakeholders in relation to EU Protected Food Schemes, See: "Bord Bia. Irish Food Board. Guide for Irish Producers to EU Protected Food Schemes PGI / PDO / TSG Designations (Draft), 19 September 2011", retrieved 2.4.2014, from http://www.bordbiavantage.ie/foodcommunity/Documents/Guide_to_PDO_PGI_TGS_Designations_5.pdf, p. 4. The current Minister for Agriculture, Marine and Food, has also suggested that these EU schemes for protected status for foods "can help to build networks among local food producers and communities to strengthen the rural economy." Retrieved 23.4.2014, from http://www.irishtimes.com/life-and-style/food-and-drink/waterford-blaa-awarded-special-status-by-eu-1.159996.

6   For the impact of the so-called e-economy on cultural heritage, see: Salomonsson 2002, esp. p. 135. For a critique of the requirements, processes, and actors involved in applications for the protection of regional food products under EU legislation, and the symbolic capital to be derived therefrom, see May 2013, pp. 278-287.

7   Here the five EU protected Irish food products are listed. See: "List of Republic of Ireland Food and Drink Products with Protected Status", retrieved 2.4.2014, from

Irish regional food", or the obvious "PGI or PDO Ireland", many pertinent results appear, including Wikipedia entries,[7] newspaper articles,[8] a document from Bord Bia Vantage,[9] and a document from the Food Safety Authority of Ireland.[10] The Waterford Blaa features quite prominently in these results using the above search data, due to the recent (2013) award of the PGI classification to this regional food.

It is only in relatively recent times that an upsurge in the number of artisan food producers in Ireland has become noticeable, and that local and regional cuisine has taken centre stage as a tourist attraction in certain areas of the country. For a small country like Ireland, the gaining of Protected Geographical Status under European Union legislation for five Irish foods, is a positive achievement. According to the online database of the European Commission's Directorate-General for Agriculture and Rural Development, an application from Ireland, which seeks to achieve PGI status, this time for Irish salmon,[11] is currently undergoing review. It is to be hoped that more such applications will be made and that protected status for many Irish foods will follow, and, as a result, that an increased understanding of their significance for the Irish tourism industry and other sectors of the economy will emerge, and give rise to a more visible online presence for them on Irish tourism and other websites.

Websites Promoting Irish Food as a Tourist Attraction

While no website specifically dedicated to promoting Irish food to food-oriented tourists planning a trip to Ireland, or for Irish people arranging a holiday at home

---

7   http://en.wikipedia.org/wiki/List_of_Republic_of_Ireland_food_and_drink_products_with_protected_status.

8   For example, Cahill, Ann, "Only Four Irish Foods Make it on to EU Quality List", *Irish Examiner*, 16.2.2011, retrieved 2.4.2014, from http://www.irishexaminer.com/ireland/only-four-irish-foods-make-it-on-to-eu-quality-list-145454.html.

9   See note 5 above.

10 "Food Safety Authority Ireland. Information Note on Protected Designation of Origin (PDO), Protected Geographical Indication (PGI) & Traditional Speciality Guaranteed (TSG), retrieved 2.4.2014, from http://www.fsai.ie/uploadedfiles/about_us/forums/artisan/pdo_pgi_tsg_info_note.pdf.

11 For the "applied" status in respect of Irish Salmon, see: "European Commission, Agriculture and Rural Development. *DOOR*", retrieved 25.4.2014, from http://ec.europa.eu/agriculture/quality/door/list.html?&recordStart=0&filter.dossierNumber=&filter.comboName=&filterMin.milestone__mask=&filterMin.milestone=&filterMax.milestone__mask=&filterMax.milestone=&filter.country=IE&filter.category=&filter.type=&filter.status.

in Ireland with a focus on regional food, appears to exist at the present time (2014), a useful current resource for such prospective tourists is the website www. ireland-guide.com.[12] This is a guide to Ireland, in which the main focus is on food and hospitality, and in which lists of recommended eating establishments and cookery schools, a "restaurant of the month", and a blog presenting a list of the "Top 10 Food Trends for 2014", feature.[13]

Food and drink also feature as part of more general tourist websites, alongside such activities as, for example, fishing, hill-walking, research into genealogy and ancestry, and general sight-seeing, associated with a touristic trip to Ireland. It is fair to say that these websites are directed at the tourist interested in just coming to Ireland and enjoying what it has to offer, rather than at someone visiting the country for a specifically food-centred experience. It is noticeable that the variety of food-related activities included on these websites has expanded significantly in recent years, and that it now ranges from offering recommendations with regard to eating and drinking establishments, to the giving of lists of food shops, food producers, food markets, food festivals, and local food trails, as well as providing articles on Irish food traditions and innovations. The general focus of these food-related activities is on regional food and cuisine, and certain food items and establishments, in different areas of the country, are presented as tourist attractions in this context.

One such general website is www.dochara.com[14] which is dedicated solely to potential visitors to Ireland and to providing information about the wide variety of activities in which they could participate. It also supplies a "guide" which the traveller can easily print before leaving for Ireland, as well as a list of foods, including fish and chips, oysters and guinness, and black pudding, which the author suggests the visitor should try to sample on arriving in the country.[15] According to this website, a visit to Ireland for most people "is not made in expectation of

---

12 This guide is described on its website as "Ireland's Leading Independent Hospitality Guide", retrieved 2.4.2014, from http://www.ireland-guide.com/.

13 "Georgina Campbell's Ireland. Top 10 Food Trends for 2014", retrieved 2.4.2014, from http://ireland-guide.com/blogs/2014/01/29/10-of-the-top-food-trends-for-2014/.

14 "DoChara" ("Your Friend"), is also described as "an insider's guide to Ireland". See "DoChara. Ireland from the Inside", retrieved 23.4.2014, from http://www.dochara.com/.

15 In addition to suggestions about iconic foods which the visitor should try while in the country, general comments on Irish food, and recommendations about what and where to eat, are also provided on the website. See: "DoChara. Where [and What] to Eat in Ireland", retrieved 23.4.2014, from http://www.dochara.com/tour/eat-sleep/where-to-eat/what-to-eat/.

having great food", and suggests that this is a reason why many visitors are surprised by the quality and variety of Irish food which they experience while in the country.[16] The section on traditional foods in Ireland on this website deals with foods such as Irish stew, cabbage and potatoes, soda bread, tea brack, and mashed potato preparations such as colcannon and champ. Only "traditional" food is mentioned on this site, which also notes that the above dishes are only rarely to be found in restaurants today, and adds that if they are actually served, they are often re-imagined and innovative versions of such traditional dishes, now prepared by well-travelled chefs.[17] The comments posted in this section of the website include some from tourists planning trips to Ireland and asking for recommendations about what and where to eat, as well as others from people of Irish decent living in different parts of the world, disagreeing with website recipes and detailing the way in which certain dishes have been made in their families for generations.[18] It should also be noted that some bloggers (for example, www.insightguides.com) and food writers, are presenting a newly-developing Irish cuisine to their readers, a cuisine that could possibly inspire a different, more food-oriented type of tourist, to visit Ireland in the future.[19]

The tourist website www.ireland.com, under the heading "Things To Do",[20] features "Food and Drink" alongside a variety of other categories such as "Angling and Fishing", "Attractions", "Christian Heritage", "Courses in Ireland", "Cycling", "Equestrian", "Genealogy and Ancestry", "Golf", "Natural Landscapes and Sights", "Literary Ireland", "Spa seekers", "Sports", "Visual Arts", and "Walking and Hiking". With regard to food and drink, this website provides a list of articles on subjects such as "Local Tastes", "The Taste of Tradition", and "Nature's Larder". These deal

---

16 Ibid.
17 The website also provides recipes and cooking instruction for some traditonal food of Ireland. See: "DoChara. Traditional Foods of Ireland. Food & Recipes from Ireland", retrieved 23.4.2014, from http://www.dochara.com/the-irish/food-recipes/traditional-foods-of-ireland/. See also Jonsson 2013, esp. pp. 63-65, in which he shows that, in the New Nordic Kitchen, Swedish chefs make tradition a basis for innovation and creativity.
18 "DoChara. Traditional Foods of Ireland", retrieved 23.4.2014, from http://www.dochara.com/the-irish/food-recipes/traditional-foods-of-ireland/.
19 See, for example, "The New Irish Cuisine" in the blog "Coddle and drisheen: what to eat in Ireland", posted by "Rebecca, 15 July 2013", retrieved 23.4.2014, from http://www.insightguides.com/inspire-me/blog/irish-food.
20 Food matters are also dealt with to some extent under other headings on this website. See: "Jump into Ireland. Things to Do", retrieved 29.4.2014, from http://www.ireland.com.en-gb/what-is-available.

with the topic of food foraging, while other articles centre on, for example, "Farmers' Markets", thus reflecting a strong current focus on local and regional produce in Ireland. The website also provides a facility for searching for information on eating establishments, cookery courses, farmers' markets, food and drink trails, food and drink visitor attractions, food festivals, and food shops, and gives links to the respective websites of all of these categories. At the time of searching the above website in the spring of 2014, it included a list of twenty-three upcoming regional food and drink festivals in Ireland, of possible interest to tourists.

Another tourist website, www.discoverireland.com, also includes "food" as a category under "Things To Do", although this time it is specifically listed under the title "Irish Food". Under this heading, four sub-sections give access to the following food-related guides (discussed briefly below): an Eating Out guide, a guide to Food Fairs and Festivals, a guide to Irish Food Trails, and information about the "Just Ask" campaign.[21]

The Eating Out Guide seems to recommend other such guides, including www. wheretoeat.ie, and www.menupages.ie – two widely-used independent restaurant review websites which are popular among tourist as well as among Irish people themselves. The list of events in the section "Food Fairs and Festivals" is much shorter than that on www.ireland.com, but further navigation leads to the same list of the twenty-three upcoming food events mentioned above.[22]

With regard to the guide to Food Fairs and Festivals, a comprehensive list of two hundred and thirty-one food fairs and festivals, food markets, cookery schools, restaurants and pubs, for browsing through or for searching using a regional criterion, is provided.[23]

Food Trails are a relatively new phenomenon in Ireland and reflect the fact that Irish food has emerged as a vibrant, innovative and international industry. Fab Food Trails (www.fabfoodtrails.ie), for example, advertised on www.discoverireland.ie, operate in the cities of Dublin and Cork. These walking tours comprise

---

21 "Just Ask" is a public awareness campaign aimed at encouraging consumers when eating out to look for information on where the food (particularly meat) on their plate comes from and to encourage chefs to provide this information on their menus. See: "Eating Out/Just Ask!, retrieved 22.4.2014, from http://www.bordbia.ie/aboutfood/eatout/pages/default.aspx.

22 The reader is encouraged to: "Tempt your taste buds… Munch your way around some of the many Irish Food Festivals taking place this year and celebrate the best of Irish food…". See "Food in Ireland. Things to Do", retrieved 2.4.2014, from http://www.discoverireland.ie/Things-To-Do/Food-in-Ireland.

23 Ibid.

six to eight tasting experiences in eating establishments around these cities, along with the inclusion of some information about the history and architecture of the areas concerned. Other food trails, such as the Dublin and Cork "tasting trails", which last over two hours, bring the partaking visitor to a range of food-related establishments, including bakeries, food halls, street markets, cheesemongers, delicatessens, and other speciality food shops, and provide them with an opportunity to meet artisan producers, some of whom have been in the business for generations, while others are relatively new arrivals on the Dublin and Cork food scenes.[24]

The "Taste of Kilkenny" food trail[25] is an extensive non-guided event, but visitors to the area can download a map and a guide to enable them to discover a range of food-themed destinations which they might wish to visit. The trail includes four food producers, an orchard, a poultry farm, a trout farm, and a cheese producer, all of which can be visited by the tourist. Also featuring on the trail are four food shops, including a bakery that has been in operation since 1838, eight restaurants, four cafés, and six "food destinations and experiences" – which include a cattle mart where the visitor can witness livestock being bought and sold, a traditional Irish thatched public house, a Georgian house (Lavistown House) in a woodland setting, with a small farm and a walled vegetable garden, where courses in mushroom hunting, gardening, and foraging are provided, Kilkenny Design which is a craft shop with a restaurant and a food hall, Mount Juliet, a country estate, with two restaurants which use local produce and herbs and vegetables picked daily in the estate's own herb and vegetable garden, and Ryeland Cookery School providing cookery workshops or full cookery courses. The trail also incorporates information on seven other local producers whose products may be encountered on the trail, including two bakers, a miller, two fruit juice producers, a fine foods producer, and an organic rapeseed oil producer. Details are also available on non-guided food trails of this kind in counties Mayo, Clare and Kerry, as well as on national trails featured on the Good Food Ireland web-

---

24 Participants in the Dublin Tasting Trail, for example, are told on the website that even though they may be familiar with the city, they "will be amazed to discover food outlets and tasty surprises they never knew existed...". See "Fab Food Trails. Dublin Tasting Trail", retrieved 2.4.2014, from http://www.fabfoodtrails.ie/dublin-tasting-trail/.

25 In addition to "Trail Kilkenny. Taste of Kilkenny Food Trail", retrieved 3.4.2014, from http://www.trailkilkenny.ie/themed-trails/taste-of-kilkenny-food-trail/speciality-shops/, the website also features a number of other themed trails in Co. Kilkenny.

site.[26] The Ireland Whiskey Trail offers a free touring map – in English, French and German – to guide the visitor to a variety of different "whiskey places", such as distilleries, whiskey pubs and specialised whiskey shops, around the country. Having encouraged the tourist to "see, taste, talk and capture the magic and enchantment of whiskey – the Irish way!", the guide also wisely advises the unwary "to drink responsibly and in moderation".[27] www.discoverireland.ie, also includes information on Bord Bia's "Just Ask" campaign, launched as a public awareness movement in 2009.[28] As well as urging consumers to seek information on the provenance of the food they are eating, and encouraging chefs and restaurateurs to provide it, it also rewards eating establishments that are "committed to showing transparency in the sourcing of the food on their menus".[29]The www.discoverireland.ie website describes the campaign

As already mentioned, the website, as being "all about promoting local food and the people behind it."[30]

A simple online search using the words "what to eat in Ireland" will yield results showing a growing community of food bloggers in Ireland. The appearance of bloggers in this context is not surprising as food blogging has become very popular in Ireland in recent years. It lately also became the subject of a discussion in the National Library of Ireland "Kitchen Archives" series of events, which focused "on how recipes and culinary skills have been communicated through the centuries in Ireland".[31] The IFBA (Irish Food Bloggers Association) was formed in order to give all those involved in food blogging, and more generally with food, a point of contact with each other, in order to enable them to share ideas and information

---

26 A wide variety of food-oriented trips (e.g., "Top Food Trips", "My Food Trip") to different parts of the country are available on the website: "Good Food Ireland", retrieved 3.4.2014, from http://goodfoodireland.ie/search/tour.

27 "Enjoy Great Irish Whiskeys on Ireland's Only Whiskey Trail" – see "The Ireland Whiskey Trail", retrieved 3.4.2014, from http://www.irelandwhiskeytrail.com/home.php.

28 See note 21 above.

29 Ibid.

30 See: "Discover Ireland. Just Ask! Campaign", retrieved 3.4.2014, from http://www.discoverireland.ie/Things-To-Do/Food-in-Ireland.

31 See the National Library of Ireland event, 20 November 2013 – "From Spoon to Screen: The Whys and Hows of Food Blogging", retrieved 3.4.2014, from http://www.nli.ie/en/list/current-events.aspx?article=549c9928-1f0d-4bb8-87a5-c97b62d46887 – which was chaired by food writer and blogger Aoife Carrigy, and also inlcuded the well-known blogger and TV chef, Donal Skehan.

about food and food-related events.[32] Currently, there are about four hundred and fifty different food and drink blogs listed on their website.[33] While some of these blogs are written by people living in Ireland but who may not necessarily be dealing with Irish food,[34] or by Irish people living abroad and writing about their food experiences,[35] nevertheless, Irish food itself has a strong presence on some of the blogs. These include the Good Food Ireland blog which states its position as follows: "Our passionate local and seasonal food ethos creates a culinary picture of our country, giving you a glimpse into our way of life. We reach out to a food community who share our enthusiasm for local and sustainable food, for food travel, for all things Irish and for the best authentic food experience that Ireland has to offer".[36] Also relevant in this context is the blog http://foodfight.ie/,[37] and that by Donal Skehan – a popular food blogger, cookbook author, food photographer, and television chef – entitled Donal Skehan's Home Cooked Kitchen Blog (www.donalskehan.com).[38] It is clear from these blogs that their audiences are both domestic and international, indicating that food blogs, and online writing about food, draw audiences from all over the world, and thus provide a channel through which food-oriented tourists can learn about Irish food. For example, the Good Food Ireland blog includes posts about local fruit farmers,[39] and Donal Skehan frequently posts about Irish food producers under the title "Irish Food

---

32 "IFBA. Irish Food Bloggers Association", retrieved 3.4.2014, from http://www.irish-foodbloggers.com/about/.

33 The food blogging community in Ireland is described as being "vibrant", in "IFBA, Irish Food Bloggers Association. Blogroll", retrieved 3.4.2014, from http://www.irishfood-bloggers.com/blogs-2/.

34 See for example the blog: "A Mexican Cook. Mexican Food and How to Cook it in Ireland", retrieved 20.4.2014, from http://amexicancook.ie.

35 For example, the blog, written by an Irish immigrant in London, "A Healthy Slice of Happiness", sub-titled "An Irish Foodie's (mostly healthy!) Adventures in London Town", retrieved 29.4.2014, from http://healthyeatinglondon.wordpress.com.

36 The blog further adds: "Our food and travel blog brings you stories and food happenings from around Ireland, tells you about top food places to eat or stay and unleashes Ireland's best kept secrets to the world at large". See: "Good Food Ireland Blog, retrieved 3.4.2014, from http://goodfoodireland.ie/blogs.

37 Mulley, Damien, retrieved 3.4.2014, from http://foodfight.ie/. According to its website, "FoodFight.ie aggregates all the tastiest content from around the Irish blogosphere. We also feature original content written by some of Ireland's top food bloggers."

38 Skehan, Donal, retrieved 3.4.2014, from http://www.donalskehan.com/.

39 See: "Good Food Ireland Blog. Berry Nice", retrieved 3.4.2014, from http://goodfood-ireland.ie/blog/berry-nice/5727.

Folk".[40] The Irish Food Guide Blog recently posted about "The 20 Best Irish Food Finds to Watch Out For in 2014".[41] Food-related events and festivals which could be of interest to tourists, and indeed even the reason for their visit to the country, are often promoted on blogs – Ken McGuire, for example, who writes the food blog http://anygivenfood.com,[42] often mentions such events.

Conclusion

As the esteem in which Irish food products are held internationally continues to grow, assisted by the gaining of the prestigious Protected Geographical Status recognition under EU legislation for a number of such products, the online presence of Irish food in general is also increasing and becoming more visible. Therefore, potential visitors to Ireland will find that information about Irish food and beverages can be easily accessed on a variety of general websites providing information about the country. In this way, it is possible for potential visitors to Ireland to learn about local and regional foods, including those with Protected Geographical Status, and also about what is regarded as traditional Irish cuisine, to enable them to plan food and drink-related activities in different areas of the country, as part of their visit. These pursuits could include involvement in food festivals, following guided or unguided food or drink trails, and making visits to recommended restaurants. By following food blogs, the potential tourists will also become aware of the latest food trends in Ireland, particularly regarding the creative use being made of traditional recipes by internationally-trained chefs, and they will also discover a range of craft-food producers and products. Above all, they will have the opportunity to enjoy good food in a variety of relaxed social settings, including public houses, as thirty-four such hostelries on the island of Ireland feature in the new *Michelin Eating Out in Pubs Guide* for 2014.[43]

---

40 For example, Skehan, Donal, "Irish Food Folk: McGeough's Butchers …", 24.4.2014, retrieved 29.4.2014, from http://www.donalskehan.com/.

41 Gallagher, Zack, "The 20 Best Irish Food Finds to Watch Out For in 2014", 8.1.2014, retrieved 3.4.2014, from http://www.irishfoodguide.ie/2014/01/the-20-best-irish-food-finds-to-watch.html.

42 McGuire, Ken, "Reminder: Meet The Cheesemakers", 2.4.2014, retrieved 3.4.2014, from http://anygivenfood.com/reminder-meet-cheesemakers/.

43 Keenan, Dan, "34 Irish Pubs Listed in Michelin Good Food Guide", *The Irish Times*, 1.11.2013, retrieved 24.4.2014, from http://www.irishtimes.com/news/consumer/34-irish-pubs-listed-in-michelin-good-food-guide-1.1580843.

List of References

Printed

Jonsson, Håkan, "The Road to the New Nordic Kitchen – Examples from Sweden". In: Lysaght, Patricia (ed.): *The Return of Traditional Food*. Lund Studies in Arts and Cultural Sciences 1: Lund 2013, pp. 53-67.

Köstlin, Konrad: "Tourism, Ethnic Food, and Symbolic Values". In: Lysaght, Patricia (ed.): *Food and The Traveller – Migration, Immigration, Tourism and Ethnic Food*. Intercollege Press: Nicosia 1998, pp. 108-114.

May, Sarah: "Making 'Traditional Food' – Local Interpretations of a European Protection-System". In: Lysaght, Patricia (ed.): *The Return of Traditional Food*. Lund Studies in Arts and Cultural Sciences 1: Lund 2013, pp. 278-287.

Salomonsson, Karin: "The E-economy and the Cultural Heritage". *Ethnologia Europaea* 32(2), 2002, pp. 125-144.

Internet

"A Healthy Slice of Happiness", sub-titled "An Irish Foodie's (mostly healthy!) Adventures in London Town", retrieved 29.4.2014, from http://healthyeatinglondon.wordpress.com.

"A Mexican Cook. Mexican Food and How to Cook It in Ireland", retrieved 20.4.2014, from http://amexicancook.ie.

"Bord Bia. Irish Food Board. Guide for Irish Producers to EU Protected Food Schemes PGI / PDO / TSG Designations (Draft), 19 September 2011", retrieved 2.4.2014, from http://www.bordbiavantage.ie/foodcommunity/Documents/Guide_to_PDO_PGI_TGS_Designations_5.pdf, p. 4.

Cahill, Ann, "Only Four Irish Foods Make it on to EU Quality List", *Irish Examiner*, 16.2.2011, retrieved 2.4.2014, from http://www.irishexaminer.com/ireland/only-four-irish-foods-make-it-on-to-eu-quality-list-145454.html.

"Department of Agriculture, Food and the Marine. Waterford Blaa Specification", retrieved 22.4.2014, from http://www.agriculture.gov.ie/media/migration/agri-foodindustry/geographicalindicationsprotectednames/WaterfordBlaa311013.pdf.

"Department of Agriculture, Food and the Marine. Products with Protected Geographical Indications", retrieved 22.4.2014, from http://www.agriculture.gov.ie/gi/pdopgitsg-protectedfoodnames/products/.

Digby, Marie Claire, "Waterford Blaa awarded special status by EU", *The Irish Times*, 19.11.2013, retrieved 23.4.2014, from http://www.irishtimes.com/life-and-style/food-and-drink/waterford-blaa-awarded-special-status-by-eu-1.1599966.

"Discover Ireland. Just Ask! Campaign", retrieved 3.4.2014, from http://www.discoverireland.ie/Things-To-Do/Food-in-Ireland.

"DoChara. Ireland from the Inside", retrieved 23.4.2014, from http://www.dochara.com/.

"DoChara. Where [and What] to Eat in Ireland", retrieved 23.4.2014, from http://www.dochara.com/tour/eat-sleep/where-to-eat/what-to-eat/.

"DoChara. Traditional Foods of Ireland. Food & Recipes from Ireland", retrieved 23.4.2014, from http://www.dochara.com/the-irish/food-recipes/traditional-foods-of-ireland/.

"Eating Out/Just Ask!, retrieved 22.4.2014, from http://www.bordbia.ie/aboutfood/eatout/pages/default.aspx.

"Enjoy Great Irish Whiskeys on Ireland's Only Whiskey Trail" – see "The Ireland Whiskey Trail", retrieved 3.4.2014, from http://www.irelandwhiskeytrail.com/home.php.

"European Commission, Agriculture and Rural Development. *DOOR*", retrieved 25.4.2014, from http://ec.europa.eu/agriculture/quality/door/list.html?&recordStart=0&filter.dossierNumber=&filter.comboName=&filterMin.milestone__mask=&filterMin.milestone=&filterMax.milestone__mask=&filterMax.milestone=&filter.country=IE&filter.category=&filter.type=&filter.status.

"Fab Food Trails. Dublin Tasting Trail", retrieved 2.4.2014, from http://www.fabfoodtrails.ie/dublin-tasting-trail/.

"Food and Drink Industry Ireland", retrieved 22.4.2014, from http://www.fdii.ie/Sectors/FDII/FDII.nsf/vPages/Food_Industry_in_Ireland~sector-profile?OpenDocument.

"Food Safety Authority Ireland. Information Note on Protected Designation of Origin, Protected Geographical Indication & Traditional Speciality Guaranteed (TSG), retrieved 2.4.2014, from http://www.fsai.ie/uploadedfiles/about_us/forums/artisan/pdo_pgi_tsg_info_note.pdf.c.

"From Spoon to Screen: The Whys and Hows of Food Blogging", retrieved 3.4.2014, from http://www.nli.ie/en/list/current-events.aspx?article=549c9928-1f0d-4bb8-87a5-c97b62d46887.

Gallagher, Zack, "The 20 Best Irish Food Finds to Watch Out For in 2014", 8.1.2014, retrieved 3.4.2014, from http://www.irishfoodguide.ie/2014/01/the-20-best-irish-food-finds-to-watch.html.

"Georgina Campbell's Ireland. Top 10 Food Trends for 2014", retrieved 2.4.2014, from http://ireland-guide.com/blogs/2014/01/29/10-of-the-top-food-trends-for-2014/.

"Good Food Ireland", retrieved 3.4.2014, from http://goodfoodireland.ie/search/tour.

"Good Food Ireland Blog", retrieved 3.4.2014, from http://goodfoodireland.ie/blogs.

"Good Food Ireland Blog. Berry Nice", retrieved 3.4.2014, from http://goodfoodireland.ie/blog/berry-nice/5727.

"IFBA. Irish Food Bloggers Association", retrieved 3.4.2014, from http://www.irishfoodbloggers.com/about/.

"IFBA. Irish Food Bloggers Association: Blogroll", retrieved 3.4.2014, from http://www.irishfoodbloggers.com/blogs-2/.

"Ireland's Leading Independent Hospitality Guide", retrieved 2.4.2014, from http://www.ireland-guide.com/.

"Jump into Ireland. Things to Do", retrieved 29.4.2014, from http://www.ireland.com.en-gb/what-is-available.

Keenan, Dan, "34 Irish Pubs Listed in Michelin Good Food Guide", *The Irish Times*, 1.11.2013, retrieved 24.4.2014, from http://www.irishtimes.com/news/consumer/34-irish-pubs-listed-in-michelin-good-food-guide-1.1580843.

"List of Republic of Ireland Food and Drink Products with Protected Status", retrieved 2.4.2014, from http://en.wikipedia.org/wiki/List_of_Republic_of_Ireland_food_and_drink_products_with_protected_status.

Melke, James: "Lough Neagh Eels the New Champagne", The Guardian.com, 6.9.2011, retrieved 8.7.2014, 2014, from http://www.theguardian.com/uk/2011/sep/08/lough-neagh-eels-are-new-champagne.

McGuire, Ken, "Reminder: Meet The Cheesemakers", 2.4.2014, retrieved 3.4.2014, from http://anygivenfood.com/reminder-meet-cheesemakers/.

Moore, Oliver, "Making Ireland's Unique Foods Stand Out in the Market Place", Georgina Campbell's Ireland, retrieved 2.4.2014, from http://www.ireland-guide.com/article/making-irelands-unique-foods-stand-out-in-the-marketplace.9521.html.

Mulley, Damien, retrieved 3.4.2014, from http://foodfight.ie/.

"Potato Awarded Special EU Status". Belfast Telegraph.co.UK, 10 July 2014, retrieved from http://www.belfasttelegraph.co.uk/news/local-national/northern-ireland/potato-awarded-special-eu-status-28707657.html.

"Skehan, Donal", retrieved 3.4.2014, from http://www.donalskehan.com/.

Skehan, Donal, "Irish Food Folk: McGeough's Butchers ...", 24.4.2014, retrieved 29.4.2014, from http://www.donalskehan.com/.

"The Ireland Whiskey Trail", retrieved 3.4.2014, from http://www.irelandwhiskeytrail.com/home.php.

"The New Irish Cuisine" in the blog "Coddle and drisheen: what to eat in Ireland", posted by "Rebecca, 15 July 2013", retrieved 23.4.2014, from http://www.insightguides.com/inspire-me/blog/irish-food.

"Trail Kilkenny. Taste of Kilkenny Food Trail", retrieved 3.4.2014, from http://www.trailkilkenny.ie/themed-trails/taste-of-kilkenny-food-trail/speciality-shops/.

"Waterford Blaa Awarded Special Status by E.U.", The Irish Times, 19.11.2013, retrieved 23.4.2014, http://www.irishtimes.com/life-and-style/food-and-drink/waterford-blaa-awarded-special-status-by-eu-1.1599966.

www.discoverireland.com, retrieved 23.4.2014.

www.discoverireland.ie, retrieved 23.4.2014.

www.ireland.com, retrieved 23.4.2014.

www.menupages.ie, retrieved 23.4.2014.

www.wheretoeat, retrieved 23.4.2014.

Manon Boulianne and Claudia Laviolette

Virtual Food Representations. An Analysis of "Local Food" Discourse in Quebec

Local food provisioning is a public issue in Quebec, for the State as well as for businesses, farmers and citizens. Self-provisioning through community gardening and, more recently, through other forms of urban agriculture, has become a social movement, and is gradually being institutionalised in municipal planning and in other public agencies. Direct food marketing strategies, such as farmers' markets, had almost disappeared from Quebec's "foodscape" between the end of World War II and the 1980s, but from the mid -1990s, they have increased steadily in number. Other types of direct food marketing – and thus, also, of local food provisioning modalities and practices – are growing in popularity. This is the case with community-supported agriculture (CSA), with U-pick (pick-your-own), farm and roadside stands or boutiques, and with the online orders and delivery services provided by individual farms. In addition, regional tourism agencies have been developing "gourmet" routes for tourists and residents of Quebec Province. In doing so, they promote agro-tourism as a way of getting to know, and appreciate, local or regional foods and foodways, as well as the farmers who produce fresh fruit and vegetables, and those firms which process them.

Large and small retail stores are also promoting "locally" produced or processed food. Some of these are totally dedicated to the marketing of local food in order to support small or organic producers. Other retail stores may, for economic or political reasons, choose to source part of their stock directly from producers, or to use the popularity of "local" food mainly as a marketing strategy, in order to attract consumers who are supportive of "local" food and producers. Within the small stores sector, there are specialised shops (bakeries, butchers' shops, artisanal-cheese factories, smokehouses, health food stores, organic food shops or specialty stores selling local or regional food or produce) where at least part of what is sold originates in short food supply chains or is prepared on the premises. There are also a few independent stores, generally referred to as "neighborhood grocery stores".

One of the most unique developments in the province of Quebec has been the emergence of virtual – or online – markets, which first appeared in Quebec in 2005 under the leadership of the NGO "Friends of the Earth". The Sherbrooke chapter of the organisation created the first "Regional Solidarity Market" (*Marché de solidarité régionale*), a model that inspired other organisations throughout the Province, where there are now thirty such online markets in existence. Like CSA partnerships, they involve fixed, weekly delivery time-slots for different groups of members, who constitute a buying club of sorts. Unlike the situation in CSA, however, members choose, through the market website, the products they want to purchase on any given week of the year. Effectively, that means that members order (or choose not to order) at will. An annual membership fee is charged, and a percentage of the total cost of any order is taken by the organisation to subsidise its managerial activities, which include dealing with suppliers, membership, ordering products, storage, and deliveries. The *Marché de proximité de Québec* (MPQ), the online market which is discussed in this paper, was founded in 2007. It consists of more than six hundred active members and its main objective is to provide urban consumers with the opportunity to buy a variety of healthy and nutritious food products. This food is produced by growers, breeders, and processors in neighbouring areas, who share common economic and environmental values, and who represent an alternative food-production strategy to corporate food processing and agriculture. Located in the inner part of Quebec City, in a former school that shelters a variety of environmentally friendly NGOs, the MPQ opens its premises to consumers from 3.30 p.m. to 7.00 p.m., on Tuesdays to Thursdays o each week. Volunteers help the co-ordinators / managers – the only two paid employees – to assemble the requested food items from counters, refrigerators and freezers in order to have them ready for collection by those who ordered them. These items appear on a list created through the market's Internet website, and members can pick and order the products and quantities required from this list. Only the foodstuffs that have been ordered by the consumers are delivered to the MPQ by the producers, who generally do the deliveries themselves.

Some use is made of the Internet in all of the aforementioned food-marketing strategies in order to promote ideas, products and services, and the provisioning schemes on which they are built. In the case of online markets, the Internet is more than an informative and advertising tool in this connection, as it lies at the centre of their operations and of the encounter between producers and consumers. How is "local food", a social and cultural construct (Blake et al. 2010, DuPuis / Goodman 2005, King et al. 2010, Ilbery / Maye 2006) described in these virtual marketing spaces? This is what we examine in this paper, through a specific case study and a comparative discourse analysis. Data is taken from an ongoing research project which deals with local food provisioning initiatives in the Quebec City Metropolitan Area (Boulianne et al. 2011). By utilising an inductive method of analysis, we examine the websites of thirty-eight producers and retail stores located in Quebec city, and discuss the relative importance of attitudes to health, food quality, the environment, and production and distribution processes, evident in their online "presentation of self". In what follows, we describe briefly the methodology relied on, and then proceed to show the outcome of our analysis. The results point to the existence of significant differences with regard to how the abovementioned issues are treated in the websites of the selected businesses. Differences are also evident in the way in which these websites relate to culture, based on how they market the food they offer to consumers.

Methodology

At the present time (2014), the *Marché de proximité de Québec* (MPQ) relies on thirty-one food suppliers. Each of these suppliers has a page on the MPQ website, where information about each particular business and the products offered for sale to members of the buying club, is displayed. Twenty of the suppliers also have their own individual websites, which are much more comprehensive than those in the MPQ site. It is the content of these individual websites that we included in the sample, except for the website of one business that does not offer food products. Thus, nineteen websites pertaining to the MPQ suppliers of food products were analysed. The MPQ sample included eight growers (four organic vegetable growers, three livestock farms that provide fresh meat, and a blueberry grower), and eleven organic food processors (who produce miso, jams, grains, butter, cheese, sunflower oil, maple syrup, medicinal plants, pasta, flours, and coffee). Almost three quarters (N=13; 68%) of these businesses clearly identify themselves, on their websites, with a specific territory. Sometimes they mention the locality, region or the province where production occurs and the quality of the soil which produces the foodstuffs, using comments such as, "On the family farm in Lotbinière, located on biodynamic loam-sandy-clay, we passionately grow garden produce, microshoots and large crops". Elsewhere, they specify that the products they offer for sale are made in Quebec ("From [the sunflower] culture to the bottling process, Champy oil is entirely Québécois"[1]), or they remark on the priority they give to the local sourcing of their raw material, or the importance they afford to buying local products: "Favouring sustainable development, the Seigneurie des Aulnaies purchases its organic grains almost exclusively from producers from Saint-Roch-des-Aulnaies" or, stating the matter even more plainly, "We favour the use of local produce".

---

1   All citations from the websites, which originally appeared in French, were translated by the authors.

As part of our analysis, we also constructed a sample of the websites of nineteen retail stores selling food products. The retailers included in the sample incorporated eight businesses that buy and process fresh produce for sale as artisanal products (three bakeries, three butchers' shops, one jam processor, and one artisan-cheese factory), as well as seven specialty stores dedicated to the sale of local and regional products. Also, among the abovementioned retail stores, a health-food store and a cheese specialty shop are to be found, as well as two neighbourhood grocery stores. The sample is taken from a list of retail stores that offer a certain selection of food distributed through short food supply chains. On the CMQ territory, these amount to more than a hundred. The sample is not randomly chosen, as diverse kinds of stores were included, for the sake of qualitative analysis. Together they provide an approximate reflection of the diversity of the "population" of local food stores found in the greater Quebec metropolitan area. As in the MPQ suppliers' sample, we also found that their websites included a number (N=12) of references to the territorial origin of the products offered for sale, although, in this case, these consisted of just very short comments (N=6, vs 3 in the suppliers' sample), such as " Made in Quebec" or simply "made here", and there were very few statements (N=2, vs 7 in the other sample) about the importance of, or giving priority to, the sourcing of "local" products.

The content of the websites of the food suppliers and retailers examined consists mostly of text, although we also paid attention to the visual aspects of the sites, which give a clear impression of the impact their owners want to make on their public. We paid special attention to the mission statements of the businesses concerned and the ways in which "local food" and, more generally, the food products offered by each business, were presented. Using an inductive approach, a coding system was created. We found that, as a result of our analysis of the websites in our sample, five main topics could be identified. These concerned health, quality, environment, cultural heritage, and economy (see Table 1). Content relating to cultural heritage and the economy of food production and distribution, is the most pervasive, while the topics of health, product quality, and the environment, appear less frequently in these websites and are strongly associated with specific types of food businesses.

Discussion

As shown in Table 1, health issues are explicitly mentioned by nine suppliers of the MPQ. Comments (six) mainly refer to the nutritive virtues of specific foods or ingredients. For example, it is said of a particular brand of cold-pressed sunflower oil that it is "high in unsaturated fats… low in saturated fats… an excellent source of omega-9 with its 55-65% of oleic acid (monounsaturated), and a good source of omega-6 with its 26% to 36% of linolenic acid (polyunsaturated), [which] contributes to keeping harmful cholesterol levels low, and which reduces cardiovascular and age-related diseases, as well as the risk of certain cancers …". Other MPQ providers describe their products as "functional foods", "nutraceuticals", "probiotics", "antioxidants", as having a "high fibre content", or, more generally, as being of "high nutritive quality". Other issues related to health are also mentioned by some of the MPQ suppliers: three of them comment on food allergies or intolerances (two offer gluten free processed food); three also declare that they can fulfil the expectations of enthusiasts of different food movements – veganism, crudivorism (raw-food), and "living food" (see Table 1: "Explicit food choices"). Health issues are much less present in the analysed sample of websites of retail stores. Only two make some statement about it, including the one which is entirely dedicated to selling natural and healthy foods. The website of the other store describes, in a detailed fashion, the nutritional qualities of the blackcurrant – the store owner's and processor's star ingredient – and insists on the fact that their products are preservative free.

Table 1. Online self-representation of 38 local food providers in Quebec, Canada

Topic	Number of MPQ providers that mention this topic on their website		Number of "local" retail stores that mention this topic on their website	
Health	Nutrition	6	Nutrition	2
	Food allergies or intolerances	3		
	Explicit food choices	3		
Environ-ment	Organic	15		
	Protection of ecosystems, maintenance of "nature's equilibrium" or biodiversity	3		
	Animal welfare	4		
	Independence from external outputs	5		
	Sustainable development	4	Sustainable development	1
Quality	Premium quality	4	Premium quality	7
	Natural aspect of food	4	Natural aspect of food	1
	Diversity	1	Diversity	7

Topic	Number of MPQ providers that mention this topic on their website		Number of "local" retail stores that mention this topic on their website	
Cultural heritage	*Terroir*	6	*Terroir*	8
	Authenticity/tradition	4	Authenticity/tradition	8
	Transmission of savo*ir-faire*	1	Transmission of *savoir-faire*	5
	Public education and the enhancing of rural heritage	8		
Economy	Family business	4	Family business	1
	Small/human scale	2		
	Artisanal	5	Artisanal	9

Table 1 also shows that the topic of the environment is much more present on the MPQ providers' websites than in the analysed sample of the retail stores' websites. In fact, in the latter case, only one reference was made to the environment and this was by a food co-operative whose mission was to market the products of small farms in Quebec. This co-operative, which opened in 2012, unfortunately went into bankruptcy in 2013. Its website, while the business was in existence, was replete with criticism of globalised food systems and, above all, with the ideas that had guided the co-operative's main promoter and founder: "Its activities, which aim to mesh the producer, users and citizens, will promote socio-economic development. All of that in compliance with sustainable development principles, equity, local traditions, and territorial and community anchoring". Conversely, our comparative analysis reveals that the MPQ suppliers, unlike the retail stores, usually describe the production process as being organically certified, "natural", or environmentally friendly.

Another topic identified in our double sample of websites relates to quality in general, and then to more specific food qualities. Mention of "high quality" products, of "tasty", "fresh", and "natural" or "naturally-made" food, is found in similar proportions among the MPQ suppliers and other businesses, although their number and content vary according to more specific categories. The naturalness of the components of the food on offer, their origin, or the processes used in their production, are stated by four MPQ providers, compared to only one – the natural food specialty store – on the retailers' side. For example, farmers who process the milk of their herds into butter declare that their "cows and goats are naturally fed", and the producers of stone-ground whole-wheat flour explain that their mill "respects the ingenuous manufacturing of flour by the force of the water and the river". The last topic related to quality – "diversity" – is almost absent from the MPQ suppliers' websites, with the exception of a vegetable grower's reference to "quality and diversity" in its mission statement. On the contrary, this quality is put forward by a third (N=7) of the retail stores which insist that consumers will find many options from which they can choose, either among a different variety of food products or among specialty foods such as breads, meats, cheeses or artisan beers. On exploring their websites, one finds comments about "our wide range of", or that "you will be impressed by its range", or that you will have "lots [and] lots of choice", when referring to the products offered for sale, and photos that exemplify these assertions are also to be found on the particular websites.

A fourth theme found in the sample under study is cultural heritage. It is manifested through references to *"terroir"*, "authenticity", "tradition", and the transmission of *savoir-faire*, public education and the enhancing of rural heritage. *Terroir* is mentioned in more than one third of the websites we examined (N=14): six from the MPQ providers, and eight from retail stores. While, in the latter case, references to *terroir* are used to refer to the local, regional or provincial origin of food products, without identifying any of its particular characteristics, three of the MPQ providers associate certain qualities of the food they produce with a specific *terroir*. For example, one of the websites mentions that "[The artisan cheese maker] creates unique cheeses, representative of her *terroir* and of her goats. Naturally, she keeps to herself the secret of the manufacturing [process] of her farmstead organic cheeses, which are hand ladled with the beauty of a traditional and artisanal gesture".

References to authenticity and tradition are twice as numerous in our sample of the websites of retail stores, than in those of the MPQ providers. In the first case, eight businesses put forward the idea that (at least some of) the products they offer for sale are produced in an "authentic" fashion, or in a traditional way. One of them, a cheese factory, is reproducing what is considered to be the first domestic cheese made by French settlers, established on the Island of Orleans, in seventeenth-century New France, and, hence, the "most ancient cheese on the continent". All of the other businesses, either of retailers or of the MPQ providers, which remark on tradition or authenticity, also offer manufactured products, and all of their comments are related to the production process. Some insist that the recipes used ("some of our recipes come from family ancestors!"), others that the technical dimensions of the manufacturing process (".... The vinegar factory is equipped with a typically traditional aging and ripening room"), and others, still, that the tools or machinery used ("... technology used in watermills at the beginning of the industrial era", for example), are all old, traditional and authentic.

Five retailers assert that their activities contribute to the transmission of *savoir-faire*, old or new. Two of them, owners of a vinegar and a cheese factory, respectively, who also run boutiques, have been mentioned in the preceding section. The *savoir-faire*, which they purport to pass on, is more than a century old, and this is also the case with a tomato wine maker whose products, resulting "from a family recipe kept secret during four generations", are sold in a specialty boutique that focuses on *terroir* foods. In the other cases, *savoir-faire* is the result of recent innovations. In comparison, only one website of the MPQ suppliers – that of an artisanal butter manufacturer – mention the transmission of *savoir-faire*. On the other hand, however, the topics of public education and the enhancing of rural heritage are much more present on the MPQ suppliers' websites – having been mentioned by eight different businesses – than on those of the food retailers. Actually, two of the businesses are registered as museum institutions by Quebec's Ministry of Culture. The others are farms that either receive kindergarten or school groups for a visit lasting a couple of hours, or that offer agro-tourism services where guests can stay for several days, thus enabling them to gain "an authentic experience of life on the farm", or that arrange workshops, conferences or consultations on topics related to agriculture, cooking, and health.

The last category of topic that emerged from the analysis of our double sample of websites is related to the economy of food production and distribution. At its core, we find claims that aim to distance the businesses surveyed from their industrial food production counterparts. Specifically, the business websites surveyed make explicit reference to either the family dimension of their business (which, *per se*, does not imply that this is a non-industrial venture, but rather that it is often perceived as such by the public), their "small-scale", or "human-scale" production or, first and foremost, the fact that they are involved with artisanal production. The mention of the family dimension of the business is found in the websites of rural farms, four of whom are MPQ suppliers, as are the statements that insist on the small scale of the business enterprise. Artisanship, on the other hand, is more often mentioned by retail stores (half of them refer to it at least once in their website). As was the case with the "diversity" of the products sold in the retail stores, the artisanship element seems to be regarded as being of particular interest to clients. This topic of artisanal production is, in a number of ways, strongly related to what was, earlier on, classified under the heading of "cultural heritage". Thus businesses that use the artisanal argument generally also refer to the elements of tradition or authenticity incorporated into the food products offered for sale.

Conclusion

With regard to discourses on food products presented on the Internet in respect of the MPQ suppliers and retail stores, it is evident that the different main topics that emerged as a result of our analysis of the websites in question, are unequally treated by businesses that are part of the MPQ, and our sample of retail stores that stock "local" food. Topics that are most commonly found on the MPQ suppliers' websites are related to health and lifestyle, the environment, production processes, and the relation between humans and territory. Regarding health, a salient feature is the provision of information on the benefits to health that their products are said to bring to consumers. The environment is dealt with in terms of references to organic, environmentally-friendly and sustainable processes of production, as well as the preservation of nature. Finally, the importance of preserving what we could define as healthy relations between humans and the territory they occupy or live from, is manifested through the aforementioned themes. The environment is an obvious theme in that regard, and the websites analysed often describe the specific and sometimes elaborate efforts being made by the people who grow or process cereals, vegetables and fruit, raise livestock or process milk, grains or herbs, in order to maintain rural economic activities in different regions, and to provide a food supply consisting of nutritious and tasty products for their fellow citizens.

Leaving aside our systematic compilation of things said and unsaid in the various websites, it becomes clear at a more general level, that for the MPQ suppliers, their work, the land they live on, and the food they produce and offer to the online-market members, are intimately related to, and infused with, meaning. This kind of complex commitment to food products was also found in a number of the retail stores included in our sample, although in this case, references to premium quality, the diversity of the food products on offer, *terroir*, authenticity, and tradition, were much more commonly found than in the MPQ sample, and often appeared to be more of an eye-catching marketing tool rather than forming a part of a statement about the role retailers and producers have in regional economies and in the preservation of cultural heritage.

As a concluding remark, and in relation to the importance and meaning of the Internet for the MPQ members, we observed that it is a basic component of this buyers' club. Orders must be made through the Market's website, and most of the interactions between consumers and producers of the MPQ are, indeed, "virtual". That said, it is important to point out that unmediated (face-to-face) social interaction between consumers has been, and still is, essential to the recruitment and renewal of members, and that it figures among the most appreciated aspects of this venture. Ultimately, suppliers' websites are not necessarily consulted by the market members with regard to their mission statement or outlook, or the quality of the products on offer. Their shared core ideas about what agriculture should be like, and about the kinds of food that are worth buying are, first and foremost, circulated by word of mouth – outside the market and during the delivery sessions which provide an opportunity for members to chat between themselves and with the market co-ordinators. Overall, it is this mix of virtual and face-to-face interactions that creates the trust that links together the different categories of members (consumers, producers and co-ordinators / managers) who make up the MPQ. A member stated the matter as follows:

> "Here, at the *Marché de proximité*, there is an element of trust that means that we don't even mention the question of profit. I trust the price that is asked, and that this is what it is worth to produce it [product] without compromising the Earth. The way I see it, I try to live, they try to live, and we meet each other [through the Market]".

(Quote from a MPQ consumer)

List of References

Printed

Blake, Megan K. / Mellor, Jody / Crane, Lucy K.: "Buying Local Food: Shopping Practices, Place, and Consumption Networks in Defining Food as 'Local'". *Annals of the Association of American Geographers* 100(2), 2010, pp. 409-426.

Boulianne, Manon / Després, Carole / Doyon, Sabrina: "Manger 'local' dans la CMQ: relocalisation des systèmes alimentaires et ville durable". Research project presented to the Social Sciences and Humanities Research Council: Ottawa, October 2011.

DuPuis, E. Melanie / Goodman, David: "Should we go 'Home' to Eat?: Toward a Reflexive Politics of Localism". *Journal of Rural Studies* 21(3), 2005, pp. 359-371.

Ilbery, Brian / Maye, Damian: "Retailing Local Food in the Scottish–English Borders: A Supply Chain Perspective". *Geoforum* 37(3), 2006, pp. 352-367.

King, Robert P. et al.: *Comparing the Structure, Size, and Performance of Local and Mainstream Food Supply Chains*. Economic Research Report Number 99, United States Department of Agriculture (USDA), Economic Research Service. Washington D.C. 2010.

Internet

Équiterre: « Pourquoi adhérer aux paniers bio? » , retrieved 12.7.2014, from http://www.equiterre.org/solution/paniers-bio.

Naoto Minami

Communication of Food Information by Means of the Internet in Contemporary Japan

For thousands of years humankind has collected and exchanged information about food and cooking and communicated it to the next generation, both orally and in writing. In the past, such information was essential for survival because most people suffered from chronic nutritional deficiency. While the medium of information exchange among the lower classes of society was mainly oral, various cookery books were written for the upper classes who were in a position to enjoy good meals. In modern times, however, the differential between the food-related information available to the lower and upper classes in society has gradually decreased. In the twentieth century, the democratisation of information was advanced by the proliferation of food magazines, and restaurant guides such as the *Michelin* Guide and the Zagat Survey; in the twenty-first century, this process is being globally accelerated by means of the Internet.

This paper identifies some fields of investigation arising from the discussion of the advancement of communication about food by means of the Internet. It focuses on information about restaurants and eating out, as well as on home cooking. Communication regarding the former is mostly carried out via commercial websites, while communication with regard to the latter is based both on commercial websites and on social and personal networks. This article examines some examples of the online communication of information about food and cooking in contemporary Japan, on both commercial and personal levels. The results are considered in terms of the possible effects which such online food-related information and communication may have on Japanese food culture.

The Evolution of Food Information in Japan

In Japan, food information became socially significant in the early modern Edo period from the early sixteenth to the mid-nineteenth century. Because early modern Japan was one of the most up to date societies in terms of literacy, many cookery books were produced for the upper classes of this society, as well as for ordinary citizens in urban areas.[1] This led to the development of traditional Japanese food culture, which included sushi, tempura, and tea ceremony dishes (Kaiseki cuisine).

Later, when the 1868 Meiji Revolution led the forces of modernisation and westernisation of Japanese society, this changing situation also influenced its food culture. During this period, information about new varieties of food, such as European food and westernised dining, was introduced and extended through new media, such as women's magazines and cookery books. Until the early Showa period in the 1930s, it was a mixture of Japanese and westernised food culture that was discernible in Japanese urban society.[2]

After World War II, Japan experienced rapid economic growth, particularly in the 1960s and during the bubble economy of the 1980s. During this period, the seeking after food information became hugely fashionable among all groups in Japanese society. This desire for food information was catered for largely through the print media, by means of popular magazines, women's magazines, books specialising in gourmet food, and restaurant guides. This flood of food information reached its highest level in the late 1980s, when the Internet age had just begun.

Characteristics of Internet Information

Food is one of the most popular topics of communication on the Internet (Kobayashi 2014, p. 6). In this sense, food and the Internet are closely connected with each other. The exchange of information on the Internet has some distinct characteristics. Three Internet-connected phenomena which I consider to be the most important in terms of their relation to food, cooking or dining out, are the following:

1) Interactivity of information: A sender of information can expect a reply from the recipient, and someone who posts information on the Internet can expect a response from other users; thus, information creation on the Internet often takes the form of an interactive exchange.
2) Forming new types of communication networks (personal/social, anonymous, mass, etc.): senders and receivers of information can form various connections on the Internet – among existing friends, and among numerous anonymous users.

---

1   There are various studies about the cookbooks of the Edo period in Japan. One of the standard studies is by Harada 1989.
2   For cookbooks during this period, see Ehara / Higashiyotsuyanagi, 2008.

3) Publication of highly personal information: Personal information is often exchanged online among friends as well as between anonymous strangers.

The existing situation in Japan in relation to Internet-provided information concerning, firstly, restaurants and dining out, and secondly, home cooking, are dealt with below.

Restaurant-related Information

This section discusses the so-called "gourmet sites", i.e. websites featuring information about various restaurants, which have been proliferating on the Internet in Japan in relatively recent times. There are several Japanese gourmet sites, the two largest and most typical of which are Guru-Navi and Tabe-Log, and these are now assessed and analysed.

Guru-Navi (http://www.gnavi.co.jp/)

Guru-Navi, one of the oldest Japanese gourmet websites, was founded in February 1996. As there is an English-language version of the site (www.gnavi.co.jp/en/), it is more accessible than some other Japanese gourmet sites, to Internet users abroad.

In terms of the administration of the site, the main content of the Guru-Navi website consists of information supplied by restaurants themselves by way of an advertisement, for which each restaurant pays a membership fee. Member restaurants may be offered advice about the management of content by Guru-Navi, if necessary. Consumers can browse information on the website without being a member, but membership, which is free, often confers certain privileges or concessions on consumers in some of the member restaurants. Generally, users play a passive role on this site (Taki 2006, pp. 23-27; "Guru-Navi" 2009, pp. 86-90; Kawaguchi 2014, p. 12).

In terms of the scale of the site, the number of registered restaurants paying the full membership fee was approximately 52,000 in March 2014, which is not regarded as being particularly large. Conversely, the number of users, i.e. monthly visitors to the site, reached about 42 million so far this year (cf. "Kurohune" 2014). Figure 1 shows the homepage of the Guru-Navi Kyoto website featuring the dish of "Hamo".[3]

---

3   "Hamo" is a kind of fish which has a shape similar to that of an eel but which has a much more delicate taste. The "Hamo" dish is a Kyoto specialty.

Fig: 1 The dish "Hamo" as featured on the Guru-Navi Kyoto website (with permission).

GURUNAVI - Japan Restaurant Guide   1/3 ページ

ぐるなび GURUNAVI   Like 2.1k   Follow   94 followers   Restauran

Kyoto Restaurant Guide

An old capital city with a 1,000-year-old I
traditional comes alive
Colorful arrangement, subtle flavor, and s
taste. You must exert all five senses to er
culinary culture of Kyoto. It is a crystalliz
history and culture of Japan. Time passes
elegantly here, and refined estheticism...
Restaurant Guide »

GURUNAVI **Special Feature**

›Japanese Beef, you must taste!

›When visit japan enjoy taste Sushi!
›Japanese Sukiyaki and ShabuShabu, you must taste!
›Japanese Sashimi, you must taste!
›Restaurant Feature;You can find Restaurant meal with
English, Chinese, Korean menu

       ›All See

Quick Searcl

All Area

Japanese

more

Please feel free tc
inquire. Gurunavi
cierges are happ
find you a restau

We accept questi
Send e-m

**Eat s
in Ja**

Restaura
by GURl

Find out
Restaur

Japan Foodie

Let's e

Search Restaurants by Location   Map of Japan

 ›Tokyo
Capital of Japan, the global
mega city

 ›Osaka
A city for epicurean
extravagance

 ›Kyoto
An old capital city with a 1,000-
year-old history where
traditional comes alive

 ›Hokkaido
Treasure box of fresh
ingredients grown in rich soil of
the magnificent northern land

 ›Kanagawa
A resort in a city

 ›Aichi
Global center for automobile
industry

 ›Hyogo
Leading the food culture of
Japan with gifts from two seas

 ›Fukuoka
The largest city in Kyushu

Search Restaurants by Category

›Japanese	›Sushi	›BBQ Meat/Horumon	›Western/European
›Shabushabu	›Izakaya	›Italian	›Sushi/Fish/Seafood
›Yakiniku/BBQ	›Teppanyaki	›Indian	›Buffets
›Kaiseki	›Okonomiyaki	›Asian/Ethnic	›French

Tabe-Log (http://tabelog.com/)

Tabe-Log was established in March 2005, about ten years after the Guru-Navi gourmet website was set up. However, in 2010, the former overtook the latter in terms of user numbers. The popularity of Tabe-Log seems to stem from its method of administration.

Users can browse information about restaurants on Tabe-Log without being a member, but membership, which is free, allows them to contribute their own word of mouth reviews and evaluations of restaurants, to the site. The evaluation consists of five rankings, from one (worst) to five (best), which are related to "taste", "service", "ambience", "value for money", and "drinks selection". Further, an average evaluation score is given for every restaurant on the site, which serves as a reference point for users in their choice of restaurant. Thus, users play the main role on Tabe-Log (Kawaguchi 2014, pp. 12-13; "Kakakukomu" 2009, pp. 48-50).

Restaurants themselves can offer information by way of advertisements, if they become a member of Tabe-Log, with or without paying a fee. Restaurants that are paying members can display their advertisements in a favourable section of the site ("Kakakukomu" 2009, p. 50), and consumers can register the names of their favourite restaurants on the site also.

This style of administration has enabled Tabe-Log to advance its position among gourmet sites. In 2010 it became the largest gourmet site in terms of user numbers, and these numbers continue to increase. The number of monthly visitors to Tabe-Log is about 53 million (2014), which is one million more than the number of visits of this kind to the Guru-Navi site. The number of word of mouth reviews of Table-Log has also increased, reaching 5.24 million this year (2014). The number of restaurants registered on Tabe-Log is also high – about 770,000 (2014). However, this number includes non-members, who are automatically registered when a user contributes a review of a restaurant (Cf. note 5 above).

It can be confirmed that Tabe-Log utilises the advantages of Internet communication, particularly with regard to the interactive exchange of information, more successfully than Guru-Navi does, because it makes the best use of its high level of customer reviews. As a result, Tabe-Log overtook Guru-Navi in terms of user numbers in 2010, and in the following year, presumably as a consequence of this situation, Guru-Navi itself also began to introduce word of mouth restaurant evaluations ("Rebyu de" 2011; "Kuchikomi Saiten", 2011).

Problems Arising from Gourmet Sites

An examination of some of the problems, which seem to be on the increase, associated with gourmet sites, provides useful insights about the advantages and disadvantages of Internet facilitated communication.

Firstly, there is the possibility that word of mouth evaluations could possibly be manipulated. In fact, in 2012, it came to light that many such reviews on Tabe-Log had apparently been manipulated by agents who, it was claimed, had been paid by restaurant owners, eager to get higher evaluation scores, to do so. To counteract any such problem occurring, Tabe-Log has introduced preventative measures, such as improving the methods of evaluation which it employs, for example ("Netto ni Afureru" 2012; "Netto Kuchikomi" 2012).[4]

Secondly, there is the phenomenon of so-called "food porn". This does not refer to pornography per se, but is related rather to the fairly new trend among restaurant goers, that of taking photographs of the food served, in order to post it online, something which may cause discomfort to chefs and other customers. Some of these photographs might be taken just for pleasure, and some for the purpose of sharing them among friends who enjoy eating out. Thus, the act of taking a photograph of restaurant food stems from, and is encouraged by, Internet facilitated communication.[5]

Both of these problems – the manipulation of the evaluation of restaurants and food porn – are, perhaps, inherent aspects food information communicated via the Internet, because this is a medium which allows and enables interaction, on a global scale, to take place. Therefore, it is likely that, as the exchange of information about eating out becomes even more frequent on the Internet, further problems may well arise.

A Hypothesis

The following is a review of the evolution of methods of communication about restaurants in the twentieth and twenty-first centuries. In the early twentieth century, the *Michelin* Guide, which had been founded in France, became the most

---

4   The fact that some word of mouth reviews were apparently manipulated came to light in January 2012, and many newspapers and TV channels in Japan reported on it. The case is explained on the "Tabelog" page of Wikipedia (Japanese version). For Japanese Wikipedia see: http://ja.wikipedia.org/wiki/%E3%83%A1%E3%82%A4%E3%83%B3% E3%83%9A%E3%83%BC%E3%82%B8, retrieved 11.10.2014; for the relevant Tabelog page see: http://ja.wikipedia.org/wiki/%E9%A3%9F%E3%81%B9%E3%83%AD%E3% 82%B0, retrieved 11.10.2014.

5   "Food Poruno" 2014, presents some different opinions about this phenomenon.

trusted form of restaurant information available. It provided ordinary people with access to data about top-class restaurants. Then, in the late 1970s, the Zagat Survey began to be published in the USA. This Survey advanced the popularity and the openness of access to restaurant information through its system of reader contributions and evaluations. Finally, in 2005, Tabe-Log, a website which facilitates the interactive exchange of information through its word of mouth reviews, came into existence in Japan.

The communication of information about eating out has undergone significant advancement and acceleration by means of the new medium of the Internet. Moreover, the continuing growth in the area of food information exchange on the Internet can be expected to lead to an intensification in the development of new types of communication networks (peer networks, anonymous networks, etc.), as well as in the tendency towards self-publication of highly personal information on electronic social media. Thus, the communication of information about food is beginning to intrude into the territory of private life. The new electronic media have already significantly advanced the methods of information communication about eating out, and, thanks to the Internet, this tendency is likely to accelerate still further in the future. This year (2014), Yelp, a global word of mouth website, was launched in Japan. As a result, competition among Internet-based gourmet sites is likely to intensify even further.

Next, we move to the topic of home cooking.

Information about Home Cooking

The posting of highly personal information can also occur during the exchange of information about home cooking on the Internet. This section analyses two Japanese home cooking sites – "Cookpad", the largest Japanese home cooking site, and "Oh! Bento Labo", a very small but intimate site. This analysis advances the discussion about food and the Internet.

Cookpad (http://cookpad.com/)

Cookpad was founded in 1997, originally as a limited liability company, and later, in 2004, as a joint-stock company. In 1998, it began to post recipes which had been contributed by a limited number of members, who were paying a monthly fee of \500, on its website. In 1999, free membership was introduced. As a result, the number of recipes which were being contributed began to increase rapidly – from 510 in 1998 to 6,900 in January 2000. In 2006, Cookpad was transformed from a closed community site for lovers of cooking, to an open site and, since then, it has dramatically advanced in scale (Kobayashi 2014, pp. 6-7).

In February 2012, Cookpad had a total of 610 million browsers per month, and 15 million active users per month. This meant that, on average, one user browsed the site 40 times per month. The number of users rose to over 20 million in July 2013. The cumulative number of contributed recipes reached 1.2 million by April 2012, which rose to over 1.5 million in July 2013. Recently, Cookpad has begun to integrate advertising for supermarkets and other food companies into its website (Kobayashi 2014, p. 9; "Cookpad: Rehsipi de" 2012, pp. 62-66; "Cookpad: Kigyo ni Yoru", 2014).[6]

The large number of recipes (over 1.5 million) on Cookpad is one reason for its success as a website. However, the sheer volume of recipes might also be a cause of confusion for the user. In order to avoid this situation, Cookpad has developed a convenient search programme, which enables users to find an appropriate recipe quickly. For instance, they can search for recipes based on an ingredient, a kind of meal (breakfast, lunch or dinner), a type of dish (Japanese, Western, Chinese, Indian, etc.), or on cooking time. The website also allows quick browsing even during the busiest period of user activity, that is, from 4 p.m. to 6 p.m. daily (Kobayashi 2014, pp. 7-8; Uesaka 2009, pp. 15-20).

Another reason for Cookpad's success is that almost all of the recipes on the site are posted by amateurs and housewives who enjoy cooking. This has the advantage of making the recipes easy to follow and this is of particular benefit to Cookpad. However, another advantage has emerged, particularly for some female contributors – the gaining self-realisation, self-assertion or self-satisfaction, when their favourite recipes are praised by browsers who have successfully tried out them out and enjoyed them (Kobayashi 2014, p. 8-9; Uesaka 2014, pp. 15-17).

But this can also be considered as presenting Cookpad with an image problem. Users of the site include married and unmarried women. More than 95% of the people who use the site are women, and based on a calculation undertaken in 2012, 57% of Japanese women in their twenties, and 76 % in their thirties, use this site (Uesaka 2014, pp. 15-17). Conversely, it is relatively unknown among Japanese men of all generations. This is indicative of a gender bias relating to cooking, which may also suggest the existence of discrimination in terms of the allocation of domestic duties in contemporary Japanese society. Such socialised gender roles may be sustained or exacerbated through the use of Internet sites such as Cookpad.

---

6   Kobayashi 2014, p. 9; "Cookpad: Rehsipi de" 2012, pp. 62-66; "Cookpad: Kigyo ni Yoru", 2014.

Oh! Bento Labo (http://oh-bento-labo.com)

Though Cookpad is a joint-stock company managed in the same way as a business, there are many cooking websites which are managed on a personal basis. An example of such a site is the strangely-named "Oh! Bento Labo" website. The word "o-bento" is the polite version of "bento" in Japanese, just as "o-sushi" is the polite version of "sushi".

Bento is a typical Japanese lunch style. Many office workers and students take their "bento", prepared by their mothers or wives (occasionally fathers or husbands), to their office or school almost every day. Therefore, there are various "bento" websites, such as "justbento.com", "aibento.net" and "lunchinabox.net". Here, we focus Oh! Bento Labo.

This site was launched in February 2011 by its founder, Kiko Matsumoto, as a Facebook community page. Currently, the site has about 30 active members, from Japan and other countries, who contribute their favourite "bento" recipes and photographs to the site on an almost daily basis, as well as posting comments and chatting with each other. This site hosts a very small, intimate community. Oh! Bento Labo is unique among the many Japanese "bento" sites, in having published a book in 2013, which includes dozens of "bento" recipes and photos, along with a personal story about each family featured (Matsumoto 2013).

The implications arising from the existence and function of this type of private site dedicated to "bento" cooking and preparation, is worthy of consideration. The act of preparing "bento" for one's children and husband/wife can be viewed and presented as a typical expression of familial love and relationships (Arai / Sugimura / Katamura 2011, pp. 37-47). The members of the Oh! Bento Labo website often present information about personal matters, such as familial love, to the outside world. Some people, however, view this as a growing trend towards excessive personal exposure on the part of those who post such information. This seems to express a phenomenon characteristic of information on the Internet, which is, that personal information, which was formerly kept private within closed, intimate circles, now tends to be networked and to be propelled into the public sphere by those most intimately concerned. Indeed, this seems to be a central element of social networking and of Internet society today.

Conclusion

Since the end of the twentieth century, the evolution of the exchange of information about food and dining has reached a new stage, thanks the Internet. Enormous amounts of food information, whether about restaurants or home cooking, have been, and continue to be posted on the Internet and on other social networks. A great deal of personal information about food now flows into the public sphere. The dividing line between the personal and the public becomes obscure when exchanging information about food and dining on the Internet. The concept of the "public sphere", as expressed by Jürgen Habermas, thus seems to be open to question in this context

Internet society has various merits and demerits. In terms of food information, its many advantages can be appreciated. For example, a huge amount of restaurant-related information is available to those searching for a reputable restaurant in which to entertain their clients or to enjoy a good meal themselves; in addition, anyone wondering what to cook at home can easily find an appropriate recipe on the Internet.

However, there are unexpected pitfalls involved in Internet communication, such as the apparent manipulation of word of mouth reviews, and the disappearance of the separation between the private and public spheres of life, which may cause unexpected conflicts among people exchanging related information.

The amount of information about food on the Internet will surely continue to increase in the future. Therefore, careful consideration should be given to the optimum methods by which this medium can be utilised.

List of References

Printed

Arai, Mitsuko / Sugimura, Rumiko / Katamura, Sayaka: "Homemade Bento in the Modern Style: Its Diversity and Background with Special Reference to Recent Phenomena, Character Bento, Bento Danshi and Bento's Day". *Bulletin of Hokkaido Bunkyo University* 35, 2011, pp. 37-47.

"Cookpad: Kigyo ni Yoru Reshipikeisai no Honkakuka e" ("Cookpad Starts Posting Recipes Presented by Food Companies"). *AduerTimes* 28. 8. 2014.

Ehara, Ayako / Higashiyotsuyanagi, Shoko: *Kindai Ryorisho no Sekai* ("A Survey and Catalogue of the Cookbooks in Modern Japan"). Domesu Shuppan Press: Tokyo 2008.

"Food Poruno Mitsu no Aji" ("Food Porn: A Taste of Honey"). *Asahi Shinbun* (Newspaper) 23. 4. 2014.

"Guru-Navi: Shokuzai ni Shoki o Kensakuchu" ("Guru-Navi: Searching for a Chance by Means of Food Materials). *Nikkei Business 7*. 9. 2009, pp. 86-90;

Harada, Nobuo: *Edo no Ryorisi: Ryoribon to Ryori Bunka* ("History of Cooking in Edo Period: Cookbooks and Dining Culture"). Chuokoronsha Press: Tokyo 1989.

"Kakakukomu: Inshokuten o Kaiin Jugo Mannin de Hyoka" ("Kakaku-Com: Evaluation of Restaurants by 150 Thousand Members"). *Nikkei Business* 29. 6. 2009, pp. 48-50.

Kawaguchi Ishiya, "Internet to Shokuji" ("Internet and Dining"). *Vesta: Magazine of Food Culture* 93, 2014, pp. 12-17.

Kobayashi, Tetsu: "Cook Pad: Sohoko Sankagata no Ryori Reshipi Saito" ("Cook Pad: An Interactive and Participating Recipe Site Model"). *Vesta: Magazine of Food Culture* 93, 2014, pp. 6-11.

"Kuchikomi Saiten Guru-Navi mo" ("Guru-Navi Introduces Word of Mouth Evaluation Too"). *Asahi Shinbun* (Newspaper) 7. 11. 2011

"Kurohune Kuchikomi Saito Raishu" ("The World's Biggest Site "Yelp" Lands in Japan Today"). *Asahi Shinbun* (Newspaper) 9. 4. 2014.

Matsumoto, Kiko: *Minna no Oh! Bento* ("O! Bento for Everyone"). Nitto Shoin Press: Tokyo 2013.

"Netto ni Afureru Uso Rebyu: Tabelog kara Hakkakusita Jittai" ("False Word of Mouth Reviews Piling up on the Internet: The Truth Disclosed by the Tabe-Log's Case"). *Aera* 23. 1. 2012. pp. 17-19.

"Netto Kuchikomi Nigai Aji" ("Bitter Taste of Word of Mouth Reviews on the Internet). *Asahi Shinbun* (Newspaper) 27. 1. 2012.

"Rebyu de Netto o Seisu: Tabe-Log ga Guru-Navi ni Katta Riyu" ("Dominating on Internet by the Power of Word of Mouth Reviews is the Reason Why Tabe-Log Beat Guru-Navi"). *Aera* 26. 9. 2011, pp. 23-26.

"Cook Pad": "Reshipi de Ryutsu Kakumei" ("Cook Pad: A Marketing Revolution by Recipes"). *Nikkei Business* 23. 1. 2012, pp. 62-66.

Taki, Hisao: *Guru-Navi: No. 1 Saito eno Michi* ("Guru-Navi: A Way to the No. 1 Site"). Nihonkeizai Shinbunsha Press: Tokyo 2006.

Uesaka, Toru, *Roppyaku Mannin no Josei ni Sijisareru Cook Pad Toiu Business*" ("Cookpad as a Company Supported by 6 Million Women"). Kadokawa SSC Communications: Tokyo 2009.

Internet

aibento.net, retrieved 26. 9. 2014.

"Cookpad", retrieved 26. 9. 2014, from http://cookpad.com/.

"Guru-Navi", retrieved 26. 9. 2014, from http://www.gnavi.co.jp/.

justbento.com, retrieved 26. 9. 2014.

lunchinabox.net, retrieved 8.10.2014.

"Oh! Bento Labo", retrieved 26.9.2014, from http://oh-bento-labo.com.

"Tabe-Log", retrieved 26.9.2014, from http://tabelog.com.

www.gnavi.co.jp/en/, retrieved 10.10.2014.

Fionnuala Carson Williams

The Use of Proverbs in the Promotion of Food on the Internet

There is a long-standing link between food and proverbs. It is an established tradition for recipe books to employ proverbs to promote food and, to quote a fairly recent example, we find *Laughter is brightest where the food is*, used as the frontispiece to a book published in 2012 in North America (*The Meatlover's Meatless Celebrations. Recipes and Menus for Everything from New Year's Eve to Summer Picnics, Birthday Bashes to Christmas* [O'Donnel 2012]).

The use of proverbs in connection with food is, no doubt, in large part because of the ability of proverbs to advise in a memorable and catchy way but also, in many cases, because of their association with that which has been tried and tested over generations and an association with wholesomeness, the family, home cooking, and so on. Proverbs, of course, move with the times and, as we shall see, more up to date examples can also be found to go with new, innovative and fast foods.

A further reason for the use of proverbs in the promotion of food must surely be that many proverbs in themselves are intimately concerned with food: in any corpus a number which informs us about the food culture of the people who use them will always be found. Looking at some twentieth-century ones collected from oral tradition in Ireland, for instance, we can find proverbs about cooks, food production, *Long churning makes bad butter*, utensils, *A blunt knife shows a bad housekeeper*, and table manners, as well as about particular foods like butter, porridge, bread, meat, fish, fruit and vegetables and drinks, in particular, milk, tea and wine (Carson Williams 2000, pp. 22-33).

Well over thirty years ago Barbara and Wolfgang Mieder published an article about proverbs in advertising in the *Journal of Popular Culture* (Mieder / Mieder 1977, reprinted 1981). There they pointed out that researchers had shown that effective copy consists of short, simple sentences and that proverbs fit this requirement, as well being suitable because of their authoritative air (Mieder / Mieder 1981, p. 310). Their examples came from local and nation-wide magazines and newspapers of the USA where, just as today, and in much the same way, as Wolfgang Mieder's more recent article, again focussed on the print media, demonstrates (Mieder 2005), proverbs were being used in the promotion of food (Mieder / Mieder 1981, p. 319 and throughout). The earliest example that Barbara and Wolfgang Mieder gave was from 1929 and was by the Coca-Cola Company using an altered form of a well-known proverb, *All roads lead to Rome* > *All roads lead by Coca-Cola signs* (Mieder / Mieder 1981, p. 313), while McDonald's, when launching its "Quarterpounder" hamburger in 1974, used a proverb in its conventional form, *Man does not live by bread alone* (Mieder / Mieder 1981, p. 316). In addition to the work of Barbara and Wolfgang Mieder on proverbs in advertising Stephen D. Winick has discussed in detail their concomitant intertextuality, and therefore the importance to advertising, that proverbs carry (2011).

My short study shows that proverbs and proverb-like sentences are now also being used in advertisements on the Internet to promote food. This is not only by manufacturers of individual foodstuffs, which include alcohol, and both organic and fast food, but even by a supermarket to promote itself. Only certain foods will, however, be advertised on the Internet. One can see that some will only ever have a local appeal and companies manufacturing them will, no doubt, be primarily concerned with reaching that local market through television and the print media rather than the Internet. Some of their advertisements do, none the less, reach the Internet through YouTube and social media, and some products are deliberately promoted there by their manufacturers.

The supermarket mentioned is now the second largest retailer in the world both by profits and revenues (http://en.wikipedia.org/wiki/Tesco, retrieved 30.7.2014). The first shop, which was a grocery business specialising in food and drink, was founded in England in 1929 with the first supermarket opening in 1956; the company now has supermarkets in twelve countries (ibid.). It has been using a conventional proverb, *Every little helps*, as its strap line in all types of advertising that has appeared in English for around twenty years and this has transferred to its advertisements on the Internet (Ramchandani, retrieved 30.7.2014, from http://www.theguardian.com/media/2006/Sep/04/mondaymediasection.advertising). The proverb is practically always seen after the supermarket's name large or small, whether on the facades of its buildings or on till receipts in reality or online. As I perceive it, the proverb is used to try and promote the idea that this supermarket always attempts to be cheaper than its rivals. The supermarket is Tesco, that most successful international company which, among the international supermarkets, enjoys the largest central European market of them all (http://www.tescoplc.com/index.asp?pageid=356, retrieved 26.7.2014). In Poland, for instance, it has 450 stores which attract five million customers a week (ibid.). The proverb, *Every little helps*, is well known and is current and commonly used in the everyday English of Ireland. Naresh Ramchandani, writing in *The Guardian*, a quality, daily newspaper published in London, sings its praises as a very effective and attractive choice and points out that it is "short, rhythmic, memorable and refreshingly down to earth" and also that, in contrast to slogans used by other similar supermarkets, it is modest and, above all, flexible, stretching to cover new aspects of the things that the company provides (Ramchandani, retrieved 30.7.2014, from http://www.theguardian.com/media/2006/Sep/04/mondaymediasection.advertising). As well as indicating a little more value it can also indicate a little more quality, a little more service and cover such developments as home deliveries – a little more convenience – and the company's green policy – a little more environmental responsibility (ibid.). I notice that it even serves to cover the fact that the firm donates something to charity when a customer uses a cash machine at one of its outlets "We Donate every time you use a cash machine at Tesco Every little helps" (http://www.tesco.com/cashmachines, retrieved 30.7.2014). Ramchandani concludes her article by saying "Tesco is a brand for everyone and so is the slogan. Tesco is a brand that does nearly everything and so does the slogan. I challenge you to find me – or write me – another that stretches so wide but stays so strong" (ibid.). In English *Every little helps* can have a widespread application. It is not used in Polish. (When Tesco was opening up in Poland one marketing company making a pitch to market it there "realized that *Every little helps* wouldn't work — it didn't make sense" (Patrick Acheson, employee of the Polish marketing company, personal communication per Nick Acheson 11.8.2014.)

By contrast the fast food outlet, the Four Star Pizza company, does not base its current advertisement on the Internet on an old-style, homely proverb, but rather on the modern short and pithy *Size matters* (http://www.fourstarpizza.co.uk, retrieved 29.7.2014). This proverb originally appears to have had a sexual connotation, or at least an underlying one, but is now used more generally despite this. The company uses a variation on it to promote its side orders, *Sides matter!* thereby creating an arresting proverb which no doubt appeals to its young customers (to be seen also, for example, on the Four Star Pizza flyer from the branch at 377 Beersbridge Road, Belfast, and distributed door-to-door in 2014). The new-style proverb works well because it recalls the original *Size matters*, which various food companies have employed to create the impression that their pizzas are large, satisfying and therefore good value for their young, hungry consumers. As with many altered proverbs, it is a pun on the original with the leading word changed but sounding similar (Litovkina et al. 2008, p. 251). The company, Four Star Pizza, is not alone in using this particular proverb alteration. The dinner menu of the restaurant "Steak 44" in Phoenix, Arizona, is displayed online showing its side orders under the same heading "Sides matter" (http://www.steak44.com/uploads/steak_44_anchor_Dinner_menu-4-28-14.pdf, retrieved 29.7.2014). Four Star Pizza, set up in Dublin in 1988 and now operating throughout Ireland, strives to project an American image, in particular, a New York city image (http://

www.solocheck.ie/IrishCompany/Four-Star-Pizza-Holdings-129459, retrieved
1.8.2014); its website – through which food can be ordered, says "To bring you
a truly authentic NYC experience our dough is still freshly made every day" and,
besides *Sides matter* – uses other American-sounding expressions on its Internet
advertising, such as *we've been round the block a few times* and, in promoting
its pulled pork, *to go the whole hog* (http://www.fourstarpizza.co.uk, retrieved
29/07/2014). In response to an email from me, I received the following information from the company:

> "We have been using slogans like this for the past 3 years since we bought the company.
> We [use] them on menus, adverts and also on our own website. I am not sure what other
> information I can give you apart from [that] we like using them; we get good reactions
> from our customer base when we do and we will continue to use them to help commu-
> nicate the Four Star Pizza attitude (email from Brian Clarke to me 31.7.2014)".

The pithy, modern, *Sides matter*, appears to be eminently suitable as part of the
marketing campaign for this fast food.

I now turn to a more specialised readymade food, only available from some
supermarkets, and serving a much narrower market. Gü is a series of desserts,
originally chocolate-based, by Noble Desserts Holdings Ltd. UK, which appeal to
luxury with their intense, concentrated flavour. In order to assist this image the
company uses a set of proverbs and sayings in advertisements on the Internet such
as *Life is fleeting; clasp it hard with both hands* and *Pleasure is everything*. The sayings, as well as being used in the company's online advertisements, are also used
elsewhere, such as on packaging. In response to a query from me, Simon Cross of
Customer Care Gü Puds [*pudding*] said: "We use a consistent tone of voice and
style across all communications, so we don't consciously choose to use 'proverbs'
any differently in online vs [versus] offline media" (email to me 28.7.2014). On the
Internet they are shown in a series of images, each saying with its own illustration.
The sayings included are:

> *Pleasure is everything*
> *Give in to happiness*
> *Reject propriety: embrace variety*
> *Prudence is sooo 1658*
> *Life is fleeting; clasp it hard with both hands*
> *Seek delight*
> *Trust your impulses*
> *Ordinary is pointless*
> *Break free*

These are simply listed one after the other, the repetition of similar ideas serving to drive home the message to be self-indulgent. The list is finished off with a classical-sounding greeting "All hail the Gü decadents!" Simon Cross describes the list thus:

> "We have our Gü Manifesto (see below) which is printed onto most of our packaging. It is used on our UK, French, German and USA packaging [the list shown above then follows] (first email from Simon Cross to me on 30.7.2014)"

He further added that the Gü Manifesto "is translated into different languages depending on the country it is going to" (second email from Simon Cross to me on 30.7.2014). Under the "Gü manifesto" Simon Cross adds quotes from the company:

> What's it all about?
> "Gü believes you should enjoy the small pleasures in life. You deserve to let your hair down, have a break and indulge in all of life's pleasures, including the indulgence of great-tasting puds"

and "propriety" (*Reject propriety: embrace variety*) comes in for a special explanation:

> What's propriety?
> "Propriety means "*conformity to established standards of good or proper behaviour or manners*." Gü wants to encourage you to do what you fancy doing and give in to the small pleasures, without feeling restrained by what you feel you should do (first email from Simon Cross to me on 30.7.2014)".

In keeping with this, *Break free*, the saying with which the Manifesto ends, recalls the song "I want to break free" released in 1984 by Queen with a controversial video (http://en.wikipedia.org/wiki/I_Want_to_Break_Free, retrieved 1.8.2014). The song and video were banned for a while in the USA; however, the long-established company Coca Cola used the song in 2004 when launching its lower calorie drink, Coca-Cola_2, in the USA on ads on radio, television and cinema (http://en.wikipedia.org/wiki/Coca-Cola_2 retrieved 1.8.2014).

The classic, *Life is fleeting*, often used in poetry, and ultimately Biblical, from Ecclesiastes, is set in here amongst other sayings of more recent coinage. In the Bible we find it as *Life is fleeting, like a passing mist* (Ecclesiastes 1:2). The Gü Manifesto version runs: *Life is fleeting; clasp it hard with both hands*. Throwing a conventional proverb into the mix adds authenticity and the flavour of truth to the others on the list.

The date 1658, as in *Prudence is sooo 1658*, is also glossed:

<u>What does the reference to 1658 mean?</u>
"This is in fact when Oliver Cromwell, Lord Protector, died after his short time in power. He was a Puritan and lived according to these principles, including a disapproval of social pleasures (first email from Simon Cross to me on 30.7.2014)".

Well and good, but that was lost on me. The saying, which is current and commonly heard in the English of Ireland without that date, generally means that something is very old fashioned. On checking the relevance of 1658 I did see that this was also the year that a collection of maxims called, in English, *The Art of Prudence, The Art of Worldly Wisdom*, was published by a Jesuit in Spain (http://en.wikipedia.org/wiki/Baltasar_Gracián, retrieved 26.7.2014; Gracián, 1601-1658, ibid.). Is this just a coincidence, or the result of a copywriter's findings? Copywriters certainly use proverb collections as I know from one who used to work on Guinness advertisements (Killian O'Donnell, personal communication 1970s).

In the company's photographs on the Internet the product has also been linked to two popular sayings with productive endings:

Keep calm and carry on

giving the variant

Keep calm and eat Gü

and *I*, heart logograph for "love", *NY* giving what looks like *I love Gü*, the pronunciation simultaneously more or less providing *I love you* and *I love Gü*. [*Keep calm and carry on* was created in 1939 by the British Government as a morale-boosting poster in the face of impending war; however, it was never displayed publically; a copy was discovered in 2000 since when it has become extremely popular (http://en.wikipedia.org/wiki/Keep_Calm_and_Carry_On, retrieved 1.8.2014). The *I*, heart logograph, *NY* was designed in 1977 by Milton Glaser since when, with different endings, it has circled the world (http://en.wikipedia.org/wiki/heart_(symbol), retrieved 1.8.2014)].

Not only food, but also alcohol is being promoted on the Internet through proverbs. Food adverts are available to all who access the Internet but, in the United Kingdom, at least, advertisements for alcohol are only supposed to be accessed by people over 18 years. Advertisements for Harp, a lager beer created and first brewed in Ireland, features there. One, probably the 2013 Christmas version, but currently available, plays on the fact that harps are associated with angels and shows a man with white feathery wings, an angel, coming to earth. He is in Corn Market in Belfast city centre leading late night Christmas shoppers round in a conga, a simple dance in which people follow a leader. The punch line *Look on the Harp side* is an altered proverb in which 'Harp' has been substituted for "bright", *Look on the bright side,* or, *You should always look on the bright side,* being the usual forms. Altered forms of proverb, such as the Harp one, catch attention. I am not sure of the ancestry of the proverb but it was popularised through a comic song by Eric Idle which was the conclusion to a 1979 British film, *Life of Brian* c The Harp angel on earth series continues on billboards and on television at least. On a billboard near the Queen's University of Belfast strategically placed on Posnett Street to be visible to an avenue (Botanic Avenue) much frequented by students and other young people heading into the city centre, the "angel" shows up again with the same altered proverb *Look on the Harp side* with the precursor: *You are never more than five days from the weekend.*

Finally, turning to other individual food products, let us look at Mornflake products. These are organic oat flakes and such like which are packaged in England. In February an advertisement for them began running in a prime television slot on Channel 4 (email from Catherine Sadler to me 28.7.2014). The company which makes them sponsored the very popular "Piers Morgan Life Stories" programme. Although the programme was in the evening, the ad promoted them as breakfast food. The bustling family scene of people rushing about getting breakfast is accompanied by a sung voiceover employing a number of proverbs, including *No point crying over spilt milk.* Again, like *Every little helps,* this is a well-known proverb which evokes a homely scene, a safe proverb which is in everyday use in English as a metaphor. In the advertisement, however, it is used literally after one character bumps into another in the morning rush. In answer to my query about using proverbs, Catherine Sadler, their Marketing Coordinator, told me: "With the sponsorship indents we have gone down the 'proverb' route as we thought this gave the viewers a light hearted [thing to] watch and hopefully one that is memorable" (ibid.). The advertisement does not, however, appear to be on the Internet but, instead, a different one minus proverbs (http://www.youtube.com/watch?v=Ew6_DlzmdvY, retrieved 26.7.2014)

It is usual, and makes economic and brand awareness sense, to run the same marketing campaign across all media, the Internet, television, print, and so on and, as mentioned, this is the policy of the makers of Gü and also seems to be the case with Tesco and Four Star Pizza. With the makers of Harp and Mornflake it appears to be different. Mornflake currently have their proverb-less ads on prime morning I[ndependent]TV slots during "Good Morning Britain", "Lorraine", the programme which immediately follows it, and "Let's Do Lunch With Gino and Mel" (email from Catherine Sadler to me 28.7.2014). Although morning slots are not available for adverts for alcohol while the Internet is available 24 hours, television is still apparently, even after a quarter of a century of the Internet, the best medium for reaching a mass audience and selling more goods (item about Creative Art Awards for advertisements aired on "You and Yours" a BBC 4 consumer programme, on 28 or 29.5.2014). Manufacturers are obviously aware of this and one can see that certain foods will only ever have a local market.

In this short survey I have found that proverbs, classic and contemporary, both in their original and in altered forms, and also mock proverbs, pop up throughout the Internet in the promotion of food – organic food, luxury food, fast food and alcohol as well as food-based supermarkets. In addition to their inherent appeal, proverbs can be particularly successful in promoting food on the Internet because of their internationality, although their cultural baggage (intertextuality) will vary in different cultural areas.

List of References

Printed

Carson Williams, Fionnuala: *Irish Proverbs, Traditional Wit and Wisdom*. Sterling Publishing Co., Inc.: New York 2000.

Clarke, Brian: email to author on 30.7.2014.

Cross, Simon: emails to author on 27 and 30.7.2014.

Litovkina, Anna T. / Vargha, Katalin / Barta, Péter / Hrisztova-Gotthardt, Hrisztalina: "Punning in Anglo-American, German, French, Russian and Hungarian Anti-Proverbs". In Mieder, Wolfgang (ed.): *Proverbium, Yearbook of International Proverb Scholarship* 25. The University of Vermont: Vermont 2008, pp. 249-288.

Mieder, Barbara / Mieder, Wolfgang: "Tradition and Innovation: Proverbs in Advertising". *Journal of Popular Culture* 11, 1977, pp. 308-319.

Mieder, Barbara / Mieder, Wolfgang: "Tradition and Innovation: Proverbs in Advertising". In: Mieder, Wolfgang / Dundes, Alan (eds.): *The Wisdom of Many. Essays on the Proverb*. (Garland Folklore Casebooks 1 Dundes, Alan, Gen. ed.). Garland Publishing Inc.: New York and London 1981, pp. 309-322.

Mieder, Wolfgang: "'A proverb is worth a thousand words': folk wisdom in the modern mass media". In Mieder, Wolfgang (ed.): *Proverbium, Yearbook of International Proverb Scholarship* 22. The University of Vermont: Vermont 2005, pp. 167-233.

O'Donnel, Kim: *The Meatlover's Meatless Celebrations, Recipes and Menus for Everything from New Year's Eve to Summer Picnics, Birthday Bashes to Christmas*. Da Capo Press: Boston 2012.

Sadler, Catherine: email to author 28.7.2014.

Smith, William (compiler): *The Oxford Dictionary of English Proverbs*. Oxford University Press: Oxford. 3ed. 1970; 1975 reprint.

Winick, Stephen D.: "'Fall into the (Intertextual): Proverbs, Advertisments and Intertextual Strategies". In Mieder, Wolfgang (ed.): *Proverbium, Yearbook of International Proverb Scholarship* 28. The University of Vermont: Vermont 2011, pp. 339-380.

Personal Communication

Acheson, Patrick: personal communication per Nick Acheson 11.8.2014.

O'Donnell, Killian: personal communication 1970s.

Internet

Ramchandani, retrieved 30.7.2014, from http://en.wikipedia.org/wiki/Always_Look_on_the_Bright_Side_of_Life.

http://en.wikipedia.org/wiki/Coca-Cola_2, retrieved 1.8.2014.

http://en.wikipedia.org/wiki/Baltasar_Gracián, retrieved 26.7.2014.

http://en.wikipedia.org/wiki/heart_(symbol), retrieved 1.8.2014.

http://en.wikipedia.org/wiki/I_Want_to_Break_Free, retrieved 1.8.2014).

http://en.wikipedia.org/wiki/Keep_Calm_and_Carry_On, retrieved 1.8.2014.

http://en.wikipedia.org/wiki/Tesco, retrieved 30.7.2014.

http://www.fourstarpizza.co.uk, retrieved 29.7.2014.

(http://www.solocheck.ie/IrishCompany/Four-Star-Pizza-Holdings-129459, retrieved 1.8.2014).

http://www.steak44.com/uploads/steak_44_anchor_Dinner_menu-4-28-14.pdf, retrieved 1.8.2014.

http://www.tescoplc.com/index.asp?pageid=356, retrieved 26.7.2014.

http://www.theguardian.com/media/2006/Sep/04/mondaymediasection.advertising.http://www.tesco.com/cashmachines, retrieved 30.7.2014.

Ewa Kopczyńska

Novelty with a Traditional Twist: Food Co-Operatives as Short Food Chains in the Global Network

For several decades, Alternative Food Networks (Afns) have been the subject of research and analysis by scholars of various disciplines, and they have also become an important aspect of development policies during the past twenty years (Goodman / DuPuis / Goodman 2014; Maye 2010). Today, as a response to the threats against, and the weaknesses of, industrial food production, a variety of organisations, associations, social movements, market entities, and individual enterprises, have sprung up *en masse*, with the objective of forming new, alternative food patterns. The two forms I have researched – farmers' markets and food co-operatives – are examples of alternative food networks.

The consumers' food co-operatives represent a new kind of a food supply chain, something which has existed in certain countries of Western Europe and the USA since the 1970s (Katchova / Woods 2011). It is only in the last few years that these food co-operatives also came to be set up in Poland. In this article, I aim to focus on the values and social networks of food co-operatives, as well as on the channels and types of communication which they employ. Since co-operatives refer to tradition, direct exchange and locality, I compare them to old and traditional forms of farmers' markets in order to reveal and to clarify co-operative ideas.

The theoretical framework of AFNs is linked in particular to the context of developed capitalist Western economies. When locating the research in Central and Eastern Europe, it is thus necessary to take into account the specific nature of food chains in the countries concerned. These include widespread informal food provision (Alber / Kohler 2008; Round / Williams / Rodgers 2010), traditional agriculture based on family households (Gilarek / Mooney / Gorlach 2003), "quiet sustainability" (Smith / Jehlička 2013), and small-scale food production involving procedures which often differ from those set out in European Union guidelines in this regard (Master 2012).

Farmers' markets and food cooperatives are based on short food supply chains, and on direct relations between the consumer and the producer, and they both invoke the idea of local food, sustainability, and traditional means of food production. In this article, however, I wish to demonstrate how deep the differences between the two forms are, and how distant from each other the social communities in which these forms operate also are. These differences are structural (linked to the social positions of their participants) and communicational (using different channels and domains of communication).

Farmers' markets are traditional forms of exchanging food as well as of maintaining social networks of geographically and demographically limited communities (Maroszek 1990). This tradition can be characterised as being rooted in pre-industrial agricultural communities. A co-operative is usually an informal group of consumers, which does its food purchasing together and then shares it. The quality of the food in question is high and it is bought directly from the producer, that is, from a trusted source. This exchange provides the farmer with a regular income, and the co-operative members with ongoing access to fresh, seasonal produce. However, the co-operatives' lack of a hierarchical structure, and the informal engagement of members with the organisation, indicate that a new social movement has come into existence (Bilewicz / Potkańska 2013).

Research Methods

The article is based mainly on in-depth individual interviews which were conducted in Małopolska during June and July 2013. Thirteen clients of farmers' markets, two customers of a health-food shop, and five co-operative members, were asked about their opinions, motives, customs and everyday practices concerning food provision. These interviews were accompanied by observation and visual data collection.

The interview citations used in this paper provide details of (a) the marketplace where the individual interviews were held ("Krze" – Krzeszowice; "Wie" – Wieliczka; "Kra" – Kraków; "Wo" – Wojnicz; "Brze" – Brzesko; "Pro" – Proszowice), (b) the type of AFN in question ("FM" – farmers' market, "HF" – health-food shop, "CO" – co-operative), (c) gender, and (d) age.

Communication, Directness, and Politics

Thanks to their regularity, farmers' markets allow relatively constant social relations and repeated contacts between farmers and customers to develop. The pleasure gained from social contact at the market is evident in the following statement:

> "I just like shopping there. And I think that when you have to queue [laughs] or something, then you buy this, and then you buy something else, and there is contact with the seller. And you don't need so much money or the supermarket trolley so full…
> "(Kra/FM/m/50)

The relationships at farmers' market can be seen to have two functional aspects. The face-to-face relationship between customers and traders gives them the pleasure and satisfaction of community affiliation, while that between customers themselves provides them with the opportunity to get useful information from each other:

> "It sometimes happens that you meet somebody and this is very nice. Then you can recommend to each other where the good strawberries are being sold or you can be warned that they are tasteless [laughs]." (Kra/FM/f/40)

The direct and ongoing relationship between consumer and producer (or between consumer and seller) helps both sides to operate in predictable conditions and to stay well informed about food matters. They know each other's expectations and needs. Tasting, smelling and discussing food quality are all part of the shopping ritual. Clients expect the sellers to act on behalf of the consumers by providing good quality food, and the consumers in turn show loyalty to the farmers and respect for their work by buying their goods. The seller knows that he can benefit financially by being aware of his clients' needs and attitudes, and the buyer knows that he, too, can benefit by having experience and knowledge of food production. There are very few labels on food, no instructions, and there are also many varieties, sizes, and colours of, and prices for, the products on offer. Choosing the best kind of potatoes, apples or strawberries involves practical knowledge as well as communication skills and social capital:

> "I grew up in a rural village, and I had a garden with my grandma. I know exactly what carrots and parsnips used to look like. My grandmother planted them, and very often the roots were tangled, rarely so smooth and beautiful as in children's books. So this strange form of vegetables means that they are natural… "(Krze/FM/w/ND)

On comparing the above characteristics of the kinds of relations that usually exist at farmers' markets with those pertaining to co-operatives, fundamental differences between them become apparent. A representative of the co-operative provides information and food-quality assurance in food co-operatives. In most Polish co-operatives (cf. Bilewicz / Potkańska 2013), there are a few members, who are profoundly committed to food-supply activities. They search for producers, contact farmers, and then arrange the trade. Other members order goods and participate in sharing or packing activities or they sometimes engage in internal food exchange. The path "from farm to fork" is short but involves an indirect producer-consumer relationship. The representative of co-operative makes the decision, relying on his/her consumer competence, experience, trust, values and calculations. If the quality of the product is not satisfactory, the consumers report their claims to their "agent" and he/she contacts the supplier about the matter.

"Generally we don't meet these people [producers] and ultimately we don't know how they operate. But there is a possibility, I mean the co-operative has contact with the farmers." (Kra/Coo/f/40)

The majority of Polish co-operatives are only a few years old. As such, they continue to grapple with organisational and logistical problems, and with refining their statutes, rules and regulations. The co-operative members whom I interviewed, pointed to difficulties in storing food provided by the producer before customers could collect it. The ideals of community, equality, and engagement, restrain "co-operativists" from developing and formalising a structure based on work division, paid jobs, deep specialisation, and hierarchy. They, therefore, search for social and organisational dynamics as an alternative to the above scenario. The sources of inspiration and know-how are often other co-operatives active in the country as well as those operating abroad. The network of interactions between co-operatives as groups, as well as between individual members, is strong and vigorous, and the community of consumers flourishes accordingly.

Political and social activism is a typical aspect of most co-operatives' outlook. The sharing of values is no less important than the sharing of bread and vegetables. Clients of farmers' markets are oriented towards private values (household sustainability, family well-being, caring for friends and neighbours, local tradition), but the legitimation for food co-operatives is rooted in a far-reaching social project. Buying food directly from farmers is never just about food. It is also about a new global food system, a food market without the domination of supermarkets, one based on justice, local communities, global environmental safety, small-scale food producers, and a healthier lifestyle, or, at the very least, about the development of a better society based on direct food exchange. The "political tomato" can sometimes be seen more clearly than other aspects of co-operatives' outlook, but in essence it is always there.

In summary, farmers' markets – as traditional, pre-modern short food chains – and co-operatives – as contemporary post-modern short food chains – are characterised by differing types of social relations. At farmers' markets, directness means that there is individual contact between producer and consumer, as well as sociability, trust, and a community of experiences associated with the food itself. In co-operatives, on the other hand, directness is understood as involving more lasting and exclusive relations, but it features intermediaries in the form of the leaders of the co-operative itself. Social ideas and aspects of ideology are an area of agreement, but it is the consumers themselves who are mostly part of the community of ideas. Differences are also manifested in terms of channels and forms of communication.

Talking about Food: Benches and Mailing Lists

The procedures and sources involved in the purchasing of food by co-operatives can vary a great deal. But all sides use the Internet as a tool of communication. As most co-operative members and clients live in big cities, and as they are busy with their everyday middle-aged life and middle-class professions (Soper 2008), they meet in person only occasionally. Most co-operatives use social media tools, e.g. blogs, fan pages, or discussion groups, for communication purposes. Some of them construct their own tools, such as order forms or shift schedules. All these forms facilitate the development of flexible and informal networks which can easily be kept up-to-date. In the co-operative movement, therefore, post-modern changeability, social mobility, and adjustment to new opportunities, are inter-twined with pre-modern community dynamics, face-to-face interactions, direct-ness, and locality.

Regular, even ritual-style shopping at farmers' markets is ingrained in every-day family and community life. The clients have their habits and find pleasure in following them:

"Oh, I like visiting the market so much. […] I have many friends there. […] One says this, one says that, and it's nice. So I don't hurry. It's more about talking, sitting, looking around [than buying]" (Brze/FM/f/70). The pleasure afforded by sociability is also important among co-operative members. However, they de-fine sociability as a demand that is unfulfilled in everyday life – which they find too-fast moving and based on indirect relations:

"This Bartek said that for them the vegetables play a secondary role, maybe not se-condary, but it is just as important that they do something together, that they act so-ciably. So maybe, if people all live in these virtual worlds, with their mobiles and the Internet, all this makes people want to go out of these worlds and enter the real world. So this co-operative gives them the opportunity, doesn't it? "(Kra/Coo/m/30)

At the same time e-communication is widely accepted and used as a tool for com-munication within co-operatives and between co-operatives. The opportunities provided by the Internet – the popularisation of co-operative ideas, the placing of orders, and the setting up of meetings for packing and collecting food, and also the using of a crowd-funding site (www.polakpotrafi.pl) for organising the Open Polish Co-operative Meeting this year (2014) – are leveraged by the members. In a manner similar to the use made of cyberspace by most new social movements (Castells 2012; Offe 1985; van Aelst / Walgrave 2002), cyberspace is also a natural and friendly environment for the co-operative movement. It functions effectively for linking members and adherents of co-operatives together.

When it comes to food producers, however, this is no longer the case. Most farmers in Poland are much closer to traditional communication platforms than to electronic ones. Directness, the foundation of short food chains, is difficult to accomplish in the producer-consumer arena. Distance is also built into the normative sphere. The ideals of global sustainability, environmental issues, and political engagement, often do not interfere with small-scale interests, private values, and traditional foodways, despite the common basis of both. The absence of shared experiences, and the limitations which exist in communication between co-operatives and farmers, give rise to a lack of trust between them:

> "Of course, we can also educate farmers themselves. But if he is dim, he just won't understand, so I am not sure if there is any point [in doing this]. Even if you educate him and tell him this and that, he will do it his way, just because he has always done it like this. Farmers are a bit dumb, unfortunately. [...] So it must be people from the city, who move to the village and set up their farms, and they know something." (Kra/Coo/f/50).

At the farmers market producers and clients can agree on what a good product is and how it should be produced. And this, plus the production and consumption experiences they share, could be a solid basis for communication. The ideal of directness at a traditional food market is usually casual, and rarely intense; nevertheless, it is effective. The global values of co-operatives locate their members within Internet-based worldwide circles of activists, new movements, social media gatherings, and transnational institutions. Their ideals of locality tend to make them incline towards small-scale food producers and traditional farming. In the Polish economic and cultural context, attempts to bring these aspirations together tend to be unsuccessful.

Conclusions: The Need for Trust

There is a clear difference in the types of social relations in the two short food chains which I have studied. Traditional forms of direct food exchange are distinguished from more recent types by differing visions of the food system, lack of trust, and divergences in terms of communication. Food co-operatives as an alternative form of food networks refer to post-modern, and, at the same time, pre-modern ideals of sociability, directness, locality, quality of food / life and sustainability (cf. Gorlach and Mooney 2008). Co-operative members share these values, experiences, and aims, and also a level of elementary consensus within the perspective of the foodscape exist.

The producer-consumer sphere is much more uneven, at least within the Polish context (but see also Pilgeram 2011). The remedy for a lack of trust is the emergence of a new form of agriculture, organic farming sector and the CSA ideas

(Community Supported Agriculture). A differentiation of food co-operatives in Poland can also be anticipated. They are starting to flourish, not only in metropolitan areas, but in smaller cities and towns as well. It is most likely that they will consist of groups with different ideals and aims that can more fully overlap traditional values.

We might also anticipate that at least some of farmers markets might turn into new types of "health-food markets". This change, which can already be seen in large cities, brings them closer to the expectations of new food movements. However, it may also offer a possibility for the preservation of the resources of traditional trust and respect typical of traditional food markets in contemporary alternative food networks.

List of References

Printed

Alber, Jens / Kohler, Ulrich: "Informal Food Production in the Enlarged European Union". *Social Indicators Research* 89(1), 2008, pp. 113-127.

Bilewicz, Aleksandra / Potkańska, Dominika: "Jak kiełkuje społeczeństwo obywatelskie? Kooperatywy spożywcze w Polsce jako przykład nieformalnego ruchu społecznego" ("How Does Civil Society Sprout? Food Co-operatives in Poland as an Example of an Informal Social Movement"). *Trzeci Sektor* 31(3), 2013, pp. 25-44.

Castells, Manuel: *Networks of Outrage and Hope: Social Movements in the Internet Age*. Polity Press: Cambridge 2012.

Gilarek, Katarzyna / Mooney, Patrick H. / Gorlach, Krzysztof: "Moral Dilemmas of Globalization: Polish Agriculture at the Crossroads". *Australian Journal of Social Issues* (1)38, 2003, pp. 1117-1128.

Goodman, David / DuPuis, Erna M. / Goodman, Michael K.: *Alternative Food Networks: Knowledge, Practice, and Politics*. Routledge Studies of Gastronomy, Food and Drink. Routledge: London [u.a.] 2014.

Gorlach, Krzysztof / Mooney, Patrick H.: "Agriculture, Communities, and New Social Movements: East European Ruralities in the Process of Restructuring". *Journal of Rural Studies* 24(2), 2008, pp. 161-171.

Maroszek, Józef: *Targowiska wiejskie w Koronie Polskiej w drugiej połowie XVII i XVIII wieku* ("Village Markets of the Polish Kingdom in the Second Half of 17th Century and in the 18th Century"). Dissertationes Universitatis Varsoviensis 401. Dział Wydawnictw Filii UW: Białystok 1990.

Master, Kathryn de: "Designing Dreams or Constructing Contradictions? European Union Multifunctional Policies and the Polish Organic Farm Sector". *Rural Sociology* 77(1), 2012, pp. 89-109.

Maye, Damian et al.: "Alternative Food Networks". *International Journal of Sociology of Agriculture & Food*, 20(3), 2010, pp. 383-389.

Offe, Claus: "New Social Movements: Challenging the Boundaries of Institutional Politics". *Social Research* 52(4), 1985, pp. 817-868.

Pilgeram, Ryanne: "'The Only Thing That Isn't Sustainable… Is the Farmer': Social Sustainability and the Politics of Class among Pacific Northwest Farmers Engaged in Sustainable Farming". *Rural Sociology* 76(3), 2011, pp. 375-393.

Round, John / Williams, Colin / Rodgers, Peter: "The Role of Domestic Food Production in Everyday Life in Post-Soviet Ukraine". *Annals of the Association of American Geographers* 100(5), 2010, pp. 1197-1211.

Smith, Joe / Jehlička, Petr: "Quiet Sustainability: Fertile Lessons from Europe's Productive Gardeners". *Journal of Rural Studies* 32, 2013, pp. 148-157.

Soper, Kate: "Alternative Hedonism, Cultural Theory and the Role of Aesthetic Revisioning". *Cultural Studies* 22(5), 2008, pp. 567-587.

van Aelst, Peter / Walgrave, Stefaan: "New Media, New Movements? The Role of the Internet in Shaping the 'Anti-globalization' Movement". *Information, Communication & Society* 5(4), 2002, pp. 465-493.

Internet

Katchova, Ani L. / Woods, Timothy A.: "The Effectiveness of Local Food Marketing Strategies of Food Cooperatives." Selected Paper Prepared for Presentation at the Agricultural and Applied Economics Association's 2011 AAEA & NAREA Joint Annual Meeting, Pittsburgh, PA, July 24-26.2011, retrieved 30.7.2014, from (http://ageconsearch.umn.edu/bitstream/103918/2/Food%20Coop%20 Paper%20AAEA.pdf.

Anna Mlekodaj

A Local Food Product and the Ethno-Future: The Online Case of Polish Mountaineers' Regional Cheese "*Oscypek*"

One of the symptoms of post modernity is the occurrence of basic change in the cultures of small communities which seek to preserve their distinctive lifestyles. Cultural co-existence, which has hitherto been a dynamic part of local communities, is being replaced by competition connected with a fight for survival. It appears that only those cultures, which show skill in finding their place in the reality of modern marketing, will be able to survive and be successful in the future. The launch of products with ethnic originality in the market place enables people who cultivate traditional professions connected with these goods to earn their living from this kind of entrepreneurship. However, this is only possible in the case of products which have managed to gain a brand. Guaranteed quality and, in case of food, compliance with an original recipe, have significant influence on the economic success of a particular product. A trademark accompanied by relevant procedures, including legal ones, is the main criterion for distinguishing valuable original products from various kinds of imitations or inventions which are non-genuine in nature and which are not protected by trademark legislation. A brand safeguards the essence of tradition in a product and it also limits general freedom of production to those who have legally secured the trademark. In order to produce traditional goods, representatives of a particular culture have to gain the relevant authorisation to do so, something which is confirmed by means of a certificate issued by a group of experts. A brand cannot be inherited; it must be gained through satisfying the conditions and procedures laid down for its attainment. The market launch of branded goods, which are popular among customers, has apparently become a fundamental prerequisite for the survival of a local culture in the global world (Chanock 2000, pp. 24-25).

The processes of the commodification and the commercialisation of culture, which have been progressing apace in recent decades, have served to stir up controversy because, in the opinion of some, these developments inevitably lead to a lowering of the value placed on tradition in such circumstances. The market regulates the activities of ethno-entrepreneurs according to the laws of economics. The purchase of goods can be made by anybody who can afford it, that is, by "locals", but also by "strangers" who are not ethnic citizens. Because "locals" are usually in the minority and are generally not interested in purchasing their native culture in the form of goods, "strangers" are the main target of a cultural marketing policy, which protects and promotes itself through partial commodification. In terms of a tourist's expectations when visiting a locality, a regional product should enable him to learn more about the local culture, that is, it should allow him to "taste" that culture, and to approach its real sources. As a visitor, he is seeking to cross the barrier that separates him from a perceivable "otherness" which he actually finds appealing. Meanwhile, ethno-goods destined for trade, in the free market environment, lose their aura, which originates from their ability to provide delight, thanks to contact with authentic values. Thus, an outsider who is open to experiencing and accepting "otherness" finds only its outward appearance rather than its essential core in these circumstances (Hillman 2003, p. 182).

On the other hand, culture's ability to create and to introduce to the market its own branded products proves that it is able to exist and to be successful in new economic and social conditions. The example of the Podhale Region in southern Poland shows that traditions, which can be successfully marketed, are cultivated, while others disappear. However, ethno-entrepreneurs are fully aware of the specificity of their goods and they understand that the intangible spirit of tradition is an integral part of their products. They also understand that commercial success strengthens both the sense of ethnicity and the social status of a community which is able to earn a living, thanks to its own culture, in an environment of strong market competition. Hitherto, vanishing traditions, which were mainly associated with the past and with civilisational under-development, have in many instances now become the basis for investment in the future (Comaroff 2011, pp. 30-40). This ethno-future prospective brings renewed life to areas, which, without cultural difference, would be doomed to languish on the arid peripheries of the global world.

Joining the EU gave Poland new possibilities for managing its regional cultural inheritance. Through the initiative of the Polish Government, many regions have registered their traditional culinary products with EU schemes of geographical indications and traditional specialities, called Protected Geographical Indication (PGI), Protected Designation of Origin (PDO), and Traditional Specialities Guaranteed (TSG). This means that certain traditional products, which have achieved such designations, must now be produced and prepared following specified procedures. These procedures have been an integral part of the traditions of a particular region for centuries and they are now strictly protected when they directly concern a product branded under EU law (Krawczyk-Wasilewska / Orszulak-Dudkowska 2013, pp. 113). The creation of, and protection afforded by, a brand, such as the EU product designations, can lead to the separation of certain aspects of a region's culture from the culture of the region as a whole, something which often involves the misappropriation of cultural elements, such as those connected with a traditional foodstuff, by an organised group of manufacturers. As a result of their endeavours, and supported by local authorities, hitherto popular and commonly-used names of traditional products have become reserved trademarks which can be used only by those – such as the aforementioned associations – who fulfil certain formal and organisational conditions. Those organisations which meet the requirements, which usually involve both time, effort and cost, have defined cultural privileges – they represent their region and attain the rank of guardians of tradition, for example. Moreover, they are supported by an advertising campaign, which is organised for them in order to promote the region in question, and they also promote their region themselves. The advertising campaign, which is tailored to suit the products involved, uses all possible media types to promote its endeavours, but the Internet plays the most important role in this regard.

An example of a local foodstuff functioning as an ethno-investment is a traditional sheep's cheese called "Oscypek". In the vision of the culture of the Podhale Region presented on the Internet, "Oscypek" holds one of the most prominent positions in that context, and information is also provided for "Oscypek" as an ethno-product with a reserved brand, which is supposed to enter European markets.

On 28th September 2005, a smoked variety of sheep's cheese produced in the Podhale mountain region and called "Oscypek" was listed as a traditional product by the Polish Ministry of Agriculture. Since 14 February 2008, "Oscypek" has been registered as a product with EU Protected Designation of Origin (PDO) status, thanks to an application made by the Regional Association of Sheep and Goat Farmers in Nowy Targ, and supported by the Polish Highlanders Alliance and the authorities of Tatra and Nowy Targ District. In 2007, the local Manufacturers' Co-operative called "Gazdowie" was set up in Leśnica, in the Podhale Region, and this co-operative consists of senior shepherds who meet all the EU requirements for "Oscypek" production.

Consequently, a proto-type model of "Oscypek" was distinguished in order to delineate all the features basic to the identity of this type of cheese. Thus, the traditional freedom of production, when each senior shepherd produced cheese in his own way, has now been curtailed by the necessity of fulfilling requirements defined in percentages, centimetres and grams, in order to meet official EU regulations concerning the product. Both on the web page of the Ministry of Agriculture and Rural Development (www.minrol.gov.pl, retrieved 8.7.2014) and on the application form for the registration of "Oscypek" for PDO status, which is also available in the Internet (www.oscypek.wniosek.pdf, retrieved 8.7.2014), there is a detailed description of "Oscypek" cheese:

> "[…] "Oscypek" is in the shape of a double-sided cone. Its middle part, which is the broadest, is cylindrical and decorated with hollow and convex patterns. The stripe of ornamentation is divided into three parts: the middle one (the main one) and two side ones. Length: 17–23 cm. Diameter: 6-10 cm. Mass: 0,6–0,8 kg. ["Oscypek" is a] hard, elastic pulp with a pronounced smoked aroma, and has a slightly salty taste. It has a creamy colour when cut in two, slightly darker close to the rind; a colour similar to white is acceptable. Its water content is from 42% to 50%. Its fat content in dry mass is from 40% to 60%."(www.minrol.gov.pl/pol/Jakosc-zywnosci/Produkty-regionalne-i-trady-cyjne/Lista-produktow-tradycyjnych/woj.-malopolskie/Oscypek-oszczypek, retrieved 8.7.2014).

The granting of PDO status to "Oscypek" involved the outlining of the area where this product can be manufactured for PDO purposes. Consequently, cheese production under the brand name "Oscypek" has been limited to small mountainous areas in the south of Poland, where shepherd traditions have deep roots. Senior shepherds from these areas are now allowed to produce PDO-branded "Oscypek" upon receipt of a relevant quality certificate, which is granted by the Polish Agricultural and Food Quality Inspection (IJHARS) association.

In spite of its obvious benefits, not all senior shepherds who are entitled to do so actually apply for the relevant certificate. The usual explanations for their reluctance in this regard include the high costs involved and the stringent inspections conducted by state officials who represent the EU. To encourage producers to apply for the right to produce the PDO-branded "Oscypek" legally, representatives of the Association of Sheep and Goat Farmers, the Tatrzańsko-Beskidzkiej Co-operative of the Manufacturers "Gazdowie", local authorities, and the Agricultural Market Agency, take extensive measures to promote "Oscypek" as a branded product. All of these actions are, to a great extent, conducted on the Internet and they form a part of a wider culinary discussion currently being conducted on that mass-communication medium.

"Three Symbols of Taste" Campaign

In February 2013, on the initiative of the Agricultural Market Agency supported by the Polish Ministry of Agriculture and Rural Development, an information campaign entitled "Three Symbols of Taste" was launched all over Poland. The main goal of the campaign was, and is, to promote Polish products which have been granted PDO, PGI or TSG status by the EU. The campaign's Internet web page contains, not only details connected with trademarks, product descriptions and producers, but also recipes, addresses of places where products can be purchased, and a photo gallery of the various products in question. "Oscypek" as a product, which was granted PDO status by the EU, is included in the élite group of products representative of Polish food in the wider world.

The Tourist "Oscypek Route"

On the initiative of the Tatra Agency of Development Promotion and Culture, what has been named the "Oscypek Route", has been mapped. This route leads visitors to shepherds' huts which have EU certificates entitling them to produce "Oscypek". The promotional materials available contain maps of the whole Route, and the relevant shepherds' huts are indicated on these maps. The promotional material also provides information about how to recognise "Oscypek" which has been produced according to EU norms, and also about senior shepherds who are hosts of huts on the Route. Following the "Oscypek Route" provides a visitor with the opportunity to discover a vast area of the Podhale Region. All shepherds' huts marked on the maps produce cheese according to old customs and use traditional shepherd equipment. Each senior shepherd visited by tourists is prepared to play the role of a custodian of tradition. Moreover, tourists also have a chance to accompany junior shepherds during the milking of the sheep, and to purchase "Oscypek" directly from a producer. Tourists thus enter the world of traditional shepherds and learn about their work and lifestyle directly from real life, despite the fact, or maybe thanks to it, that everything happens in the twenty-first century.

Although, the "Oscypek Route" does not have its own web page, it can be easily located by putting its name into any search engine. Some tourist web pages equip their clients with additional tools linked to modern tourism. Thus, on the web page www.tropto.com, under the heading "Oscypkowy szlak" ("Oscypek Route") it is stated:

> " […] Tropto.com guide invites you to tour along the "Oscypek Route". Using our multimedia application for smartphones you will be able to reach 10 shepherds' huts in the Podtatrze Region, the Podhale Region, and in Polish Spisz, where traditional methods of manufacture of the famous smoked sheep cheese are used. The application uses a GPS location system and a map with a suggested route, thanks to which you will easily find the shepherds' hunts, in which you can try the certified 'Oscypek'. The guide provides not only descriptions of the ten shepherds' huts but also photos, our films, audio files, and lists of the most interesting cultural and sports events in Zakopane and its surrounding areas. The application works in off-line mode too." (www.tropto.com, retrieved 9.7.2014).

At present, the "Oscypek Route" connects about forty shepherds' huts from Zubrzyca Górna in the west, across the Tatra Mountains and Nowy Targ, to Hala Wojkowa in the east. Thanks to this interesting initiative, which supports a local brand, "Oscypek" has led to the growth of cultural tourism in the Podhale Region.

e-Oscypek

"Oscypek" is a kind of cheese which is produced exclusively during the period of the year when the sheep are grazing in mountain pastures, namely from April to September, and its availability is limited to this time frame. It is thus a seasonal product and, consequently, it requires intensive marketing during the period of its availability. The Internet web page www.e-oscypek.pl serves this purpose, and it also acts as an Internet shop, as it offers for sale mainly dairy products which have been granted European quality trademarks. In the section: "About us", the hosts of the web page state:

> "Today, through our web page, the individual customer may purchase these natural and healthy regional products without leaving home. Thanks to the large-scale production of the co-operative GAZDOWIE, which guarantees constant access to fresh products, we are able to service most orders throughout Poland within 24 hours after receiving the money transfer to our bank account. e-Oscypek.pl is simply... The spring of health straight form the mountains. "(www.e-oscypek.pl, retrieved 9.7.2014).

Thanks to the virtual shop, "Oscypek" is currently purchased by and delivered to customers from countries such as Canada, the Czech Republic, France, Germany, Georgia, Italy, Kazakhstan, the Netherlands, Slovakia, Spain, Sweden, the UK and the USA.

When offered for sale on the Internet, "Oscypek" loses its cultural context. Its purchase is no longer connected with the necessity of visiting the Podhale Region or even of leaving one's home. When sent by post to any destination in the world, "Oscypek" is nothing more than just another cheese with a certain taste. Its connection to the tradition, which led to its creation, becomes vague and tends to be no longer even essential for its survival and success. The hosts of the web page seem to be aware of this situation. Thus, in order to underline the connection of the cheese on offer with the culture of the Podhale Region, they put forward the possibility of co-operation with highlander folk artists and they also express a willingness to broaden their current activities:

> "[…] If you paint, sculpt, sew or do something that sustains our native tradition, write to us. We are open to new proposals for co-operation and for the diversification of goods in our shop" (www.e-oscypek.pl, retrieved 9.7.2014).

However, the online shop has not, so far, diversified the list of goods it has on offer, and it continues to sell different kinds of cheese, among which an increasingly anonymous "Oscypek", is still the most important product. The Internet discourse about "Oscypek" creates its media image, which is tailored for the purposes of product promotion, advertising, and commerce. In the space of hypertext, an ethno-product becomes an e-product. Web pages presenting "Oscypek" are linked with others, such as culinary web pages with recipes using cheese. An Internet user can thus acquire information about "Oscypek", he can see pictures and films about its production, and read recipes for meals prepared with this cheese. Even if he has never visited the Podhale Region, he becomes a virtual consumer of Oscypek's culture. Thus, while the Internet is certainly a medium which supports ethno-investments, it is not, however, the space of their actual implementation.

List of References

Printed

Chanock, Martin: "'Culture' and Human Rights: Orientalising, Occidentalising and Authenticity". In: Madani, Mahmood (ed.): *Beyond Rights Talk and Culture Talk: Comparative Essays on the Politics of Rights and Culture.* St. Martin's Press: New York 2000, pp. 15-36.

Hillman, Ben: "Paradise under Construction: Minorities, Mythos and Modernity in Northwest Yunnan. *Asian Ethnicity* 4(2), 2003, pp. 175-188.

Comaroff, John / Comaroff, Jean: "Ethnicity, (Ethnicity) Inc." Wydawnictwo Uniwersytetu Jagiellońskiego: Kraków 2011.

Krawczyk-Wasilewska, Violetta / Orszulak-Dudkowska, Katarzyna: "Farmers' Markets in Poland: Revitalisation of Traditional Food Products". In: Lysaght, Patricia (ed.): *The Return of Traditional Food.* Lund Studies in Arts and Cultural Sciences I. Lund University: Lund 2013, pp. 113-117.

Internet

www.minrol.gov.pl/pol/Jakosc-zywnosci/Produkty-regionalne-i-tradycyjne/Lista-produktow-tradycyjnych/woj.-malopolskie/Oscypek-oszczypek, retrieved 8.7.2014.

www.oscypek.wniosek.pdf, retrieved 8.7.2014.

www.tropto.com, retrieved 9.7.2014.

www.e-oscypek.p l, retrieved 9.7.2014.

PART III:
The Internet and Food Values: Ethics, Aesthetics, Environment, Health and Lifestyle

Una A. Robertson

Slow Food: Scotland

The speed at which the Internet transmits information is a phenomenon of modern times. One such example concerns the movement called "Slow Food" which originated in Italy in 1989 as a reaction to the tidal wave of "Fast Food"[1] engulfing the globe. Using the Internet as the principal tool for research, the movement proved to be an ideal subject for this presentation.

"Slow Food is a global, grass roots organisation with supporters in over 160 countries round the world that links the pleasure of food with a commitment to the community and the environment" (www.slowfood.org.uk, retrieved 29.12.2013).[2] It came about as a reaction to a McDonalds outlet opening in the centre of Rome, perceived as yet another threat to the ever-increasing standardisation of the world's food. Three years later Carlo Petrini and a group of like-minded people formed Slow Food with the aim of defending regional traditions, good food, gastronomic pleasure and a slower pace of life. The movement has since grown to number hundreds of thousands of members in a truly international organisation – its rapid growth assisted by the Internet and the ease of communication.

Slow Food has evolved "to develop a comprehensive approach to food that recognises the strong connections between plate, planet, people, politics and culture" (www.slowfood.com/international/7/history, retrieved 31.5.2014). Today, the movement maintains its opposition to the homogenisation of taste and culture, together with the unrestrained power of the food industry multinationals and the industrialisation of agriculture. The concept of quality is fundamental, defined by three interconnecting principles – good, clean and fair: "Good", because food should primarily taste good and be what it says it is – an increasingly important point today when food fraud is a potential risk; "clean" because food should be grown and produced in a sustainable way without a negative impact on the environment; and "fair" because growers and producers deserve a fair wage for their labour.

---

1 "Fast Food": food that is prepared/served quickly, convenient/pre-cooked ingredients or ready-made meals.
2 This is Slow Food U.K.'s own website. It has been the major source of information as it provides many pages and informative links although other websites have been used to corroborate the information.

There is an international structure with headquarters in Piedmont where the network and worldwide projects are developed. To realise its projects and ambitions Slow Food created the Slow Food Foundation for Biodiversity in 2003; the Terra Madre Foundation in 2004 to support the growth of a global network of food communities and a sustainable food system; the University of Gastronomic Sciences, also in 2004, to educate future food professionals; and the Slow Food Youth Network in 2007 (www.slowfood.com/international/157/university-of-gastronomic-sciences, retrieved 5.6.2014). The movement has developed further spin-offs and projects, with each country having its priorities.

In some countries organisation is on a national level but, in each, members form local groups known as "convivia". It is they who bring the Slow Food philosophy to life by organising visits to local producers and farms, by holding conferences and discussions, film screenings and festivals, taste education courses for children and adults, and by promoting farmers' markets or supporting local and international campaigns.

Despite the rapid spread of Slow Food during the 1990s and the development of its philosophy it only arrived in the UK in 2006 and here it follows the patterns found elsewhere – as a non-profit, member-supported association, with charitable educational projects that aim to spread the Slow Food message as widely as possible. Whereas in the UK as a whole there are some twenty-five local groups, in Scotland there are currently three: West Scotland (a merger of former groups in Glasgow and Ayrshire); Aberdeenshire; and Edinburgh, second only in size to London.

As happens elsewhere, Slow Food UK runs several campaigns under its banner: Slow Fish, Slow Baby (now "Baby's Taste Journey"), Slow Kids, Slow Food on Campus, Forgotten Foods (the UK Ark of Taste) and the UK's Chef Alliance. The focus of this paper will centre on these last two.

The Forgotten Foods Programme supports small-scale quality produce threatened by industrial agriculture, environmental degradation and standardisation. Such products are often at risk of extinction: by raising awareness, it is hoped they may be rediscovered and returned to the market (www.slowfood.org.uk/ff-products, retrieved 26.1.2014). The programme is part of Slow Food's Global Ark of Taste. Worldwide this programme is currently helping to preserve some 1700 products. In the UK as a whole it amounts to about 80 items and, of these, a number pertain specifically to Scotland:

Beremeal is a flour made from Bere, the six-row local barley ideally suited to growing on land of low fertility and a short growing season; formerly widely grown, it is now found mainly on Orkney.

Peasemeal is also a flour but made from yellow field peas. They are first roasted, to carmelise the sugars, ground through three sets of stones and finally sieved.

The Musselburgh leek is named after the village outside Edinburgh where it was introduced in 1834; it fell out of favour due to its shorter, thicker white stem and longer green

"flag"; it is no longer grown commercially but seed is readily available.

Dulse is a type of seaweed also found and used in Northern Ireland. It formed part of the traditional diet for coastal dwellers being rich in vitamins and minerals and a good source of protein.[3]

Blue-Grey Cattle derive from crossing two native breeds – the Whitebred Shorthorn bull and the Galloway cow. They are renowned for their distinctive looks and the high quality, slow grown, succulent meat. Being slow to mature they are unpopular with the supermarkets that buy on price and therefore favour faster-maturing breeds.

The British Red Grouse is a medium-size game bird, native to the British Isles. It has survived only on keepered heather moors that are expensive to maintain and large areas have been lost to cheaper usage, making heather moorland rarer than rain-forest.

The Scottish islands are well represented: the sheep on Orkney's North Ronaldsay are unique in that they live on the seashore, feeding on seaweed. The meat is lean with a distinct "gamey" flavour. Shetland contributes no less than five items: the native cattle, native sheep and also the preserved mutton from those sheep, (called "reestit" mutton[4]), black potatoes and the distinctive Shetland cabbage – all adapted to their particular environment.

Alongside this list of products in danger, Slow Food UK's website also gives a "Forgotten Food Recipe Bank" (www.slowfood.org.uk/ff-recipes, retrieved 1.6.2014). Beremeal, for example, was traditionally made into barley bannocks, eaten as the main form of bread, but today an alternative would be beremeal crackers or as a dough in which to cook salt-baked carrots, both purple and orange. In former times peasemeal was the basis for "brose", a soup or thick savoury porridge, and also for bannocks, but modern usage finds it coating fish or chicken, in vegetarian pates and as a Peasemeal Soda Bread. Blue-Grey Beef Carpaccio has very thin slices of fillet served raw in a Balsamic and Citrus dressing. Other

---

3   Dulse: *Palmaria palmata*.
4   Reestit Mutton: first salted in brine, then hung in the rafters above the peat fire. Once dried, after 10-15 days, it will keep for years. Often used in soups or stews it can also be eaten cold.

"Forgotten Foods" are provided for, some of the recipes being straightforward while others are labour-intensive.

For many years there has been concern that numerous foodstuffs were being "lost" to the consumer, either because they were too localised, unreliable in cropping or unsuited to the supermarket. It is often said it is easier to buy foods from the other side of the world than it is to buy products from one's own locality.

Two points should be stressed. The first is that this concept is by no means solely a component in any recent Internet campaign. Well before the computer age authors were questioning the loss of not only traditional foodstuffs but also the amount of chemicals in our food, the loss of nutritional value, the dangers of the modern processed diet and looking for the underlying reasons for this situation. To name just a few: from the 1940s to the 1970s Doris Grant was warning of the dangers of the modern diet: "Concurrently with the deterioration of the nation's food there has been an alarming deterioration of the nation's health" (Grant 1973, p. 11); the 1980s saw Maisie Steven's book "The Good Scot's Diet (Steven 1985): what became of it" and Francesca Greenoak's "Forgotten Fruit" (Greenoak 1983). Annette Hope in "The Caledonian Feast" takes a broad look at the Scottish diet over the centuries and provides traditional recipes (Hope 1987) while Catherine Brown's "Scottish Cookery" is a working cookery book with historical insights (Brown 1985). The loss of tradition has been an ongoing concern for decades: back in the 1820s Meg Dods in her popular work "The Cook and Housewife's Manual" thought it necessary to print "A Bill of Fare for St. Andrew's Day, Burns' Club or other Scottish National Dinners" (Dods 1827, p. 65).[5]

The second point to stress is that these "Forgotten Foods" are different to the numerous regional, local or traditional foods granted protected status: either as Protected Designation of Origin (PDO), Protected Geographical Indication (PGI) or Traditional Speciality Guaranteed (TSG) (www.gov.uk/protected-food-names-guidance-for-producers, retrieved 11.1.2014). England has its registered products such as Stilton cheese and Cornish pasties along with about sixty others while for Scotland the list includes items such as Arbroath Smokies, Forfar Bridies, Scottish Farmed Salmon and Scottish Wild Salmon, Orkney Beef, Lamb and Orkney Island Cheddar, Scotch Beef, Stornoway Black Pudding, Shetland Lamb and Native Shetland Wool. The most recent addition is Dundee Cake and protected status is currently being sought for Ayrshire potatoes.

Although much is being done to preserve our edible heritage it is not only the less common varieties that are in danger. According to a recently published survey

---

5   St. Andrew's Day, 30 November; Burns' Night, 25 January (the poet's birthday).

63% of adults were ignorant of the fact that British farmers grow blueberries; 62% did not know they grew sweetcorn (maize); and 29% that cauliflower was grown locally. Added to that, 19% did not know that apples were grown in Britain and 41% denied all knowledge of British-grown strawberries – despite their celebrated connection to the Wimbledon Tennis Championships. Of those born in the 1990s, 16% optimistically thought oranges were grown here commercially.[6]

With statistics such as these, the importance of food education cannot be over-emphasised. An obvious need exists to reconnect people with the source of their food, so that not only can they make informed choices about what they eat but also understand the implications. Considerations regarding the protection of our food culture and traditions must also be taken into account, along with environmental issues.

Slow Food UK has its educational campaigns but, in addition, the Internet provides access to a multitude of related initiatives, projects, programmes, strategies, organisations and so forth – a bewildering array to cover every possible angle of our food and drink scenario. Many of these echo or even overlap the Slow Food Movement's philosophy which suggests a considerable duplication of effort and funding. Whether national in scope, regional, or purely local, all have their websites and links to other like-minded groups or umbrella organisations.

Running parallel to and in harmony with Slow Food's campaign to save our culinary diversity is another initiative, the UK's Chef Alliance, whereby chefs who share the Slow Food ethos commit to supporting it by championing small-scale producers and working within their communities to promote good quality local, seasonal and sustainably produced food (www.slowfood.org. uk/slow-food-uks-chef-alliance-celebrates-100-members, retrieved 29.12.2013). They are encouraged to use "Forgotten Foods" in their menus and to help raise the profile of traditional British products. Although this only started in the UK just over two years ago, well over one hundred chefs have already signed up to the scheme: of these twenty or so are spread across Scotland, with about half of them in Edinburgh. Menus are published on the restaurants' websites with a profile of the chefs who, without exception, speak of their commitment to using local, seasonal produce and to showcasing the exceptional quality of Scottish produce. Some have provided recipes for the Forgotten Food Recipe Bank (ibid.).

Although these menus are mostly utilising Scottish products there is some leeway in translating the word "local". For example, how "local" is Serrano ham

---

6   *The Scotsman*, 2 June 2014, p. 14: "Britons don't know their onions, say experts." Survey
    conducted by Leaf (Linking Environment and Farming).

which can only be produced in the south and southwest of Spain? Avruga caviar, made from herring roe, carries a Spanish Chain of Custody Certification; and is it really necessary to use Asparagus grown some three hundred and fifty miles away in England while the local product is growing within fifty miles of Edinburgh?

"Seasonal" is another term with a flexible definition as, for example, when a menu in early June in "Celebration of the Season" has elderberries "from the chef's own garden" to accompany a fish dish: they may be local but one has to ask "which season" as at this point in time Edinburgh's elder trees are in full flower and the berries are still in the future.[7] Another chef in a late-summer menu when Scottish produce is plentiful and at its best, includes Parmesan cheese and Puy lentils both of which carry protected status in their own countries.

Finally, a brief look at some of the numerous "traditional Scottish", "heritage" or "authentic" menus and recipes available elsewhere on the Internet, to see how closely this concept is being interpreted in the wider world. Certain examples can only lead to an element of confusion! The restaurant serving "Scottish tapas" for example; another providing a dessert based on tayberries – Scottish, yes, but hardly traditional as they are a modern hybrid fruit released in 1979[8]; Sticky Toffee Pudding is another favourite but this has an English provenance, going back to either the Lake District in the 1960s or to a Yorkshire pub in 1907.

The St. Andrew's Day menu using fresh, seasonal, and doubtless local produce until the dessert – of Creamed Vanilla Rice Pudding. But when did pudding rice qualify under those headings? The same question can be asked about the impeccably Scottish menu for a Burns' Supper that lapses from grace with an Avocado salsa served with the Hot Roast Salmon. An even more momentous question mark surrounds whisky, the national drink essential to any celebration: with increasing amounts of English barley needed to keep Scotland's distilleries running – just how Scottish is the Scotch?

Food and drink are core elements of the Scottish economy, currently worth some £13 billion a year, with plans to double the value by 2025, and the sector employs over 330,000 people.[9] But food and drink are a basic fact of life for the individual and Slow Food offers a viable alternative to the supermarket and fast food lifestyle. Critics might say the movement in Scotland has been highjacked

---

7   Elder: *sambucus nigra*.
8   Tayberries: *rubus fructicosus x ideus*, released by the Scottish Horticultural Research Institute, 1979.
9   *The Scotsman*, 6 January 2014, p. 37: "Scottish food and drink not just about humour, there are pride and passion."

by middle-class "foodies",[10] whose core activity centres on monthly gastronomic supper clubs, generally attended by the same people (www.heraldscotland.com/food-drink/opinion/is-slow-food-stuck-in-a-middle-class-ghetto.20762592, retrieved 29.12.2013). However, the horsemeat scandals of January 2013 and on-going anxieties regarding food fraud and the length of supermarket supply chains has reinvigorated the Movement.[11]

Slow Food UK's programmes touch on many interlocking facets of modern life – but a key point is "food education" in its widest sense – for infants, for children, for students and for anyone with an interest in their daily food. The Internet has enabled Slow Food to develop into a truly international movement, rapidly spreading its message around the world, promoting the pleasures of food produced locally, maintaining our food heritage and safe-guarding our edible biodiversity. The Forgotten Foods Programme and UK Chef Alliance are integral to the success of the entire Slow Food movement.

List of References

Printed

"Britons don't know their onions, say experts." The *Scotsman,* 2 June 2014, p. 14.

Brown, Catherine: *Scottish Cookery.* Richard Drew Publishing Ltd.: Glasgow, 1985.

Dods, Meg, (pseud.): *The Cook & Housewife's Manual.* Oliver and Boyd, and Bell and Bradfute et al: Edinburgh 1827.

Grant, Doris: *Your Daily Food: recipe for survival.* Faber and Faber: London 1973.

Greenoak, Francesca: *Forgotten Fruit.* Andre Deutsch: London, 1983.

Hope, Annette: *A Caledonian Feast.* Mainstream Publishing Co., (Edinburgh) Ltd. 1987.

"Scottish food and drink not just about humour, there are pride and passion." The *Scotsman,* 6 January 2014, p. 37.

Steven, Maisie: *The Good Scot's Diet.* Aberdeen University Press: Aberdeen 1985.

---

10 "Foodies": people with an obsessive interest in and knowledge of food.
11 Horse meat was discovered in a consignment of beef products sold in the UK. See: www.bbc.co.uk/news/uk-21335872, retrieved 1.6.2014.

Internet

"Is Slow Food Stuck in a Middle-class Ghetto?" *Herald Scotland*, 13 April 2013, retrieved 29.102.2013, from

www.heraldscotland.com/food-drink/opinion/is-slow-food-stuck-in-a-middle-class-ghetto.20762592.

"Protected Food Names: Guidance for Producers", retrieved 11.1.2014, from www.gov.uk/protected-food-names-guidance-for-producers.

"Q&A: Horsemeat Scandal", retrieved 1.6.2014, from www.bbc.co.uk/news/uk-21335872

"Slow Food UK": www.slowfood.com/ international/7/history, retrieved 31.5.2014.

"Slow Food UK Forgotton Food Products", retrieved 1.6.2014, from www.slowfood.org.uk/ff-products.

"Slow Food UK Forgotten Food Recipes", retrieved 21.1.2014, from www.slowfood.org.uk/ff-recipes.

"Slow Food UK's Chef Alliance Celebrates 100 members", retrieved 29.12.2013, from www.slowfood.org.uk/slow-food-uks-chef-alliance-celebrates-100-members,.

"University of Gastronomic Sciences. Getting into the future of food", retrieved 5.6.2014, from www.slowfood.com/international/157/university-of-gastronomic-sciences.

Ivanche Dimitrievski, Philippos Papadopoulos
and Rodica Arpasanu

Should the Mediterranean Diet be Viewed as a Fully-Fledged Public Discourse, or as Part of a Wider Food and Wellness Narrative? An Internet-Based Study

Defeated by westernisation processes in its native domain, the Mediterranean diet seeks asylum in the West itself. An American food magazine noted that, in the U.S., "[the] Mediterranean is moving out of the shadows of the big three ethnic cuisines [Mexican, Italian, and Chinese] and taking center stage at restaurants." (Lauren 2011, p. 1). One study of Google search trends, for example, showed a decline in the related Spanish, Italian, and Greek cuisines in the U.S. as against to the remarkable 139% increase of searches concerning the Mediterranean cuisine group (Papadopoulos / Arpasanu / Pavlovska 2014, pp. 1-20). Should this achievement be considered a sign of mature discourse, or rather a side effect of the broader interest in food and wellness narratives in this country? We shall address these questions in the light of Foucault's discourse analysis. In seeking to identify the position of the Mediterranean diet in the constellation of dominant public narratives, we shall draw evidence from American electronic 'health' and 'healthy living' magazines.

Theoretical Note

Foucault (1972) argued that discourse is "a fragment of history [...] posing its own limits, its divisions, its transformations, the specific modes of its temporality." (p. 117). Such conceptualisation requires focus on discourse as a matter of the social, historical, and political conditions under which statements come as true and false (McHoul / Wendy 1997). According to a Foucauldian perspective, therefore, one needs to move both *in* and *out* of the text, that is, to drive the analysis of the discursive through the extra-discursive. (Hook 2001, 521-547). This perspective compels us to "question" the Mediterranean diet as a discursive formation. This questioning encompasses the system by which particular objects are formed and the types of enunciations that are involved. Thus, it is not enough to consider whether a certain phenomenon is true, but rather to think about how its objects might become formed (Graham 2005). For example, one US electronic magazine article stated: "Mediterranean Diet: The World's Healthiest Diet" (Johnson 2014). Our aim here is not to question the truthfulness of this statement but, in considering the Mediterranean diet as a discursive formation, to examine how it speaks the object of "health" into existence. In so doing, we interrogate whether the Mediterranean diet is indeed a discourse or whether it appears merely as an object in a broad discourse on health and diet.

From Cholesterol to the Mediterranean Diet

Studies on the epidemiology of coronary heart disease emerged in the late 1940s in the belief that, "if clinically healthy persons were examined, queried, and followed over the years, it would be possible to identify characteristics associated with the development of clinical coronary heart disease" (Keys 1980, p. 14). These initiatives started in the United States. The related *cholesterol hypothesis*, then being revived, needed to test the idea that "the diet of a population would be reflected in the level of cholesterol in the blood which, in turn, would affect susceptibility to coronary heart disease" (Keys 1980, *loc. cit.*). Were there, as rumoured at the time, large differences among populations in the frequency of coronary heart disease?

In this period, Ancel Keys postulated that "diets rich in fatty acids were the principle cause of coronary heart disease" (Wright 2011, p. 436). From 1955 to 1958, Keys began to organise teams of clinicians and scientists to investigate this matter. His study required fieldwork that would take scientists deep into the lifestyles of rural populations of seven countries: Yugoslavia, Italy, Greece, Finland, the Netherlands, Japan, and the United States. It thus became known as the Seven Countries Study. From 1958 to the early 1970s, Keys' teams built their database, "translating cultural differences into a set of equations that could predict heart disease" (ibid., 437). Their central finding was that "saturated fat as a percentage of calories, was the most powerful lifestyle predictor of heart disease" (*loc. cit.*).

Five and ten years after the initial visits, Keys returned to the investigated sites, identifying those who had experienced a coronary heart attack. The lowest rates (0.1%) were found in rural Crete, where the population led a predominantly Mediterranean lifestyle with a diet consisting mainly of grains, pasta, legumes, fruits and vegetables, olive oil, and wine. This Cretan diet became the prototypical Mediterranean diet recognised by Keys in his work, *Eat Well and Stay Well* (Keys / Keys 1959). Today, Keys is known as the father of the Mediterranean diet. In a tribute to him, Henry Blackburn wrote: "He showed us that there is a personal responsibility to model behavior so as to provide an example of healthful living to our families and our patients" (Blackburn 2014).

The Mediterranean Diet: A Panacea

By the early 1960s, Keys denounced the excess of calories and fat characterising the average American's diet. He labelled obesity as malnutrition, "an immoral disease in contrast to the problems with the under-nutrition seen in [post-war European] countries" (Serra-Majem 2006, p. 1071). In this way, Keys directly addressed the poor consumption habits of American society. His work thus drew parallels with *diaetetick management* by the medic George Cheyne (1671-1743), who, in the eighteenth century, had problematised the "diseases of abundance" of the English élites (Turner 1982, pp. 254-269). Both diets were inspired by a typically Mediterranean lifestyle and both promoted the idea of a life of regularity, moderation, and physical exercise. Keys' dietary recommendations, therefore, were not a unique invention. There were, however, historical differences between the approaches of Keys and Cheyne.

For the working class of the eighteenth century whose reliance on cereals often meant starvation, diet was but a means of survival. The healthy body of the worker was, in fact, essential to the capitalist, whereas diet could work in the direction of eliminating "inefficient" customs of consumption (ibid.). In the eighteenth century, then, having an interest in diet was limited chiefly to the aristocratic and professional classes. Such an interest inspired a drive towards the scientific analysis of lifestyle and diet, which, through Keys' Seven Countries Study, eventually gave birth to the twentieth century Mediterranean diet. The twentieth century "obesity problem" was considered a medico-scientific risk factor. And by then, medical science showed that *every-body* – and especially "obese" Americans – was at the risk of cardiovascular disease (see Cassell 1995, 424-427; Gracia-Arnaiz 2010, pp. 219-225; Jutel 2006, pp. 2268-2276).

Consequently, the emergence and popularisation of the Mediterranean diet were in part brought about by a discourse of medicalisation. In the broader sociological sense, medicalisation consists of "defining a problem in [medico-scientific] terms, using [medico-scientific] language to describe the problem, and adopting a medical framework for understanding the problem" (Mudry 2010, p. 94). Today, electronic magazine texts on the Mediterranean diet embrace a wide range of medicalised conditions to address an even wider array of diseases, while claiming adherence to the Mediterranean diet as the solution. The following quote is one such example:

> "Studies show that the Mediterranean diet can help overcome erectile dysfunction or impotence in men with metabolic syndrome [...] metabolic syndrome is a group of conditions that put you at risk for heart disease and diabetes. These conditions according to the National Institute of Health are high blood pressure, high blood sugar levels, high

levels of triglycerides, low levels of HDL, and too much fat around your waist." (Ficarra 2014).

According to this excerpt, the Mediterranean diet, through its relationship with the metabolic syndrome, can even cure erectile dysfunction and impotence. The article also provides the medical logic for understanding this relationship: "less inflammation, better flow, better hormone levels, better erections" (ibid.) Here, both the source (i.e. the metabolic syndrome) and the treatment of the issue (i.e. the Mediterranean diet) are found in the individual. Erectile dysfunction is, in other words, the result of one's own dietary actions; and, only by engaging with the Mediterranean diet can one achieve better erections. Other means of intervention to deal with such medical matters are thus effectively closed. So: "move to Greece where you can immerse yourself in *la dolce vita* and expect to be sexually active well into your 70s." (Thompson 2014). Or, just stay at home and embrace the Mediterranean diet.

How *Mediterranean* is the Mediterranean diet?

In 1990, K. Dun Gifford founded "Oldways", a non-profit organisation aiming to "promote healthy eating and drinking, with programs that help consumers improve their food and drink choices" (Oldways 2014 [a]). In 1993, in association with the Harvard School of Public Health, "Oldways" introduced the Mediterranean diet pyramid "featuring olive oil as the principal fat, inclusion of moderate wine drinking, and recognition of the difference between plant and animal protein" (Oldways 2014 [b]). By 2008, "Oldways" updated this pyramid with the inclusion of herbs and spices for the first time and by making the fish and seafood elements more prominent. This update was approved by a scientific committee.

The Mediterranean diet of "Oldways" marked the introduction of a new theme in the discourse of diet, that of *culture*. In this case, adherence to the Mediterranean way meant following a tradition that had the semantic weight of years of heart-healthy Mediterranean people. This theme presented an alternative way in which to talk about food and drink – one which focused on *how to eat* in addition to *what to eat* (Murdy 2010; Murdy 2010, p. 94). The introduction of the cultural theme to the discourse on diet opened up yet another discursive space for the Mediterranean diet. This claim to cultural origin – that the Mediterranean diet *is* traditionally Mediterranean – resonates in the electronic magazines on the subject:

"The Mediterranean Diet Pyramid is based on the dietary traditions of Crete, Greece, and southern Italy circa 1960 at a time when the rates of chronic disease among populations there were among the lowest in the world, and adult life expectancy was among the highest, even though medical services were limited "(Boose / Segal, 2014).

The signifier *Mediterranean* as used here points to both geographical and historical-cultural descent – the texts emphasise that one should "Eat like the Romans" to point to the centuries-long Mediterranean diet. These texts maintain historical continuity as Keys did not *invent* the Mediterranean diet; he merely *discovered* what was there already, since the time of the ancient Greeks. But here, too, the attempt at construction of continuity ends, because another, and perhaps an even more crucial construction, begins:

> "To be Italian is to appreciate dark leafy vegetables, especially this [broccoli] [...] Like other cabbage family members it's a nutrition superstar, providing plenty of vitamin C, potassium, calcium and fiber as well as carotenoids and cancer-fighting indoles and isothiocyanates."("9 Healthy Foods from the Mediterranean Diet", 2014).

The rationalisation of cultural habits is evident here, echoing the ideology of nutritionism, that is, the belief that "the scientifically identified nutrients within foods or drinks determine the value of those foods or drinks within a diet" (Mudry 2010, p. 98). Broccoli is considered to be healthy because it contains x and y substances. This kind of ideology is made possible by a broader discourse of quantification, which allows the quality of food to be judged on the basis of the concentration of particular substances (Mudry 2006, pp. 49-67). And "plenty of vitamin C, potassium and fiber" means only one thing: more health. Giving the Mediterranean diet principles through a discourse of quantification, however, makes it difficult to delineate between a "traditional" and a "scientific" argument:

> "Red wine gets a thumbs-up, in moderation (one glass for women, one to two for men)"(Robinson, 2014).

Under the subtitle *What You Can Eat and What You Can't*, this excerpt discusses wine, tradition, and the concept of moderation. In the bracketed dietary advice, the excerpt quantifies moderation. Does this quantity represent a certain Mediterranean reality, or is it a scientific proposition? After all, the act of quantification draws legitimacy mainly from studies that illustrate a specific health benefit, not from tradition. The text refrains from clarifying this. Yet this is an important move, because in order to make Mediterranean lifestyles commensurable with the American discourses of diet, the qualitative aspects of the Mediterranean cultures have to be quantified (Mudry 2006, 49-67). *What is healthy* and, for that matter, *what is part of the Mediterranean diet* are consequences of such quantification. Furthermore:

"When you think about Mediterranean food, your mind probably goes to pizza and pasta from Italy, or hummus and pita from Greece, but these dishes don't exactly fit into any healthy dietary plans advertised as "Mediterranean." The reality is that the *true* Mediterranean diet consists mainly of fruits and vegetables, seafood, olive oil, hearty grains, and more – foods that help fight against heart disease, certain cancers, diabetes, and cognitive decline." (Boose / Segal 2014).

Are not pizza and pita as traditional to Italy and Greece as olive oil and hearty grains? The electronic magazine texts classify the latter as traditionally Mediterranean, while the former as "unhealthy" and, therefore, not *truly* Mediterranean. This indicates that the content of the Mediterranean diet is selected on the basis of medico-scientific discourse. In this way, tradition is restricted to what is scientifically found to be healthy; in other words, not everything that is traditionally Mediterranean is part of the Mediterranean diet. The selected content is also generalised so as to include "categorical entities" rather than "traditional" ones. For instance, *tomatoes* (not even a native European fruit!) produced in the Netherlands are as Mediterranean as those produced in Greece, and *cheese* does not have to be feta in order to be considered part of the Mediterranean diet. Thus a narrowing of the Mediterranean diet to a traditional content might disable cultural mobility. The resulting discursive object is, therefore, a Mediterranean diet which is universally adoptable, across various, and not necessarily Mediterranean, cultural contexts.

Tradition is maintained in the discourse of the Mediterranean diet, however, and for a good reason: to separate it from a modern American understanding of what Mediterranean food is. This reason is evident in the online magazine texts:

"What was once a healthy and inexpensive way of eating back then is now associated with heavy, unhealthy dishes that contribute to heart disease, obesity, diabetes, and other chronic diseases." (Boose / Segal 2014).

In this way, the discourse draws from scientific studies in order to break through related stereotypes to demonstrate the healthiness of the Mediterranean diet. This discourse pushes certain "unhealthy" aspects of Mediterranean tradition into the background, thus singling out a "pure Mediterranean diet". In this way, it opens cracks in the general, "stereotypical" American understanding of ethnic Mediterranean cuisines, and opens yet another discursive space for the Mediterranean diet to spread even further.

The Sick American

The use of scientific discourse to discuss food in relation to health results in food becoming a sort of *dual pathogen* (Lupton 1995, 477-494); that is, both a source of nourishment and a source of disease. Such a construction of food, in turn, redefines cultural habits in terms of their impact on individual health:

> "All [Mediterranean diet] components make a lot of sense from a healthy eating standpoint. Compare that to the average American diet, or the even unhealthier American junk food diet. Just incorporating some of the [Mediterranean] diet ingredients to every day eating would be a significant upgrade." ("The Mediterranean diet meal plan [Infographic]", retrieved 8.2.2014, from http://livinggreenmag.com/2013/05/15/food-health/the-mediterranean-diet-meal-plan-infographic/).

By virtue of consuming foods which are scientifically found to be unhealthy and which are presented as being "empty of nutrition" or as "disease inducing", the American lifestyle is regarded as "sickening" and Americans are regarded as a "sick population". (Zief / Veri 2009, pp. 154-179). By regarding oneself as being sick, the individual is led into adopting a scientifically approved "healthy" lifestyle. And since America is said to be a "sick population", *every-body* in America is therefore in the need of dietary reform, which the Mediterranean diet, a science-based paradigm, provides. With this, the American eater becomes a *patient* who, instead of taste, pleasure, or tradition, becomes concerned with the relationship between diet, illness, and health (Mudry 2010, p. 98). A vision of an ideal, healthy being worth striving for is suggested to this patient – a transformation made possible only by living the Mediterranean way. The success of this transformative ideology is dependent upon the existence of a self-reflective and self-regulating individual (Coveney 1998, 459-468). This means that having been exposed to the electronic magazine articles on the Mediterranean diet, the person reflects and acts upon his own eating habits in relation to those described in the articles. We now outline what such a transformation would entail.

With regards to the meal, the discourse of the Mediterranean diet calls for the reshaping of American food pyramids with respect to content, frequency of consumption, and nutritive origin; the reshaping of cooking practices which encompass the reduction of industrial processing and the intake of fresh ingredients; and the reshaping of consumption scales while adopting a continuum of limitation. With respect to the body, the discourse asks for the establishment of self-discipline concerning physical activity to counter the largely sedentary American lifestyle. Finally, with regard to self, the discourse calls for the reshaping of mental frames with regards to food (e.g. "think of meat as flavouring, not as the main dish"); the reshaping of shopping practices towards searching for nutritive wholeness, thus redefining the shopper as a buyer of nutrition rather than a purchaser of foods or food ingredients; and finally the rethinking of one's relationships with others, seeking socialisation around meals, and so addressing a "lonely, depressed self" (Sarris et al. 2014, 1-29), and the related medicalised conditions (Conrad / Mackie / Mehrotra 2010, 1943-1947).

With the aforementioned acts of transformation, the sick subject is promised freedom from the chains of a sickening American lifestyle:

> "Delicious food that's stood the test of time and helps keep you healthy for years to come. That's at the heart of the traditional Mediterranean diet" (Robinson 2014)

The promise of health, however, comes at a price. The transformation outlined above implies the sacrificing of normal everyday American life as the health gains come as a result of what is given up. But also, this transformation traps the individual in its scientific ideology. One consequence of this "confinement to liberation" is the emergence of new emotionalities in the form of, for example, guilt resulting from transgressing the inherent logic of this confinement. Another one is the increased reliance and dependence on medico-scientific expertise to interpret what is "good" and what is "bad" with regards to one's lifestyle in general and one's eating in particular. It is no wonder then that the online magazine texts evoke, and are written primarily by, medico-scientific experts and nutritionists as the authorities on and authors of the Mediterranean diet, rather than by the native Mediterranean people.

Concluding Remarks

In examining the discursive status of the Mediterranean diet, we are led back to Foucault's definition of discourse as a "group of statements in so far as they belong to the same discursive formation" and in particular, that "discourse is made up of a limited number of statements for which a group of conditions of existence can be defined" (Foucault 1972, p. 117). It is evident from the analysis of the electronic magazines that, as a discursive formation, the Mediterranean diet is located in the synthesis between tradition and medical science. In other words, magazine texts articulate statements which, identified in Mediterranean tradition and transformed through Western medico-scientific practice, are *given in medico-scientific terms*. In turn, such deliverance de-emphasises traditional aspects of the Mediterranean diet (e.g. statements reflecting hedonistic elements), while emphasising the relationship between nutrition and health. Related discourses of vegetarianism, animal welfare, environmentalism and sustainability (Freeman 2010, 255-276), as well as hedonism and cuisine (Ball 2003, pp. 1-36), (here deliberately left for further investigation) meet with a similar fate. But the medico-scientific discourse recognised in the statements does not claim them as its own. And while tradition seems to fade, it is still *maintained*. For instance, various scientists have nowadays proclaimed the healthfulness of red meat. This medico-scientific object might problematise the Mediterranean diet pyramid with respect to health, but never change the order of its food categories for, while being built upon medico-scientific practice, this pyramid reflects the traditional eating habits of the Mediterranean people, and the Cretans of the 1960s in particular. With this, medical science does not take precedence over tradition – a situation which also limits the number of medico-scientific statements which may penetrate the Mediterranean diet as a discursive formation. These two broad conditions of existence limit the number of statements belonging to the same discursive formation of the Mediterranean diet as found in American electronic magazines, on the basis of which we conclude that the Mediterranean diet is indeed a fully-fledged discourse.

List of References

Printed

Ball, Eric, L.: "Greek Food after Mousaka: Cookbooks, 'Local' Culture, and the Cretan Diet". *Journal of Modern Greek Studies* 21(1), 2003, pp. 1-36.

Blackburn, Henry: "Ancel Keys", retrieved 17.3.2014, from http://mbbnet.umn.edu/firsts/blackburn_h.html

Boose, Greg / Segal, Robert: "The Mediterranean Diet: Myths, Facts, and Health Benefits of a Mediterranean Diet", retrieved 17.2.2014 from http://www.helpguide.org/life/mediterranean-diet.htm

Cassell, Anne, J.: "Social Anthropology and Nutrition: A Different Look at Obesity in America". *Commentary* 95, 1995, pp. 424-427.

Conrad, Peter / Mackie, Thomas / Mehrotra, Ateev: "Estimating the Costs of Medicalization". *Social Science & Medicine* 70, 2010, pp. 1943-1947.

Coveney, J.: "The Government and Ethics of Health Promotion: The Importance of Michel Foucault". *Health Education Research* 13(3), 1998, pp. 459-468.

Crotty, Patricia, A.: *Good Nutrition? Fact and Fashion in Dietary Advice*. Allen and Unwin: St. Leonard's, NSW 1995.

Edwards, Lauren: "Hot Emerging Cuisines". *Prepared Foods* 11, 2011, p. 1.

Ficarra, Barbara: "Mediterranean Diet can Help Improve Sexual Health in Men", retrieved 12.2.2014, from http://healthin30.com/2010/02/mediterranean-diet-can-help-improve-sexual-health-in-men/.

Foucault, Michel: *The Archaeology of Knowledge*. Pantheon Books: New York 1972, p. 205.

Freeman, Packwood, C.: "Meat's Place on the Campaign Menu: How US Environmental Discourse Negotiates Vegetarianism". *Environmental Communication* 4(3), 2010, pp. 255-276.

Gracia-Arnaiz, Mabel: "Fat Bodies and Thin Bodies. Cultural, Biomedical and Market Discourses on Obesity". *Apetite* 55, 2010, pp. 219-225.

Graham, Linda, J.: "Discourse Analysis and the Critical Use of Foucault". Paper presented at the *Australian Association for Research in Education*, Sydney 2005.

Hook, Derek: "Discourse, Knowledge, Materiality, History: Foucault and Discourse Analysis". *Theory and Psychology* 11(4), 2001, pp. 521-547.

Jutel, Annemarie: "The Emergence of Overweight as a Disease Entity: Measuring up Normality". *Social Science & Medicine* 63, 2006, pp. 2268-2276.

Keys, Ancel / Keys, Margaret: *Eat Well and Stay Well*. Doubleday: New York 1959.

Keys, Ancel: *Seven Countries Study. A Multivariate Analysis of Death and Coronary Heart Disease*. Harvard University Press: Cambridge, Massachusetts 1980.

Lupton, Deborah / Chapman, Simon: "A Healthy Lifestyle might be the Death of You: Discourses on Diet, Cholesterol Control and Heart Disease in the Press and among the Lay Public". *Sociology of Health & Illness* 17(4), 1995, pp. 477-494.

McHoul, Alec / Grace, Wendy: *The Foucault Primer*. New York University Press: New York 1997.

Mudry, Jessica: "Quantifying an American Eater: Early USDA Food Guidance and a Language of Numbers". *Food, Culture and Society: An International Journal of Multidisciplinary Research* 9(1), 2006, pp. 49-67.

Mudry, Jessica: "The Poison is in the Dose: The French Paradox, the Healthy Drinker and the Medicalization of Virtue. *Food, Culture and Society: An International Journal of Multidisciplinary Research* 13(1), 2010, p. 94.

Papadopoulos, Philippos / Arpasanu, Rodika / Pavlovska, Aleksandra: "American Perceptions of Mediterranean Cuisine: Internet Based Research". *Food Studies: An Interdisciplinary Journal* (3), 2014, pp. 1-20.

Sarris, Jerome *et al*: "Lifestyle Medicine for Depression". *BMC Psychiatry* 14(107), 2014, pp. 1-29.

Serra-Majem, Lluis: "Foreword. X Anniversary of the Foundation of the Mediterranean Diet (1996-2006). Dedicated to Ancel Keys (1904-2004)". *Public Health Nutrition* 9(8A), p. 1071.

Turner, Bryan, S.: "The Government of the Body: Medical Regimens and the Rationalization of Diet". *The British Journal of Sociology* 33(2), 1982, pp. 254-269.

Wright, Michael, C.: "Bibliographical Notes on Ancel Keys and Salim Yusuf. Origins and Significance of the Seven Countries Study and the INTERHEART Study". *Journal of Clinical Lipidology* 5(6), 2011, p. 436.

Zieff, Susan, G. / Veri, Maria, J.: "Obesity, Health, and Physical Activity: Discourses from the United States". *Quest* 61, 2009, pp. 154-179.

Internet

Johnson, Rachel: Mediterranean Diet: "The World's Healthiest Diet?", retrieved 11.2.2014, from http://www.eatingwell.com/nutrition_health/nutrition_news_information/mediterranean_diet_the_worlds_healthiest_diet?page=4.

"9 Healthy Foods from the Mediterranean Diet", retrieved 4.2.2014, from http://www.eatingwell.com/healthy_cooking/healthy_cooking_101_basics_and_techniques/healthy_foods_of_the_mediterranean_diet?page=9.

Oldways [a]: "Founder & History", retrieved 14.02.2014, from http://oldwayspt.org/about-us/founder-history.

Oldways [b]: "Oldways Timeline", retrieved 14.2.2014, from http://oldwayspt.org/about-us/oldways-timeline

The Mediterranean diet meal plan [Infographic]", retrieved 8.2.2014, from http://livinggreenmag.com/2013/05/15/food-health/the-mediterranean-diet-meal-plan-infographic/.

Robinson, Mayer, K.: "*The Mediterranean Diet: A Total and Lifestyle Approach Continues to be One of the Best Prescriptions for a Long, Healthy Life*, retrieved 7.2.2014, from http://www.webmd.com/food-recipes/guide/the-mediterranean-diet

Thompson, Ryan: "The Mediterranean Life: It's a Healthy One...So Follow It", retrieved 13.2.2014, from http://www.menshealth.co.uk/food-nutrition/healthy-eating/the-mediterranean-life-206955.

Yrsa Lindqvist

Seasonal Food in a Virtual Basket –
A Campaign for Environmental Sustainability

Using the Internet and sharing information on social media are the most efficient ways nowadays of spreading data, organising campaigns, and advertising. In less than twenty years the virtual world has become accepted and is now a natural part of everyday life (Svenningsson / Lövheim / Bergquist 2003). Since the Internet contains "everything", so to speak, food, like other aspects of daily life, is also a significant Internet topic. Here, for example, recipes, restaurant reviews, diets for health and training, food blogs, information about the home delivery of food, can be found. This article is about a campaign for the return of seasonal food in home kitchens in Finland.

In the late 1980s, strawberries, blueberries, cucumbers, watermelons and so forth, were still seasonal products in Finland. Every season had its highlights; the first tomatoes were longed for since there were hardly any Spanish or Dutch ones available at the market. Some off-season products could be bought in certain shops, but they were not commonly available. The situation changed quite rapidly after Finland joined the European Union in 1995 as the market then opened up for global food trading to a much larger extent than had previously been the case. During the decade prior to this many Finns became familiar with Mediterranean food, Thai food, barbecue cooking, and so on, as a consequence of travelling abroad, especially on holidays, to different destinations. As a result of this combination of factors, a more international kind of food culture became popular in Finland in the closing decades of the twentieth century. Consumers got used to buying what they needed, when they wanted to have it, irrespective of season, and, over the years, this has led to a reduction in traditional season-based cooking in the home.

In 2013, the Martha Association, a Finnish women's organisation, decided to start a campaign for the promotion of seasonal food.[1] This Association, which has existed for more than a century, has, naturally enough, seen its popularity both

---

1   The following description of intentions, goals and results are based on non-published material from the Martha Association. Project number: 5767. In Finland the Martha Association is, for practical reasons, divided into two separate organisations: the Finnish-speaking "Marttaliitto" and the Swedish-speaking "Marthaförbundet". This paper deals with the Swedish-speaking "Marthaförbundet". See "The Swedish Martha Association", retrieved from http://martha.fi/english/, 2.10 2014.

rise and fall over time. Today, however, as a result of environmental awareness, both with regard to food and the economy, the Martha Association's old values have become popular once again, not least among a new, young generation of Finns. Since the Internet is an excellent medium for distributing information, the Martha Association invested in setting up an informative and a very attractive website about five years ago. At the heart of the Association's campaign to promote seasonal food was the concept of a basket filled with ingredients. But, unlike entrepreneurs in the food business who offer products and recipes which can be delivered to your door, in a basket, Martha's food basket was of the *virtual* kind (http://martha.fi/svenska/hushall/, retrieved 18.9.2014).

Fig. 1: The website of the Martha Association, as a well-established institution, offers information and support, not only for its members, but also in general terms as it provides expert advice on issues such as housekeeping, childcare, economy, and environmental subjects. "Marthas Matkorg" – the food basket campaign was in force throughout every season of the year in 2013 (http://martha.fi/svenska/hushall/, retrieved 18.9.2014).

There were several reasons for the starting of the campaign. One was that a newspaper with a large circulation in Helsinki compared the price of a basket containing "regular" food with a basket filled with organic food products. The latter, of course, was more expensive, but what the Martha Association's experts particularly reacted against was the fact that the organic basket contained grapes and many other imported products, which were not seasonal, even in Europe, at that time of the year, and thus contributing to the extra cost involved. The example showed a lack of knowledge about, and a loss of tradition concerning, season-based households. This kind of household is less expensive to support, and much more sustainable in terms of the environment that its non-seasonal counterpart, since factors such as the global transport of goods, for example, are not as heavily involved. One of the goals of the Martha project, therefore, was to enable people to increase their knowledge about better tastes, less expensive foods, and sustainability, by choosing primary seasonal products to fill the virtual seasonal baskets.

Another goal was to encourage consumers to use all of the products of nature that are available for picking or foraging for, free of charge. In the Nordic countries, everyone has a legal right of access to private land ("Allemansrätt"), for foraging purposes. This means that berries and mushrooms can be picked by anyone, anywhere, when they are in season, and fishing permission, valid everywhere in the Nordic countries, can be had for just a small fee. The tradition of growing food items at summer houses, or, if living in the countryside, in one's home garden, is still quite strong – red and black currant bushes, especially, are to be found in most backyards. At the same time, however, people have become less inclined to harvest food from nature. By offering recipes and practical advice in this regard, the Association points out that harvesting food from nature can be seen as being a part of an overall life experience, since one has to pick it oneself, and, by doing so, one gets to know about different edible products, one learns how to prepare such food, and one gets satisfaction from what are called "real tastes" of natural food products. The campaign also sought to focus on, and to notify small food producers about local food, by emphasising that this is a cultural heritage worth protecting, and also by stressing that support for local producers brings regional economic benefits, leading perhaps to further local employment in the future.

Fig. 2: During the summer and autumn seasons, the focus of the Martha campaign was on supporting local producers, as well as on the picking and the collecting of what is to be found for free in the woods, such as berries and mushrooms (The Society of Swedish Literature in Finland [Svenska litteratursällskapet i Finland] SLS 2244). (Photo: Carola Herberts.)

And, finally, a major goal of the campaign was related to the environment, as it aimed to reduce the negative effects of food production and food availability, on nature, by supporting the use of local foods.

Root Vegetables and Mushrooms

So how is a campaign like this working out in reality? Is it enough to have a fancy website and hope for the best? Actually, this is not necessarily the case. The Internet is often seen as an inexpensive and a quick way of reaching a large and diversified audience, and it *can* be, if the sharing of information via social media turns out to be successful. But the amount of information available on the World Wide Web is so enormous that a more traditional dissemination approach, that is, to actually go out and meet people face to face, can also be necessary, depending on the message, its purpose, and the intended audience. Both approaches – the sharing information about the campaign on social media, and actual hands-on courses – were planned for as part of the Martha campaign. There were plenty of occasions during which the public was instructed in the use of food from nature in cooking. Events, during which such instruction was given, were held for different target groups, and kitchen personnel in schools were also informed about the use of seasonal food (Finnish schools have offered free meals for pupils since 1948). The sharing of information about seasonal food on social media was also not left to chance. Collaboration with popular food bloggers was sought and this was successful to a certain extent.

The first virtual food basket was launched in February 2013 and it was called the "spring food basket". At that time, spring seemed very far away as the temperature was -28°C on the day on which the first press conference was held in Anton & Anton (A&A), a small grocery store in Helsinki specialising in organic and locally-produced food. There were no Finnish fresh, green, early spring vegetables available at that time, and the campaign staff had to find a new strategy. Since one of the goals of the campaign was to reduce food waste, people were encouraged to take a look in their freezers and to use the harvest from the previous year still stored there. The tradition of picking berries, vegetables, and mushrooms, for example, and of preserving them in the deep freezer for use in wintertime, is still strong in Finland at an individual level. But many people also forget to use all of the food items which they had preserved during the previous autumn. So they got a reminder to empty the deep freezer before the next harvest came round. It was not until May that it became possible to finally fill up the spring virtual food basket and to supplement the recipe bank on the website with the inclusion of recipes featuring nettles and wild herbs. During the first week of March there were 3,700 hits on Facebook and 5,900 hits on the Martha website, seven articles about the campaign where published in newspapers, and three radio stations also gave information about the project. When the new recipes became available in May, 3,000 hits where registered. In an international context, the numbers of hits may not sound so impressive, but the Swedish speaking Finns are a small community of 300,000 persons. The Martha Association felt pleased with the results.

Fig. 3: Facebook offered a quick channel of communication for reaching those who wanted information about new recipes, events like farmers' markets, meetings, and cookery courses (https://www.facebook.com/marthaforbundet?fref=ts, retrieved 17.9.2014).

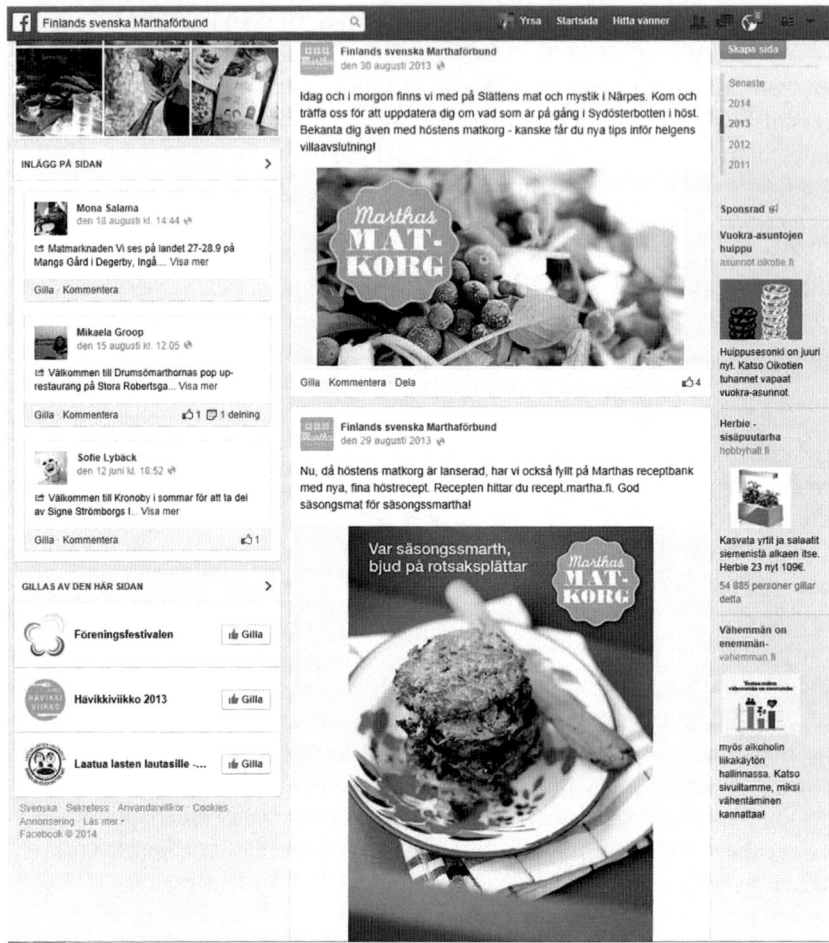

The primary products in the Martha Association's summer food basket consisted of uncomplicated summer food, and the possibility of visiting local producers was also on offer. The basket contained fresh potatoes, tomatoes, cucumbers, root and green vegetables, berries, fish and other foodstuffs connected with the summer season. As was the case with the springtime basket, the summer virtual basket was supplemented with late summer products and with recipes for mushrooms dishes, jams, and the preservation of vegetables.

The summer basket had 2,300 hits on Facebook and 4,000 unique visitors on the Martha website.

The autumn food basket was introduced in August just before what turned out to be a fantastic mushroom season. The key word was "cheap is good" and the recipes focused on everything in the surrounding landscape that was available for free – berries, mushrooms and inexpensive primary products such as cabbage and root vegetables (http://martha.fi/svenska/start/recept/index-51918?def-51918=36, retrieved 17.9.2014). About 2,000 people shared the Facebook information about the autumn virtual basket, and the Martha website had 4,000 unique visitors. The topic was discussed in three newspapers, and it featured as the subject matter of a radio broadcast from one of the major radio stations in Finland.

The last basket was that containing winter food. This final season's basket was perhaps the most challenging for the campaign's goal of helping people to use only local seasonal ingredients. Since everything *can* be bought, the consumer, especially in wintertime, needs to make a conscious decision to buy specifically local food. This basket was introduced during a national week for focusing on waste, including both food and energy waste. Again, root vegetables played an important role in the winter virtual basket and the recipes, which were provided, focused on nourishing soups and casseroles.

Seasonal Food Joy

When analysing the virtual side of the Martha Association's seasonal food campaign, there were a few points that I wanted to explore. One was about the selection of seasonal products. It is obvious that the climate of the Nordic area limits the local selection of foods available during the long winter season. But since the tradition of gathering, picking and preserving wild products is still alive, the campaign was able to connect issues of localness, waste, and economy together by focusing on last year's harvest still lying in deep freezers in many households. Root vegetables, and free forest "food" such as berries and mushrooms, are the central seasonal ingredients highlighted by the Martha project. And, of course, these are the ones that are often neglected if a more global selection is available – goji berries, for example, which are classified as a superfood, can be bought instead of the local blueberries that likewise constitute a superfood. Root vegetables and wild berries are very specific traditional seasonal foods, and it was against the lack of use of these natural ingredients that the Martha campaign wished to react.

Fig. 4: The concept of being a "Martta/Martha" is prevalent in Finnish society. It means being practical, knowing about food, economy, ecology, and about being down-to-earth – a sort of superwoman. One of the leading evening magazines in co-operation with the Finnish Martta Association, published a test on their website entitled "Do you know that in every one of us lives a small Martta? What kind of a Martta are you? Take a test and discover your knowledge of the autumn harvest" (http://www.iltalehti.fi/ruoka/201408220133118_ru.shtml, retrieved 18.9.2014).

Another aspect I wished to explore was the way in which the campaign was presented on social media. The channels used were the trendy, life-style profile websites, as well as Facebook. There was also a deal with some popular food bloggers to mention and promote the campaign. The figures relating to the number of shares, likes, and unique visitors, the campaign gained on social media, are available. But I have also noticed that there are quite a few comments about the campaign on Facebook. From these it is evident that the interactive part, and the feeling of belonging to a community as part of a joint project, was not actually achieved in this format to any great extent, while the traditional way of interacting and disseminating information – by arranging courses, evening classes, meetings, and so on – apparently succeeded far better in creating enthusiasm among the participants. The Martha Association, as the organiser of these events, was happy with the results, and also with the positive interest emanating from the broadcasting and newspaper media.

Finally, I have some reflections and questions of a more general kind resulting from the campaign and how it was presented on a variety of social media – for example: How are food-related lifestyles mediated visually? Food photography has developed over time, from a situation in which it served to provide a realistic visual presentation of food, to being more and more involved in food visualisation processes, which entail appealing to feelings, situations and places. The new social media have increased the impact of visual communication; pictures constantly surround us, while the impact of text has become less important, except for slogans and trademarks (Bergström 2012). Our minds rapidly categorise visual impressions and it is said to take just fifty milliseconds to determinate the aesthetic appeal of something like a website (Lindgaard / Fernandes / Dudekx / Brown 2006). And first impressions have long-lasting effects.

The pictures used in the Martha Association's virtual food baskets campaign are colourful, simple, and fresh. Kitchen utensils, plates and saucepans, are often a little retro in design, something that brings back memories to an older target group but which also appeals to a younger audience interested in flea markets, second hand products, and so on. The pictures agree with the Martha Association's overall image – the campaign is not visually intrusive but follows a familiar Martha Association profile. Since the Association has a reputation for being sincere, reliable, honest, and environmentally and economically focused, this campaign was totally in line with the Association's well-known strategies. Borrowing a term from psychology and marketing, especially from brand marketing, it is likely that the success of the food basket campaign can be classified in terms of a halo effect, that is, if people are satisfied with one product of a specific brand, they are likely to choose other products of the same brand (http://www.allbusiness.com/glossaries/halo-effect/4959645-1.html, retrieved 27.8.2014). So if a person supports the Martha Association's values, that person will most likely also agree with, support, and take part in, this campaign. If a person likes the Association's brochures, recipes and activities in society, he/she will probably also connect the visual impression got from the pictures to this positive image of the "Martha" brand.

Is the Internet, therefore, a medium that can effect change in attitudes and values concerning food habits? I would say yes and no. The Internet offers information, inspiration, recipes and diets, in abundance. It enables one to count calories and carbon footprints easily, but consumers probably need a trigger to cause them to search for something like the Martha Association's virtual seasonal food baskets, to inspire them to actually change their food habits. The social utility, Facebook, which was successfully used in the food basket campaign, can presumably be regarded as a channel of information acting at an individual level. By getting data on your Facebook feed, it would seem as if it is especially directed at you, or you can see from the feed that your friends are aware of something that might also be of interest to you. The Internet of itself is probably not to be regarded as a medium for changing attitudes and values as far as food habits are concerned, but, as a complement to other media, and as a means of inspiration for further engagement with food choices, seasonal and otherwise, it provides valuable information which is within easy reach of most of us on a daily basis.

List of References

Printed

Bergström B.: *Effektiv visuell kommunikation. Om nyheter, reklam och profilering i vår visuella kultur* (Efficient Visual Communication. News, Advertisement and Profiling in Our Visual Culture"). Carlsson: Stockholm 2012.

Lindgaard,G. / Fernandes G. / Dudekx C. / Brown J.: "Attention Web Designers: You have 50 Milliseconds to Make a Good First Impression!" *Behaviour and Information Technology* 25(2), 2006, pp. 115-126

Svenningsson M. / Lövheim M. / Bergquist M.: *Att fånga nätet. Kvalitativa metoder för Internetforskning* ("To Catch the Web. Qualitative Methods for Internet Research"). Studentlitteratur: Lund 2003.

Internet

"The Swedish Martha Association", retrieved from http://martha.fi/english/, 2.10 2014.

http://martha.fi/svenska/hushall/, retrieved 18.9.2014.

http://martha.fi/svenska/start/recept/index-51918?def-51918=36, retrieved 17.9.2014.

http://www.allbusiness.com/glossaries/halo-effect/4959645-1.html, 27.8.2014.

https://www.facebook.com/marthaforbundet?fref=ts, retrieved 17.9.2014.

http://www.iltalehti.fi/ruoka/201408220133118_ru.shtml, retrieved 18.9.2014.

Astra Spalvēna

Picture Me Perfect: The Aesthetics of Food in Online Photographs

The history of the visual representation of food can be said to have started with painting and with still life works of art depicting food items, especially by seventeenth century Dutch artists. The art historian, Kenneth Bendiner, has argued that most still life paintings of food from this period condemned worldly pleasure and were called *vanitas* images, in which edibles of all kinds symbolised the insubstantiality of material life (Bendiner 2004, pp. 8-15). However, food paintings could be so appealing that there was a risk that this moral caution could be buried under a mass of delicious-looking foods, which stimulated the appetite. Carolyn Korsmeyer, examining the philosophy of taste, argues that food can play an important narrative role if it forms a part of a grander painting that tells a legend, a story from the Bible, or from history, but which lacks a meaning of its own. In the modern period, food was regarded also as a subject of art, with the result that its ordinary nutritional role, and its rational and physiological functions, were removed in this context (Korsmeyer 2002 pp. 156-167).

In paintings, therefore, food has had meanings other than those connected with the depiction of real cooking or eating situations. Food depicted in photography also lost some of its previous real-life meanings and acquired new ones connected with one of the basic functions of photography – to document life. Nonetheless, food photographs in the early nineteenth century, essentially adhered to the form adopted in still life paintings. Thereafter, as food photography researcher, Helen G. V. Thompson, has concluded, the precondition of food photography's development as a separate genre was its practical use for illustrating recipes (Thompson 2014). In the first half of the twentieth century, recipes were mostly illustrated with drawings, but from the beginning of the 1950s, cookbooks tended to have black and white photos, which were gradually replaced by colour ones during the succeeding decades.

In the 1980s, food photography, with its lavish and highly-styled food images, again resembled Dutch still life painting. The 1980s was a period which witnessed continual growth in interest in food and it was also the time in which the term "foodie" emerged. Ann Barr and Paul Levy describe foodies as: "the New Man and the New Woman", an "aspiring professional couple to whom food is fashion and art", the "children of consumer boom", and an "international elite", who talk about food, experiencing it as a matter of "glamour and fun" (Barr / Levy 1984, pp. 6-7). Food photography, as part of this aspirational representation of food, showed opulent meals and abundantly-laden tables, but it was only rarely that a particular dish, and the various steps in its creation, was depicted. However, these photographic representations gave rise to the notion of an eternal feast, something which did not correspond with everyday eating habits in general. Later, the whole foodie trend became subject to strong criticism, pointing to its apparently unethical food choices, snobbery, and spiritual degradation (Myers 2014). The foodie trend also affected food photos in that seemingly simpler styles were to be observed, and the emphasis also shifted to focusing on one dish at a time or on a limited display of ingredients. As Thompson (2014) puts it, the aesthetics of food photography were revolutionised in 1990s. Instead of everything in the image being in focus, the background was now unfocused, resulting in the food in question being the centre of attention. By having the backdrop as a blur in the photo, the dish appears softer, less interested in objectivity and more concerned with artistic impression.

These techniques made food look desirable and accessible and, as a result, coffee table cookbooks emerged. In this way, cookbooks became both practical guides to cooking and objects of admiration in their own right. By the late 1990s, illustrated cookbooks became more popular than those without illustrations. In this way, food photography, as a separate genre, gained commercial potential, and this was further developed by new kinds of professionals such as food photographers and food stylists.

With the emergence and popularisation of digital technologies, the situation changed considerably, because it became possible for amateurs to photograph food. In the age of analog photography, it was mostly professionals who took food pictures. Consequently, food appeared only occasionally in family photographic albums – usually when food lovers captured magnificently-laid tables or delightful-looking foods. With the advent of digital technologies, however, the whole process of photography became virtually accessible for everyone without the requirement of having special skills or professional equipment. Consequently, virtually every mundane subject was thought to be worthy of being photographed, thanks to the capacious memory cards of digital cameras, as well as the generous storage spaces in computer hard drives, instead of the just thirty-six shots in a roll of film, or the one hundred pages of a family album. Nowadays, built-in cameras in mobile devices allow people even further possibilities for capturing any place, situation, or indeed, any food item or meal, in an instant.

The social impact of these changes is now an object of study. José van Dijck, who carries out research on new media, focuses on how photos function in virtual space, and asks whether this new situation has an impact on memory and identity. Van Dijck argues that the taking of photographs seems to be no longer primarily an act of memory intended to safeguard a family's pictorial heritage, but rather that it is increasingly becoming a tool for an individual's identity formation and for the communication of that identity. Cameras serve as tools for mediating quotidian experiences other than rituals or ceremonial moments, and this broadens the range of objects photographed. Pictures are shared on social networks, not so much as objects of interest but rather as indicators of personal experiences (van Dijck 2008, pp. 2-6).

Most of the food photographs online circulate in the community of the next generation of foodies who, by means of them, express their aesthetic views as well as their values, beliefs, and their broad range of interests. Although online food photographs do not have any material quality, nonetheless their functions are shaped by the particular online medium used.

Online food blogs, which contain large collections of food photos, also include opinions and comments about food-related issues, as well as illustrated recipes and reflections on the culinary achievements of the blogger. In recent decades, as food blogging has become increasingly popular,[1] the significant aesthetic quality of the pictures in some blogs has enabled such blogs to be singled out and to attract addition attention from a range of browsers. As a consequence, many food bloggers focus particularly on photos. Unlike blogs, online food forums on the other hand, which are created mainly for the sharing and the discussion of recipes, normally consist of short, mostly anonymous posts, which include food pictures for practical purpose, without necessarily having high aesthetic standards in mind. Media sharing sites allow their users to work with their photographs, the most popular in this category being the mobile photo-sharing service Instagram (see instagram.com/, retrieved 10.10.2014), which enables its users to take pictures and videos, apply digital filters to them, and share them on a variety of social networking services. Instagram functions as a social network itself in which the photos can be sorted by keywords (hashtags) and examined in these categories. Social media offer a wide range of functions for food pictures. The characteristic feature of food photos here is that they are evaluated only by appearance. In Fa-

---

1   The first food blog, by cookbook author David Lebovitz, dates to 1999, and in 2002, the *Julie / Julia* project, which opened up food blogging for a huge number of foodies, was launched (Suthivarakom 2014).

cebook, food photographs are mostly used to communicate, to create a story, and to make an impression with regard to oneself.

The international Digital Marketing Agency "360" carried out research about why people put food pictures online, and the reasons they gave were as follows: 25% make a food diary and document everyday meals; 22% document self creations, showing off a finished product or the process involved in its creation; 16% document special occasions; 12% are interested in food art; 10% share the photos of a moment with friends or family; 8% write food / restaurant reviews; 4% teach with recipes, and 3% exhibit extreme food (extremefood.com/, retrieved 10.10.2014) (Digital Marketing Agency "360" 2014). These percentages give an insight into some of the reasons why food photos are posted online; the fact that practical and rational reasons are among the last to be listed is worthy of note.

In order to examine the functions of online food photographs, the approach of visual semiotics developed by Roland Barthes is used in this article. Barthes put forward the idea of layered meanings, involving denotative meaning – i.e. that which is depicted in the picture – and connotative meaning – i.e. the ideas and values that are associated with the things, places and people depicted in the picture; in other words, the factors which allow and enable these associations to be made (Barthes 2009, pp. 131-187; van Leeuwen, 2011, pp. 92-118).

Roland Barthes has used this approach in his essay "Ornamental Cookery" in which he analyses food presentation in the French magazine *Elle*. Barthes concluded that the particular kind of presentation involved revealed ideological meanings, since the depiction of luxury foods and the high level of decoration included, creates an impression of magical, "idea"-cookery, which helps working class readers to forget everyday concerns about how to get food and how to pay for it (Barthes, pp. 89-91).

In this paper, the focus is on the content of the food pictures only, with no account being taken of their verbal context. The main sources which I have used, are Facebook, Instagram and food blogs, all of Latvian origin. However, it is probably true to say that many features of the food pictures discernible in these media are also common globally.

To decipher the denotative meaning of photographs further, the content of the pictures in question is described, as well as the particular ways in which the pictures are presented. Food in this context can refer to foodstuffs, which represent the ingredients of a prepared dish, or a dish itself. Dishes are depicted either ready for serving – in cooking pots, baking trays, and so on, or ready for eating – that is, garnished and on a plate, sometimes with a spoon or fork inserted in the food, or simply left on the plate, or showing food that is already half eaten. Usually, there are one or two portions included in the picture. Sometimes drinks are placed next to the dishes to complement the food, but also to create a complete picture of the meal.

The dishes shown in the photographs are often decorated – either very simply to represent home cooking, or in a more elaborate restaurant-type fashion. Garnishing can make food visually appealing, even festive, and it can also serve to distinguish it from everyday fare. The art of decorating food is to contrast different forms and colours – by the manner in which the different ingredients are arranged on a plate or by scattering chopped greens over a plain dish, or by having a side dish of colourful vegetables, fruits or berries. The elaborate restaurant-style of decoration involves the dripping and the trickling of sauces on dishes, the spreading of cream, and the vertical arrangement of ingredients used. Various figures might be carved – egg mice, cauliflower sheep, letters or numbers, and so on – to please children.

The use of decoration is intended to make food look beautiful. However, a different approach might also be observed, that of preserving the natural appearance of the dish by not using any form of decoration whatsoever. In this scenario, paying attention to the setting of the table with beautiful crockery and cutlery, flowers, and table decorations, and also to the manner in which the food is served, could make the food pretty. A white background is often used to highlight a dish, the photo might be taken from above to give the dish a central position, and close-up shots may also be used in order to lift out every detail of the dish in question. However, Instagram photos represent just the opposite kind of aesthetic: they are often blurry, low key, with dark hues; they embody hipster aesthetics; and they are usually taken using a phone camera.

If the photo shoot takes place indoors, the most common place used for this purpose is either the blogger's home or kitchen, or a restaurant. Photo shoots taken out of doors include locations such as, beautiful landscapes as a background for the serving of the meal (often a picnic taking place by the sea or a lake), woods, or the home vegetable or fruit garden. The home garden is sometimes chosen as a location in order to show where the food came from, as are woods, and sometimes also the local market is used in this context. In cases where the food photos deal with celebrations of one kind or another, people are usually shown sitting around a table, but the food in these pictures is rarely the central object of the photo. In typical food pictures, people are not often included, and if they are, it is mainly just the upper part of the body that is involved in the photos. In restaurant scenes, for example, it usually only the torso of the person sitting opposite the photographer that can be seen, while in cooking scenes, it is usually only the hands which handle the products, and the utensils used in the cooking process, that are visible.

In most cases, the composition of objects in pictures is thoughtful; there are no accidental details, something which might occur if the prepared dish was taken out of the kitchen and brought to another, more attractive location, or if the food was placed against an impressive background for photographic purposes. The objects included, as well as the ways in which they are arranged, convey messages associated with ideas and values. To decipher these messages, a range of objects and the narratives associated with the photos, are further examined. Consequently, it might be implied that several concepts in particular are regarded as being positive – for example, country life, home cooking, the sharing of a meal, or the making of everyday life beautiful, to mention but just a few.

Although food pictures are mainly set indoors, there is a specific way in which the countryside is depicted, even idealised in food photos. Harvesting scenes are often used as a background for spectacular photos. Here gardens and woods are often the backdrop used for piles of golden pumpkins, for carrots with green tops and with earth still attached, for baskets of large mushrooms, or for bowls of freshly-picked berries. The ability to grow one's own food, or even knowing where the food one eats comes from, is seen as a personal achievement, and the joys of simple living are represented in pictures which depict a rustic environment, simple clothing, and retro-style objects. The food also looks rustic – natural in form and colour, cut into big chunks or not carved at all, and often served directly from baking trays, or by simply putting it on a piece of paper.

The growing popularity of food blogs confirms that people do cook at home and that they are interested in sharing their skills with others, and in showing off their achievements. Apart from visually artistic blogs, there are many more created with the intention of demonstrating how a particular dish is made, so that a constructive approach when photographing the dish is required. Ordinary tableware, simply-set tables, as well as the involvement of family members, help to create a sense of a homely atmosphere. These kinds of pictures set out to document ordinary life, and among the meanings which can be inferred from them is that everyone can cook. However, the making and the serving of a homemade meal are still considered an achievement; hence it is photographed and shown to others. But the next step in food blogs is to progress to showing photos of dishes garnished and photographed in imitation of the work of professional chefs and photographers, in order to achieve pictures similar to those in food magazines and in coffee table cookbooks.

Many food photos reveal the convivial and the communal character of a meal. A photo of a shared meal can indicate a special occasion when gathering around the table, and it can also encapsulate the togetherness of the group. Also cooking for friends, family, or a partner, has a positive value attached to it – whether it is a home-made dinner for a big family, or a cake decorated as a present for a parent or a child, or a St. Valentine's breakfast for a loved one, or a table set for two with candles and flowers, that is involved – as all of this points to the cook as being a caring and a loving person. Homemade and joyfully-decorated food for children is testimony to being regarded as a perfect mother. Cooking and eating together is a way of expressing feelings and emotions.

The making of beautiful food and the photographing of it, resemble any spare-time project that is done out of sheer pleasure. Eating can also be a leisure activity, such as when trying out a meal in a famous restaurant or when tasting national cuisine while travelling. Many blogs are devoted to food, but also involve home, garden, and any other everyday activities and objects, which are beautifully presented. This situation serves to demonstrate that everyday life can be beautiful, and that paying attention to ordinary activities can be worthwhile and rewarding.

These positive messages do not reveal the natural state of things; they are more mythological in character. Food in this context represents ideas and values, and fulfils roles other than being a product for consumption. A few further examples of such roles are now provided.

Food as Art

Cooking could be regarded as a way in which to express creative potential. The act of garnishing and decorating a dish makes food similar to an art form. Some decorations represent current fashions, others might be considered to be old-fashioned, thus acknowledging the existence of earlier aesthetic trends and conventions, while others still might represent particular schools in terms of cooking modes and the garnishing of food, like *nouvelle* French cuisine or modern Scandinavian cuisine, for example. The composition, as well as the colours and forms used, are important in food photography, since the dishes function as exhibits to be evaluated by others. Food has to be beautiful to be worth photographing. This makes food an aesthetic object thus eliminating its existential character in this context.

Food as Part of a Gender Myth

The authors of food blogs are very often women, and, by presenting everyday life as being picturesque and rewarding, they carry on the myth of the ideal woman who manages everything, from arranging perfect meals in a beautiful living space, to caring for children, and achieving career success. Cooking is still considered to be a feminine domain, but food can reflect gender bias in other ways as well.

Specific kinds of foods are metaphorically associated with men and women, with reference to alleged natural characteristics of both genders. Sweets and cakes are connected with women, who not only make them, but who are also said to eat them, or to crave them, and who show off the sweet life with friends in cafés and cake shops. Men, on the other hand, are mostly depicted roasting meat, as well as posing with caught fish or shot game. Thus, the gender stereotypes are used not only to indicate that women have a light, sweet nature, but also as means of imposing a duty on men to be strong and to bring home the mammoth.

Food as a Status Symbol

The publishing on social media of photos of food that is considered a luxury – that is, dishes made with expensive, or even, non-seasonal ingredients, and which require complicated and time-consuming preparation – is a means by which people try to upgrade their social status. The same rationale can be said to lie behind the posting of photos of exotic foods from far-off lands, as the implication is that those who took and posted the photos could afford to make expensive trips to unusual destinations.

Homemade food can also be considered a luxury as it can involve time-consuming shopping and preparation, as well as requiring strong financial resources. On the other hand, shop-bought convenience food, and easily-accessible junk food, if used, would often be less expensive than homemade food, and would also be capable of providing the required amount of nutritional calories.

Food as a Part of Identity

Social media offer people the possibility to document the details of their lives – by making pictures of their activities and by sharing them with others via online networks. The documentation of everyday meals creates the idea of a real or an imagined life. A lifestyle story, for example, or a particular version of it, can be told or hinted at on Facebook via pictures of food[2], showing, for instance, a TV dinner for one; a meal eaten while on an exotic trip; a party with friends, funny looking food seen somewhere, a fancy restaurant dinner, a lavish market scene, and so on. A similar story might also be told by using clothing items in a fashion blog, but it is easier and less expensive to upgrade ones social status by using images of food rather than of clothing, cars or real estate, in one's personal blogs.

---

2   For a sample Facebook profile, see Baltā 2014 (htpp://www.facebook.com/inga.balta.5?fref=ts, retrieved 21.5.2014).

To conclude, online food photography documents food but it also documents the society in which the photos are taken and its current views and values. In still life paintings, food has a mostly symbolic function, but in photography, which also has a documentary function, food is more than just an object for fulfilling existential needs; it also conveys social and cultural messages. This article offers a summary of these messages but this is a topic which merits further exploration.

List of References

Printed

Barr, Ann / Levy, Paul: *The Official Foodie Handbook*. Ebury Press: London 1984.

Barthes, Roland: *Mythologies*. Vintage: London 2009 [1957].

Bendiner, Kenneth: *Food in Painting. From the Renaissance to the Present*. Reaktion Books: London 2004.

Korsmeyer, Carolyn: *Making Sense of Taste*. Cornell University Press: Ithaca and London 2002 [1999].

Van Dijck, José: "Digital Photography: Communication, Identity, Memory". *Visual Communication* 1, 2008, pp. 57-76.

Van Leeuwen, Theo: "Semiotics and Iconography". In: van Leeuwen, Theo / Jewitt, Carey (eds.): *Handbook of Visual Analysis*. Sage: Los Angeles et al. 2011 [2001], pp. 92-118.

Internet

"Baltā Inga", retrieved 21.5.2014, from https://www.facebook.com/inga.balta.5?fref=ts.

Digital Marketing Agency "360": "Online Food & Photo Sharing Trends", retrieved 21.5.2014, from http://www.360i.com/reports/online-food-photo-sharing-trends/.

www.extremefood.com, retrieved 10.10.2014)

"Foodspotting", retrieved 10.10.2014, from www.crunchbase.com/organization/foodspotting.

"Instagram", retrived 10.10.2014, from instagram.com.

Myers, B.R.: "The Moral Crusade Against Foodies", retrieved 3.6.2014, from http://www.theatlantic.com/magazine/archive/2011/03/the-moral-crusade-against-foodies/308370/.

"Pinterest", retrieved 10.10.2014, from https://www.pinterest.com/.

Suthivarakom, Ganda: A Brief History of Food Blogs, retrieved 14.01.2014, from http://www.saveur.com/article/Kitchen/A-Brief-Food-Blog-Timeline.

Thompson, Helen G. V.: "It Isn't a Little Subject – A History of Food Photography", retrieved 4.6.2014, from http://helengraceventurathompson.com/blog/historyoffoodphotography/?page_id=5.

Rafał Pilarek

"Cabane à Sucre" on the Internet

The subject of this article is the role of the Internet in promoting traditional Canadian restaurants called *cabanes à sucre* ("sugar cabins"). Before dealing in detail
with this aspect of the paper it is worth taking a closer look at the history and rich
tradition of "the maple feasts" in Quebec. Canadian cuisine as a whole reflects all
the complexity and geographical peculiarity of the country itself. Populated by immigrants of various cultural origins, Canada is a melting pot of culinary flavours,
customs, and tastes. The Atlantic provinces, which were colonised by the French
over a period of four centuries, still retain French cuisine traditions, which were
enriched over time by methods of preparing wild game, fish and maple syrup
meals borrowed from the Mi'kmaq Indians, First Nation people, indigenous to
the Maritime Provinces and the Gaspé Peninsula of Quebec, Canada. Most of the
first settlers who came to Quebec had their origins in the northeast of France, in,
for example, the Charente-Maritime region to the north of Bordeaux (Copeland
2007, pp. 117, 119). The immigrants, who were used to rural hardships in their
homeland, coped well with the severe climate of New France, and because of it,
they quickly mastered the technique of extracting syrup from the maple trees.
This was a necessary survival technique – for both for the Indian people and the
colonisers – as maple syrup constituted the only source of carbohydrates that was
available during the long, severe Canadian winters. In this way, it became a symbol
of endurance and continued existence for both groups of people. The exceptional
significance of the maple tree in Canada is evident from the fact that by 1700 the
maple leaf had already apparently become a national symbol of Canada (www.
pch.gc.ca/eng/1363626184104/1363626227047, retrieved 4.03.2014). As in past
times, maple syrup still constitutes one of the most recognisable food products
of Canada and it has become a key element of the culinary culture of the country. Against this background, the traditional Canadian restaurants called *cabanes
à sucre* will now be discussed.

Maple syrup is known as a natural sugar. It is produced by the evaporation of
water from the sap drawn from the trunk of a maple tree (Latin: *acer saccharum*).
It is a purely natural product which is rich in sugars, minerals, and vitamins,
and which has anti-bacterial properties just like honey (www.agmrc.org/com-
modities_products/specialty_crops/maple-sugar-profile, retrieved 16.06. 2014).
Canada is one of the leading producers of maple syrup, three-quarters of which

is generated in the country's largest province, Quebec. Outside of Canada, maple syrup is also produced in the U.S. states of Vermont, Maine, New York, Pennsylvania and Ohio (ibid.).

The first people to produce maple syrup and maple sugar were the native Indian people inhabiting the northeastern regions of North America (Lips 1971, pp. 259; Herd 2010, pp. 16-17). Maple tree products had deep symbolic significance for them, as, according to numerous legends, they were believed to be a gift offered to humans by the Gods (Lawrence / Rux 1993, pp. 54-55). The harvesting period for maple syrup, which falls at the end of February and at the beginning of March, was looked on – despite the amount of additional work involved – as a time of fun and enjoyment. Gatherings, accompanied by various rites and ceremonies, would take place in specially prepared wigwams maintained specifically for that occasion (Taylor 1994, pp. 237). The most famous of the festive events which took place at this time was known as the Maple Dance, which was held during the first spring full moon (Eagleson / Hasner 2006, p. 15). The syrup produced by the native Indian people served mainly as a valuable addition to their meals. It was used to sweeten fruits, vegetables, cereals and even fish. Mixed with water, it was served as a nutritional energy drink (Taylor 1994, p. 237).

In the early stages of the colonisation of the northeastern part of North America, the native Indian people passed on their knowledge about maple syrup production to the newcomers from Europe (www.library.uvm.edu/maple/history/timeline.php, retrieved 4.3.2014). French and English colonists continuously perfected maple production techniques by introducing new tools and processing methods. A significant technological breakthrough took place in the 1970s when, in order to collect the juice from the trees and to transfer it to a processing destination, plastic pipes were used for the first time, by means of which, together with the help of vacuum pumps, the juice was collected in a storage area, then brought to a room with an evaporator in a *cabane à sucre*, where the production of the syrup was be carried out (Duncan 2003, pp. 12-14).

In North America, the forest farms which produce maple syrup are called "sugarbush" or "sugarwood" farms, while the buildings where the maple sap is boiled are called "sugar houses", "sugar shacks", "sugar shanties" or "sugar cabins". In the French-speaking region of Quebec, which has the longest tradition of maple syrup production, these buildings, which also function as maple restaurants, are commonly called *cabanes à sucre* ("sugar cabins") (www. web.archive.org/web/20060429074616/http://ohioline.osu.edu/b856/, retrieved 28.02.2014).

The tradition of holding "maple feasts" in Quebec dates back to the early nineteenth century, when wooden sheds began to be erected as canteens for lumberjacks and farm workers labouring in the maple orchards. These simple buildings made of hewn piles were also a place where farmers, together with their families and neighbours, could come to taste maple products (www.nytimes. com/2009/02/08/travel/08explorer.html?pagewanted=all&_r=0, retrieved 28.2. 2014). The popularity of these maple gatherings increased after the Second World War, when the "maple shacks" began to draw visitors from the big cities and when Canada became an ever more popular destination for foreign tourists (Fig.1).

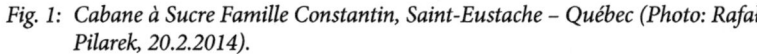

Fig. 1: Cabane à Sucre Famille Constantin, Saint-Eustache – Québec (Photo: Rafał Pilarek, 20.2.2014).

The most important part of the family gatherings in the *cabanes à sucre* is a meal consisting of traditional dishes such as pea soup, country sausage, pancakes, homemade pickles, omelette with ham or bacon, eggs, and the traditional French Canadian *tourtière* – a pork pie. The main culinary attraction of a *cabane à sucre* is, however, maple syrup, which is regarded as an irreplaceable addition to most dishes. These culinary gatherings, often involving hundreds of people, are accompanied by performances by folk artists. In addition to the traditional meal, a *cabane à sucre* offers its guests other attractions, such as culinary workshops in which the participants can make their own maple lollipops known as *tire d'érable*, horse-drawn sleigh rides, snowmobile tours, cross-country skiing in the maple forest, as well as massages and dance courses (Fig. 2).

Fig. 2: Horse-drawn sleigh ride, Cabane à Sucre Famille Constantin, Saint-Eustache (Photo: Rafał Pilarek, 20.2.2014).

The tradition of family gatherings in the *cabanes à sucre* remains an important part of the cultural and culinary heritage of Quebec. The "sugar shacks" located in the vicinity of the maple orchards are also one of the biggest tourist attractions of the region. With these considerations in mind, the provincial authorities, as well as numerous non-governmental organisations, are taking action to support this form of social activity. Nowadays, in addition to traditional media and education, the Internet has an ever-increasing role in promoting the traditions of *cabanes à sucre*. Information about the "sugar shacks" as attractive places for family vacations appear on many Canadian Internet sites devoted to tourism. Of particular note in this regard is the official government of Quebec portal: QuébecOriginal – www.bonjourQuebec.com, which provides extensive information on, among other things, the culinary traditions of the province. *Cabanes à sucre* are also mentioned on the pages of other travel portals such as www.quebecregion. com, www.quebecvacances.com, and www.tourisme-montreal.org, as well as on the Quebec tourist information websites.

Currently, in the French-speaking province, there are more than two hundred *cabanes à sucre* in operation, located mainly around the two largest cities, Montreal and Quebec (www.artdevivre.restomontreal.ca/le-printemps-arrive-allons-a-la-cabane-a-sucre/, retrieved 4.3. 2014). Maple restaurants are mostly family-run businesses, where culinary traditions are handed down from generation to generation. The "maple inns" are associated with the Association des Restaurateurs Cabane à Sucre du Quebec. Their website, www.laroutedessucres.com, is a veritable compendium of knowledge about maple syrup production and about its use in traditional Canadian cuisine. Additionally, the website publishes a detailed list of all *cabanes à sucre* operating in the province and provides a practical search engine that is useful for selecting and locating the various premises. Similar information appears on the website: www.siropderable.ca, which is the official website of the federation of maple syrup producers in Quebec (Fédération des Producers Acéricoles du Québec). This organisation is very active in promoting maple syrup in Canada and around the world. The portal www.cabaneasucre.org is particularly popular among fans of maple syrup and traditional gatherings in the *cabanes à sucre*, and currently has 190,000 users. Here also a list of all currently operating *cabanes à sucre*, is to be found, as well as practical recipes, links to sites related to the tradition of maple syrup, and many other interesting facts connected with the "sugar shack" gatherings. In addition, the portal provides a direct link to the blog, www.lesfillesdelerable.ca, containing information about current cultural and educational events related to maple culture. Maple syrup also has a presence on Facebook in the form of a group called *J'aime l' érable* ("I like/I love maple") with nearly 13, 000 members (as of 30 March 2014), as well as on Twitter and YouTube.

It should be emphasised, nevertheless, that the main sources of information on the functioning of the *cabanes à sucre* are the individual websites of the restaurants themselves. According to the Association des restaurateurs de cabanes à sucre du Québec, out of the 233 "sugar shacks" in operation (www.laroutedessucres.com, retrieved 19.03.2014), 153 have their own websites. This data suggests that nearly 66%[1] of *cabanes à sucre* owners treat the Internet as a desirable and effective marketing tool. Most of the websites provide an extensive service, including a detailed description of the activities offered by their respective establishments. Only a very small number of restaurateurs use the simplest forms of online advertising, e.g. business cards and brochures.

A review of *cabane à sucre* websites reveals that most of them are of high quality as regards their content, design and user-friendliness. One feature in particular that stands out is the artistic design of the websites, which in many cases corresponds to the individual character of the restaurant being presented. In addi-

---

1 According to the author's calculations based on data published by the Association des Restaurateurs des Cabane à Sucre du Québec.

tion, the *cabane à sucre* websites contain, in most cases, extensive photo galleries, which further enhance the attractiveness of this medium. The user-friendliness of the websites also deserves praise in most cases. This has been achieved by the skilful highlighting of key elements, the careful selection of typography, and by an efficient system of navigation. There are, however, certain reservations about the websites that deserve mention, especially the fact that only some websites are tailored to the needs of people with disabilities. This would seem to be a significant drawback for the websites and businesses in question, since this cohort currently represents from 8% to 10% of Internet users (www.web.archive.org/web/20060429074616/http://ohioline.osu.edu/b856/, retrieved 26. 3.2014).

In the case of the more extensive *cabane à sucre* websites, users navigate by way of individual links / tabs on the homepage of the restaurant. A typical *cabane à sucre* website will begin with a "Welcome" or an "About us" page. This part of the site usually contains information about the location, standard, size, and history of the "sugar house". In the case of a restaurant which boasts a particularly rich tradition, this information is usually presented under a tab / link marked "history". An essential part of every *cabane à sucre* website is the menu that also includes the current price-list of dishes. All the necessary information on the additional attractions offered by the "maple shack" can be found by Internet users under the tab / link, "attractions" or "suggestions". In addition, each of the *cabane à sucre* websites allows users to make online reservations.

Most of the "maple inns" in addition to their restaurant activities, also sell regional products based on maple syrup. These products can be purchased on the spot or through the website of the restaurant under the tab / link, "Products" or "Souvenirs". In summary, it should be stated that maple syrup has become an indisputable trademark of Canada. The proof of this is the fact that this product belongs to the group of souvenirs that are most frequently purchased by visitors to the country. The popularity of maple syrup in many parts of the world is evident from the rising annual exports of this product, mainly to the U.S., Japan, France, and Germany. It should be noted that maple feasts are popular among both Canadians themselves and tourists to the country, and they are organised mainly in the eastern part of Canada. The evidence for this observation is the immense number of publications, blogs, discussion groups, and photographs, published on this subject on the Internet.

In summarising the above considerations it can be concluded that, currently, Internet websites are the most common and effective form of advertising for the traditional *cabane à sucre* restaurants in Canada, the profits of which reached 144 million Canadian dollars in 2013. (www.newswire.ca/en/story/737941/the-economic-importance-of-quebec-maple-production, retrieved 28.2.2014). The role of the Internet in promoting *cabanes à sucre* is not limited solely to commercial issues. The global net plays an important role in cultivating and promoting the cultural traditions of the region both nationally and internationally. The Internet is also an excellent platform for an exchange of views on a *cabane à sucre* experience, as well as on the emotions and sensations experienced as a result of participation in maple syrup culture. The role of the Internet in this respect is all the greater, as the sugar gatherings in Quebec are a unique combination of tradition, fun and friendship.

List of References

Printed

Copeland, Colette: "Kuchnia" ("The Kitchen"). In: Rudnicki Bogdan (ed.): *Kanada*. Mediaprofit: Warsaw 2007, pp. 117, 119.

Duncan, Dorothy: *Nothing More Comforting: Canada's Heritage Foods*. Dundurn Press: Totonto 2013.

Eagleson, Janet / Hasner, Rosemary: *The Maple Syrup Book*. Boston Mills Press: Richmond Hill, Ontario 2006.

Herd, Tim: *Maple Sugar. From Sap to Syrup. The History, Lore, and How-to Behind this Sweet Treat*. Storey Publishing: North Adams MA. 2010.

Lawrence, James M. / Rux, Martin: *Sweet Maple: Life, Lore and Recipes from the Sugarbush*. Houghton Mifflin Harcourt:Willowdale, Ontario 1993.

Lips, Ewa: *Księga Indian* ("The Book of the Indians"). Wiedza Powszechna: Warsaw 1971.

Taylor, Colin F.: "Indianie Regionu Północno-Wschodniego" ("The Indians of the North-East"). In:

Collins, Richard (ed.): *Indianie Ameryki Północnej* ("The Indians of North America"). Muza SA: Warsaw 1994.

Internet

Agricultural Marketing Resource Center: "Maple Sugar Profile", retrieved 16.6.2014, from http://www.agmrc.org/commodities__products/specialty_crops/maple-sugar-profile/.

Association des Restaurateurs de Cabanes à Sucre du Québec: *Liste des Cabanes à sucre*, retrieved 19.3.2014, from http://laroutedessucres.com

Fédération des Producers Acéricoles du Québec, retrieved 16.6.2014, from http://www.siropderable.ca/accueil.aspx.

Government of Canada: "Canadian Heritage", retrieved 4.3.2014, from http://www.pch.gc.ca/eng/1363626184104/1363626227047.

J'aime l'érable: "Le sirop d'érable et les produits d'érable du Québec", retrieved 16.06.2014, from http://jaimelerable.ca/.

"Les filles de l'érable", retrieved 16.6.2014, from http://lesfillesdelerable.ca/.

Maple: "O syropie" ("On the Syrup"), retrieved 16.6.2014, from

http://www.maple.com.pl/web/index.php/main/index/pg/o-syropie.

The New York Times. Travel section: "Tapping the Flavors of a Quebec Sugar Shack", retrieved 28.2.2014, (www.nytimes.com/2009/02/08/travel/08explorer.html?pagewanted=all&_r=0, retrieved 28.2. 2014).

The Ohio State University: "Maple Production and Processing Facilities", retrieved 28.2.2014, from http://web.archive.org/web/20060429074616/http://ohioline.osu.edu/b856/.

"Pour des idées de vacances et de sorties au Québec", retrieved 28.2.2014, from http://www.quebecvacances.com/.

PR Newswire: "The Economic Importance of Quebec Maple Production", retrieved 28.2.2014, from www.newswire.ca/en/story/737941/the-economic-importance-of-quebec-maple-production.

Quebec City and Area", retrieved 28.2.2014, from http://www.quebecregion.com/en/.

Quebec: "Guide to Attractions, Events and Vacation Packages", retrieved 28.2.2014, from http://www.quebecindulge.com/.

Restomontreal: "C'est le printemps, allons à la cabane à sucre!", retrieved 4.3.2014, from http://artdevivre.restomontreal.ca/le-printemps-arrive-allons-a-la-cabane-a-sucre/.

Site touristique officiel du government du Québec: "QuebecOrginal", retrieved 28.2.2014, from http://www.bonjourquebec.com/.

TAAT technologie cyfrowe: "Jak ocenić jakość wykonania strony internetowej?" ("How to Evaluate the Quality of an Internet Website Design?), retrieved 26.3.2014, from http://web.archive.org/web/20060429074616/http://ohioline.osu.edu/b856/.

The University of Vermont: "Maple History Timeline", retrieved 4.3.2014, from http://library.uvm.edu/maple/history/timeline.php.

PART IV:
Food, Gender, Identity and the Internet

Rogéria Campos de Almeida Dutra

When Men go to the Kitchen: Food and Gender in Brazilian Websites

Introduction

Eating habits are experienced in their traditional forms through the invisible dynamics of everyday life which include, *inter alia*, gestures, rites and codes inherited from family and local tradition. However, the modernisation of society through industrialisation and increasing urbanisation, which intensifies people flows and information exchange, favours the adoption of varied feeding habits, which can be more freely established and moulded along a personal trajectory.

The dialogue between these dimensions – traditional cultural patterns and personal choices – gives rise to singular food combinations, through a constant negotiation of reality that occurs in the context of complex industrial societies, which not only aggregates heterogeneous groups but also produces them. While some members of this sector of society prioritise links with the broader tradition in order to maintain their inherited habits, others, with a higher predisposition towards innovation and the expansion of the gustatory universe, use dietary practices as an alternative route to individualisation. It is worth remembering, however, that social reality is a dynamic and also often a contradictory process, with no clear divisions between "traditional and modern" forms to be seen, as there is no automatic association between certain values and certain social groups. In short, no specific food pattern exists in a cultural vacuum, since any such configuration is subject to a constant exertion of influence stemming either from the media or from people's friends and relatives (Simmel 1971; Hannerz 1980; Fischler 2000).

Luis C. Cascudo (1983) drew attention to the "inviolability" of the popular diet, as opposed to the upper class one, which is frequently "opened to every breath of elegant variation". Although some caution is necessary when making generalisations of this kind, these differences are essentially confirmed by Bourdieu (1979) who reflected on how taste can transform food preferences into distinct and distinctive signs. Social differences and inequalities are reflected in dietary practices in society, such as in the opposition between the upper class "taste of luxury", based on the freedom of choice, and the lower class "taste of necessity", which is modest in its economic limitations. It is as if one part of society was selected for the "extraordinary" and festive dimensions of food while the other was confined mainly to a state of the everyday frugality of life (Goody 1982). The transmission of culinary practices and their associated recipes can occur in a variety of ways. Such transmission is often triggered by means of "live" education, that is, face-to-face relationships in which those who "learn to do", cook by watching (and remembering) those "who know how to do", in action. This kind of cultural heritage transmission is, or was for a long time, a part of the process of the socialisation of most women in society (Halbawachs 1984). However, other ways of passing on culinary knowledge and skills have developed over the last three centuries. In addition to culinary manuscripts – eminently feminine objects and part of families' heritage – the development of the press with the advent of modernity, as well as the expansion of formal education, brought cookbooks into being. Thus, by applying a formal language to the largely informal knowledge of the kitchen, the diffusion of culinary knowledge in the public sphere was made possible by this form of written transmission. Cookbooks democratised access to culinary formulas and taste sensations, as well as facilitating the authorship experience for many culinary experts. The expansion of the print media enabled cooking recipes to spread, once they had conquered space in newspapers and women's magazines.

Recipes tend to circulate among those who have an interest in and somehow deal with cooking in one way or another, either practising it on a daily basis or during leisure time. The advent and development of the virtual network, over the last twenty years or so, has given added impetus to the exchange of culinary information, as it has provided Internet users with greater freedom of choice in terms of accessing and sharing culinary data. A process of constant redefinition of values accompanies the accelerating pace of change that occurs in complex industrial societies. The co-existence of multiple orientations results in the "construction" of different dietary patterns with different signs providing the experience of varied gustatory delights.

Men in the Kitchen

The act of cooking leads to the provision of much more than a meal once it indicates social relationships. Messages about how women and men are supposed to act in our society and the roles which they are expected to play, can be depicted by our food culture. In this context, the pioneering study of Bantu culture in Africa, by Audrey Richards ([1932] 2005) in the first half of the twentieth century, provides a good example of the importance of food-centered activities and food-cultural meanings, to the construction of gender relations and identities. Richards showed that in Bantu culture, gender hierarchies were maintained through differential control over, and access to, food. In fact, study of small-scale tribal societies has pointed to the existence of a classical division of labour in which most of the cultivation work is allocated to woman while hunting is assigned to men. Based on his studies of the eating habits of tribal societies of North and South America in the mid twentieth century, Levi-Strauss (2006) associated the boiling of food with the feminine universe in opposition to the roasting of food with the male universe.

Concerning activities associated with food provision and preparation, there is a clear traditional gender division of labour evident in our society. Men's economic status is demonstrated by their control over food provision, while women are credited with controlling the cooking and serving processes. Despite modern women's involvement in production activities, both inside and outside the home, their day-to-day lives are portrayed in ways that emphasise their internal domestic responsibilities. This situation does not, however, indicate that men are completely removed from cooking activities but rather that they are hardly ever associated with home-cooking arenas. In other words, they are usually involved in cooking in the public domain as professional cooks and entrepreneurs. In early modern times in Europe – in France, Spain and Italy – male cooks were one of the main groups employed at court and by the aristocracy. The culture of gastronomy offered men the opportunity to become famous, by serving the aristocracy and transforming the culinary art into a specialist field of endeavour. They became famous through the authentic discourse and doctrine of gastronomy (Sarti 2012). After the French Revolution, a great number of cooks who had formerly served the aristocracy opened restaurants in urban centres, thus making their skills accessible to an emerging bourgeois group. The emergence of the restaurant as a public space consolidated male cooking as a profession, and male chefs still prevail in professional kitchens today (Spang 2000).

It has also been observed, however, that nowadays men are becoming increasingly involved in all aspects of meal preparation in the home. A study conducted by researchers at the University of Michigan about the lifestyle habits of a group of men and women born between 1961 and 1981, has noted that male American youths spend more time shopping for and cooking food, watching cooking shows on TV, and talking to their friends about food and cooking, than was formerly the case (http://healthland.time.com/2012/04/30/generation-x-men-spend-more-time-in-the-kitchen, retrieved 18.8.2014). They are learning basic culinary skills, as well as becoming cookery buffs and information consumers.

If cookbooks have been instrumental in contributing to the provision of cooking information to the general public, the growing number of online cooking websites indicates that the Internet has become a much broader and less expensive source of information about cooking, than cookbooks ever were. The next section will discuss how the study of online Brazilian cooking sites dedicated to men shows that male interest in the kitchen is steadily increasing.

Male Cooking Sites

Brazil is the fifth largest country, and has the seventh highest rate of Internet usage, in the world. It is also experiencing a growing interest in the Internet as a medium of communication as well as a means of obtaining general information. Online cookery websites vary as regards content and presentation and have different approaches to the culinary universe. They range from sites depicting traditional regional cuisine to those dealing with practical and ordinary kitchen cooking. The sites are a means by which culinary knowledge can be accessed by a growing middle class sector, consisting of people who spend their time between work, and household tasks such as cooking. In common with others in the developing world, these people, who have been engaged in obtaining formal education, have spent the greater part of their lives away from the traditional domestic domains, where traditional culinary knowledge is transmitted informally by word of mouth and by example.

Although traditional cultural values in our society are identified in terms of the hierarchical family model, in which clear divisions of gender roles, with household activities dedicated to women, are evident, the makeup of urban middle class families has been changing. Single parent households are on the increase, as are the number of adults living alone, and families consisting of two working spouses. Contrary to the prevailing culture of *machismo*, which states that traditional feminine activities serve to compromise perceptions of masculinity, Brazilian men, at least those who are younger and residing in urban areas, have become more involved with cooking and cooking culture in the home.

Having analysed a total of twenty Brazilian culinary websites and blogs dedicated to the male public, this exploratory research has revealed that there are three major trends, or different approaches to male cooking, evident in these websites. The first group of sites is dedicated to first-time male cooks. The names of these sites are indicative of men being out of place in a feminine domain: "Men in the Kitchen" (http://www.homemnacozinha.com/, retrieved 18.8.2014), "Briefs in the Kitchen" (http://www.cuecasnacozinha.com/, retrieved 18.8.2014), and "Husbands in the Kitchen" (http://maridonacozinha.com.br/, retrieved 18.8.2014) Their aim is to introduce the male public to the culinary universe by presenting step by step instructions to basic cooking and to a practical cuisine. By finding it necessary to teach men how to cook ordinary Brazilian dishes, such "Boiled Black Beans", these websites demonstrate, not only that cooking some "obvious" Brazilian recipes – part and parcel of informal domestic learning – has not been a part of male education, but also that at the present time, immediate contact for men with familiar cooking references, actually exists.

The second group of websites, with names such as "Deep Plate" (http://prato-fundo.com/, retrieved 18.8.2014), emphasises the pleasure associated with eating and, consequently, with cooking. They talk about cooking as a means of achieving refinement, as a way of exploring new skills, of improving taste, and of enjoying the art of conviviality. They promote cooking as leisure activity and offer recipes which are suitable for occasions when friends are invited to home gatherings. The sites also suggest that cooking is a comfortable and socially valued activity for men. Information and suggestions about alcoholic beverages have a special place in these websites, thus confirming that drinking is still regarded as a traditional symbol of male identity.

The third group is composed of websites which specialise in offering recipes linked to fictional characters inspired by epic adventures of the Middle Ages. Here can be found, for instance, a recipe for Lembas Bread (a nutritious bread wrapped in leaves in "The Lord of the Rings" story). There are also sites and blogs dedicated to "Nerd Kitchen" which include some junk food recipes. Dealing mostly with a young male public, they also refer to "ogre cooking", that is to say, to a culinary form without "frills", or to the "true culinary", or "war culinary" form. This differs from sophisticated gastronomy by presenting big sandwiches and creative solutions for day-to-day hunger. Some of these culinary blogs show men cooking informally in small common kitchens with sinks overflowing with dirty bowls and plates. The sites also present improvised recipes with ordinary ingredients – such as toasted bread with sausages prepared in the middle of the night or a basic pasta for dinner – which can be a "salvation board" when men must try hard in order to get some nourishment.

In addition to presenting recipes and cooking hints, all of these websites use photos to illustrate not only the completed dish, but also the various steps involved in its production, so that the user can cook it successfully by following the pictures. It is important also to highlight the communication mechanisms offered by the cooking websites to their users, such as mailing lists and comment boxes designed to enhance and encourage conversation and online forums. These mechanisms strengthen the creation of virtual networks. and stimulate the sharing of experiences and information with other bloggers, based on a common interest in cooking. Food blogs, in particular, contribute greatly to the diffusion of cooking experiments, once this web format permits personal publishing and creative writing. The sidebar on these websites, listing other sites frequently visited, serves to enlarge this network and to maintain a continuous form of contact between its followers.

In terms of the cultural construction of gender roles, the exploratory research undertaken for this paper demonstrates the way in which male web users in particular, have been dealing with food and cooking in Brazil. Although modern values are influencing gender perspectives in food-centered activities, dietary pattern differentiation still persists. Thus alcohol products, as well as red meat, continue to serve as indicators of maleness, whereas products such as vegetables, fruit and sweet foods are not commonly found in male cooking sites. It is also evident that emphasis is being placed on the pleasure of eating and on large food portions, in these male-oriented websites. Men cook for fun, for friends and close family gatherings, or for themselves; they prepare dishes, not ordinary meals on an everyday basis. It is thus evident from these websites that men have been using food in their personal and collective performances as a grounding force for self-expression.

In her study of male cookbooks, Colleen Eils (2010) reports that the male cookbook genre reproduces traditional portrayals of gender roles. It deals with the mainstream belief that men must justify being in the home kitchen, and it presents a kind of cooking style that forms part of an authorised masculinity – a kitchen on men's own terms, defined by male exceptionalism as cooks. Cooking as a male professional in a kitchen, and dealing with prestigious cuisine, can be considered a safe space for masculinity. However, the occupying of an uncomfortable feminised space, such as a home kitchen, demands cultural value negotiation: thus men are only expected to cook domestically in authorised circumstances.

Cooking websites directed at Brazilian males follow this tendency. They offer men the opportunity to be exceptional cooks at home by providing details about special dishes for non-ordinary occasions. However, these websites also contribute to the idea of male cooking autonomy in the home kitchen. By describing cooking as a matter of survival for guys who need to feed themselves, they acknowledge that the reality of day-to-day living for many men is not necessarily that of marrying at a young age, or of being fed by women.

The investigation of male cooking websites provides an opportunity for the examination of popular representations of domestic space, as well as for finding out about cultural trends in the transmission of cooking knowledge. Food habits are being moulded by forces other than those which are local, and familiar, once urban young men have the possibility to build their own food universe by combining different ideas and influences concerning food.

List of References

Printed

Bourdieu, P. *La distinction. Critique social du jugement.* Editions de Minuit: Paris, 1979.

Cascudo, Luis C. *História da Alimentação do Brasil.* Itatiaia: Belo Horizonte 1983.

Fischler, Claude: *L'Homnivore.*, Odille Jacob: Paris 2001.

Goody, Jack: *Cooking, Cuisine and Class: A Study in Comparative Sociology.* Cambridge University Press: Cambridge. 1982.

Hannerz, Ulf: *Exploring the City. Inquiries towards an Urban Anthropology.* Columbia University Press: New York 1980.

Halbwachs, Maurice: *Les cadres sociaux de la mémoire.* Albin Michel: Paris 1984.

Levi-Strauss, Claude. *A origem dos modos à mesa.* Cosac Naify: São Paulo 2006.

Richards, Audrey: *Hunger and Work in a Savage Tribe: A Functional Study of Nutrition among the Southern Bantu.* Routledge: London 2005. First published 1932.

Sarti, Raphaela: "Melhor o cozinheiro? Um percurso sobre a dimensão de gênero da preparação da comida (Europa ocidental, séculos XVI-XIX)" ("A Male Cook, Is this Better? An Overview of the Gender Dimension of Cooking [Western Europe, 16th to 19th centuries]"). *Cadernos Pagu.* (39) jul/dez 2012, pp. 87-158.

Simmel, George: *On Individuality and Social Forms.* University of Chicago Press: Chicago, 1971.

Spang, Rebecca: *The Iinvention of the Restaurant. Paris and Modern Gastronomic Culture.* Harvard University Press: London 2000.

Internet

Eils, Colleen G: "'Storm in the Kitchen!' Popular Representations of Masculine Domesticity

in the Male Cookbook Genre". MA Thesis Report, The University of Texas at Austin 2010. Retrieved May 25.5.2014, from http://repositories.lib.utexas.edu/ bitstream/handle/2152/ETD-UT-2010-05-1444/EILS-MASTERS-REPORT. pdf?sequence=1.

http://healthland.time.com/2012/04/30/generation-x-men-spend-more-time-in-the-kitchen, retrieved 18.8.2014.

http://www.homemnacozinha.com/, retrieved 18.8.2014.

http://maridonacozinha.com.br/, retrieved 18.8.2014.

http://pratofundo.com/, retrieved 18.8.2014.

Laura Solanilla and F. Xavier Medina

Gastronomy and Social Networks: Heritage and Food Blogging in Catalonia

This article presents the results of research which analysed the relationship between cuisine and identity in Catalonia in the context of new digital practices. The aim of the research was to test whether social networks, mobile devices, and the popularisation of ICT (Information and Communications Technology) were becoming factors associated with the recognition of culinary practices as elements of identity in contemporary Catalonia. The results show that these new online practices are transforming the definition of Catalan cuisine and reformulating it in accordance with new contemporary values.

Historical and Cultural Background

Catalan cuisine is one of the best historically documented cuisines in the world. The first known cookbook in the Catalan language is the Book of (the three books known as) *Sent Soví* (14th century), which is also one of the most ancient European cookbooks in the vernacular language (Grewe 2003). Towards the end of the fifteenth century (c. 1485), Master Rupert de Nola in Naples wrote *Llibre del Coch* (cf. Leimgruber 1996), also in Catalan. Throughout the modern era, and especially during the reign of the Borgia family in Rome, dishes prepared in the "Catalan way" became popular in different European courts.

From the eighteenth century onwards, Catalan cuisine suffered a withdrawal period which lasted until well into the nineteenth century. In 1835, the anonymous *La cuynera catalana* ("The Catalan Cook") appeared (cf. Queralt 2009). This was not just a cookbook, as it also described, in a very didactic manner, hygiene protocols for the table, in food preservation, and even for domestic economy. This book is important from the perspective of this paper because, for the first time, the word *cook* and the adjective *Catalan* appear together – in its title.

In the early twentieth century, the writer Ignasi Domènech, having contributed to the promotion of French *haute cuisine* among the Catalan bourgeoisie, published his book *La Teca: la veritable cuina casolana de Catalunya* (1924) ("A Meal: The True Homemade Cuisine of Catalonia") (cf. Domènech 2005). It soon became a classic wedding gift for middle-class young couples. But the explicit relationship between *cuisine and identity* and the emergence of the concept of a *national* Catalan cuisine appeared for the first time in 1928 with the publication of *Llibre de la cuina catalana* ("Book of Catalan Cooking") compiled by the journalist and politician Ferran Agulló (cf. Agulló 1990). During the Spanish Civil War (1936-1939) both works sank into oblivion and they have only recently come to attention once more. This War led to destruction, poverty and hunger in Catalonia, as a result of which food became an obsession for a large segment of society.

The Loss of Traditional Cooking (1960-1970)

During the Franco dictatorship (1939-1975), the concept of Catalan cuisine was banned. Nevertheless, some authors who published books and articles on "Spanish Cuisine" made timid references to "regional Catalan cuisine" – for example, *El Libro de la cocina española* ("The Book of Spanish Cuisine"), by Néstor Luján and Juan Perucho, published in Barcelona in 1970 (Luján & Perucho 2003).

Catalan traditional cuisine had virtually disappeared from restaurant menus by the late 1950s, to be replaced by a Spanish standard menu or by a typical mass tourism one – which included gazpacho, paella and other such dishes. During the 1960s, Josep Pla, a Catalan journalist and author, was commissioned by *Destino* (a lifestyle magazine) to write a series of articles on the traditional cuisine of the Empordà (the most northeastern part of the Catalan region). In 1971 he published a compilation of his work under the title *El que hem menjat* ("What we Ate") (Pla 2005). This was during the late-Franco period and just before political transition, after which people spoke once more about Catalan cuisine as a feature of Catalan identity. Pla had witnessed the loss of Catalan traditional cuisine and suggested that this arose from [new] lifestyles, tourism predation, and the country's general fragility due to a lack of power structures, or due to powers which were often more symbolic than real (Fàbrega 2002, p. 19).

In 1977, Manuel Vázquez Montalbán, in the Prologue to the first edition of *L'art del menjar a Catalunya* ("The Art of Eating in Catalonia") stated:

> "[...] Among the ruined signs of Catalan identity, there is Catalan cuisine. About 50% of the Catalan landscape is occupied by posters advertising housing estates while the remaining 50% is taken up with posters promising the traveller a gastronomic paradise that has only two arrival paths: Bread with tomato and ham and grilled rabbit with al-lioli. [...] It is true that there is a priority order and that the Espriu's goal of "Saving the words" appears to me fundamental in times gone or going by. But I deem lawful every parallel effort to save a plot of identity that deserves a spot in the collective memory of our people." (Vázquez Montalbán, 1977, p. 8).

The Flourishing of Contemporary Catalan Cuisine (1980s–)

Since the 1980s, Catalan cuisine has undergone a singular transformation. This arose because of the rediscovery of traditional dishes, on the one hand, and the emergence of the first sparks of culinary creativity, on the other, through figures such as Josep Mercader (1926–1979), the "father" of modern Catalan cuisine at Motel Empordà restaurant in Figueres (Girona).

By the 1980s, Catalan cuisine, which had re-emerged from virtual oblivion, had taken its place on the identity agenda. Seven years before, Vázquez Montalbán himself had referred to the danger of Catalan cuisine becoming extinct and he had alerted people to the risk of it being considered almost as an archaeological or folk relic. He revised his assertion, however, in the Preface to the second edition of *The Art of Eating in Catalonia*, stating that:

> "[…] I may say, and should say, that the panorama of Catalan cuisine has changed radically. […] It would be an unpardonably foolish thing not to realise the most relevant factors which have influenced the obvious recovery of the Catalan culture of cooking and eating. Although it did not have much of a presence in restaurants, and was relegated to foci of local resistance, or was actually a dying practice in the home, Catalan cuisine made a remarkable recovery, one that has resulted in the opening of restaurants offering Catalan cooking, the new qualification in Catalan cuisine for chefs, the reprinting of an abundant literature on cooking, the demand of the consumer, and the emergence of a new generation of amateur chefs." (Vázquez Montalbán, 1984, p. 8).

In relation to the recovery of traditional cooking, several books on Catalan cuisine appeared in the 1990s, e.g. Josep Lladonosa's *El gran llibre de la cuina catalana* ("The Great Book of Catalan Cuisine") (Lladonosa 1991) or Jaume Fàbrega's *La cuina catalana* ("Catalan Cuisine") in nine vols. (Fàbrega, 1995). This development led to Catalan cuisine seeking World Intangible Heritage status from UNESCO, and to the edition of the *Corpus del Patrimoni Culinari Català* ("Corpus of the Catalan Culinary Heritage") published for the first time in 2006 (*Corpus del Patrimoni Cultural Català* 2006; 2nd ed. 2011).

The idea of a "Traditional Catalan Cuisine", as a *Heritage* item, actually existing as a feature of Catalan identity, and as something deserving of being preserved and nurtured, is currently widely accepted. It is indeed supported by scholars and by the work carried out within the Corpus of Catalan Culinary Heritage project. But, today we live in a crossbred Catalonia. Our culinary habits are being transformed day by day by a series of social factors (e.g., who cooks what and why? working outside home, new robots and utensils…) that also involves contact with other culinary cultures, as well as the impact of globalisation (including the influence of the Internet on food habits), immigration, and so on. Even though our cuisine, as a part of our culture, is continuously evolving, nowadays the rhythm of transformation is subjected to an ever-increasing degree of acceleration.

At the same time, however, there is also a growing trend towards taking a stance in relation to food ethics, involving, for example, the recovery of local products, eating on a seasonal basis, Km. Zero transportation of food products, and so on. Catalonia is actually an important gastronomic tourist destination, which has a very high internationally-recognised cuisine and well-regarded chefs (e.g. Joan Roca, Ferran Adrià or Carme Ruscalleda). And this importance is expressed both locally and internationally through the mass media and, not least, through the Internet, which is one of the most important ways of developing communication networks and relationships nowadays.

It is in this complex framework that we find very lively and very active food blogging groups which choose to write in Catalan as a sign of identity. These groups of culinary bloggers consider themselves to be a community (Catalan *gastrosphere*) and to share symbolic and identity elements in relation to culinary practices. In the following sections, the role of this virtual gastronomic community in the construction of today's broad understanding of Catalan cuisine is examined and analysed.

Food Blogging in Catalonia

In the course of the last three years an increasing number of food bloggers have chosen to use the Catalan language when writing their blogs, but no analysis has been carried to date about who these bloggers are, or why they are writing in Catalan. Questions which arise, therefore, include: Is there a relationship between these Catalan food-blogging practices and national identity-building processes?

In order to answer these and some other queries, a survey – consisting of 22 open-ended questions, that was intended to find out more about the profile of food bloggers who wrote in Catalan, as well as about the kind of content they offered and the sort of relationships, both online and on site, that existed between them – was undertaken. The survey was carried out between 6 March and 15 April 2013. We had 173 answers from 395 identifiable blogs (44% of responses). Here are some of the results – which are as yet unpublished.

Food Bloggers' Profiles

Most of the blogs (149) were individually authored and only 21 had more than one author. In the case of single authorship blogs, women were overwhelmingly represented in this context as 70% of such blogs were by women as against 18%

by men. In absolute numbers, there was a total of 76% female authorship (150) and 24% male authorship (47), of which 77% represented individual authors. The age profile of the blog authors is also relevant. 34% were aged between 36 and 45 years, 29% between 26 and 35 years, 24.5% between 46 and 55 years, 5% were less than 25 years old, while 7% were aged between 56 and 65 years, and 0.5% was over 66 years old. With regard to their educational level, the majority (61%) held a Bachelor level diploma; 17% had Upper Secondary Education level diplomas, while another 17% had Masters or PhD level degrees. Only 5% held a Basic Compulsory Education level diploma.

Concerning their cookery training, 28% stated that they did not have any such training, 67% indicated that they had some training in this area, 3% had taken professional courses, and 2% worked as cookery teachers. The most popular kinds of training courses undertaken consisted of occasional workshops (93%), while 11% took long-term training; 7.3% got training once a week, and 6.5% got training once a month.

Subject Matter

According to the research results, a large number of Catalan blogs were set up between 2010 and 2012, with December being the most popular month for doing so, and July being the least popular in this regard. When providing an answer to question #10: "How often do you update it?", 32% stated that they did not update the blog regularly, 30% did so once a week, 22% did so more than once a week, 11% updated it every 15 days, and 5% said that they updated it once a month.

The primary purpose of the survey was to find out whether the bloggers had a particular standpoint in relation to the Catalan language, and on protecting Catalan traditional cooking by means of blogging. More than 78% of respondents stated that they engaged in traditional cooking; 73% indicated that they made "Sweets and Pastries" recipes, while 33% said that they had made cooking innovations; 23% had chosen diet and ecological cooking, and 19% referred to a tupperware meal. Only 10% said that they talked about wine-tasting and wine and food matching in their blogs, and 11% made recipes for *Thermomix* (the popular cooking robot). If we probe the meaning which bloggers associate with the term "traditional cooking", we find that 81% associated it with (elaborate) family recipes, while 58% saw it as referring to attempts to recover traditional Catalan recipes. When answering the questions about traditional cooking values, 89% regarded Catalan cuisine as being a part of the culture and heritage of Catalonia, while 64% believed that Catalan cuisine deserved international recognition as Cultural Heritage.

Images and photography are very important features of their blogs for food bloggers. Almost half of the bloggers included in the survey believed that photography added value to the content of their blogs, and 98% took original pictures for this purpose. 11% had done a course in food photography and, finally, 35% of users posted photographs in another platform such as Flickr, Instagram or Pinterest. Catalan food bloggers also had, in this sense, a strong presence on social networks. The most important such network was Facebook with an 86% presence, while Twitter had a 58% presence, followed by photo networks such as Instagram with 23%, Pinterest with 20%, and Flickr with a 13% presence.

One of the more interesting questions included in our survey was, "Why do you write your food blog in Catalan?", since all Catalan speakers are also competent in Spanish. If the bloggers had chosen to write in Spanish that would probably have meant that the blog would have more followers and be more popular. So, was there some ideological reasons for choosing Catalan as their blogging language? One of the comments in this regard was as follows:

"I'm proud to write in Catalan... I couldn't write in any other language... It's my language and my culture, as gastronomy also is. It's an identifying feature of my blog. I speak Catalan, I think in Catalan, and I cook in Catalan... it allows me to be coherent with myself... I simply do as I feel."

In the second case, the decision to use Catalan as the language of blogging is not only a matter of personal taste, it is also done out of a sense of belonging to a nation and responsibility:

"Catalan is ours, as is our responsibility … to standardise the use of the language on the Net. The traditional recipes (…) must be explained in our own language. The goal of the blog is to spread Catalan culture. (…) It was a way of introducing our culture (language and cooking) to my friends from the States [USA], [and] to support and promote our language…"

The answers to the question: "What are the main disadvantages of writing in Catalan?", were also very revealing. For instance:

"... Certain logos offer free items if you change your blog into Spanish, but I have not done this... the number of readers is less... it is difficult to disseminate a blog in Catalan because it creates rejection in many people. It reduces the possibility of visits, comments, of sharing it on social networks.... But I honestly don't mind; I think if I had a business I would be forced to make two blogs, one in Catalan and another in Spanish, in order to sell more. Some people don't visit it for this reason. It can be a disadvantage for a non-Catalan person, but I added a translator. Occasionally, I have duplicated a post also in Spanish, I reduce the circle [by writing in Catalan]… some disadvantage regarding the impact outside Catalonia, but I don't care. "

Relationships

Food blogging also changes relationships and opens up a new range of personal interaction possibilities. These relationships may be face to face or in the online sphere. In the virtual world, the most common types of interactions are concerned with making comments on other blogs and with participating in cooking challenges.

In the first case, according to the survey results, almost 50% of bloggers very often made comments, while only 14% never made a comment. 37% said that they seldom made comments because of the lack of time, but they would like to be able to make them more frequently. With regard to cooking challenges, 47% never engaged in them, but 24% did so regularly, while 28% seldom participated in them. Most bloggers (63%) kept their culinary activity in the virtual world and did not participate in on-site activities, but most of them expressed a wish to do so. 7% were, nevertheless, very active and participated regularly in pursuits (cookery workshops, tasting products, having meetings with food bloggers...). 32% said that they were activity organisers in the culinary area. The last question in the survey was about whether having a blog had led to a change of acquaintances. More than half (66%) stated that that was certainly the case, while only 21% said they have not changed their relationships because of having a blog, and 10% pointed to a difference between face to face and online relationships.

Conclusion

Concepts such as heritage and tradition have been transformed by new online social practices. It can thus be said that social networks, particularly those arising from the popularisation of mobile devices and ICT, are actually playing a significant role in the recognition of culinary practices as elements of identity in contemporary Catalonia.

However, institutional concepts of culinary heritage seem sometimes to be at variance with perceptions of it based on amateur practice (in this case, Catalan gastro-bloggers). The existing tension, between heritage-building processes emanating from the top down and from the bottom up, becomes evident especially in this context, as the bloggers look not only for cultural expression, but also for a very practical role for it in their everyday lives: "I began to be a food blogger because my children needed a place to find family recipes".

This opens interesting possibilities for future research, where, for example, public/private tensions, commercial/amateur practices, tradition/innovation and global/local concepts, depict some unique features marked by social networks and cultural practices related, for example, to leisure (but not only to this). Gastro-blogging in Catalan is more than just a blogging exercise when compared to that of other cultures. As one of our informants remarked: "For me, the blog is a place for conscience." Another gastro-blogger said: "I think it's great, any initiative that puts Catalan cuisine in the place it deserves." For these bloggers writing in Catalan, therefore, eating is an expression of culture, identity and habits concerning themselves in terms of postmodern societies. And the Internet is helping to transform the definition of Catalan cuisine, heritage and culture, and to reformulate it in accordance with new contemporary values, spaces, uses and challenges.

List of References

Printed

Agulló, Ferran: *Llibre de la cuina catalana*. Alta-Fulla: Barcelona 1990.

Corpus del Patrimoni Culinari Català. RBA/Institut Català de la Cuina i la Cultura Gastronòmica: Barcelona 2011 (2nd Edition).

Domènech, Ignasi: *La Teca: la veritable cuina casolana de Catalunya*. Cossetània: Valls 2005 (First published 1924).

Fàbrega, Jaume: *La cuina catalana*. 9 vols. L'Isard: Barcelona 1995.

Fàbrega, Jaume: *El gust d'un poble. Els plats més famosos de la cuina catalana*. Valls, Cossetània, 2002.

Grewe, Rudolf (ed.): *Llibre de Sent Soví / Llibre de totes maneres de potatges de menjar. Llibre de totes maneres de confits* (critical edition by Joan Santanach i Suñol). Barcino (Els Nostres Clàssics, B 22): Barcelona 2003.

Leimgruber, V. (ed.): *Libre del coch, del Mestre Robert* (o Rupert de Nola) Curial: Barcelona 1996.

Lladonosa, Josep: *El gran llibre de la cuina catalana*. Empúries: Barcelona 1991.

Luján, Néstor / Perucho, Juan: *El Libro de la cocina española. Gastronomía e Historia*. Tusquets: Barcelona 2003 (First published 1970).

Pla, Josep: *El que hem menjat*. Destino: Barcelona 2005.

Queralt, Carme (ed.): *La Cuynera catalana* (Introduction and critical Edition by Carme Queralt). Cossetània: Valls 2009.

Vázquez Montalbán, Manuel. *L'art del menjar a Catalunya*. Edicions 62: Barcelona, 1977.

Internet

Foodblogging in Catalonia (in catalan)
http://www.slideshare.net/lsolanilla/gastrosfera-cat-24662510?

Magdalena Tomaszewska - Bolałek

Homo Gourmand and Homo Cooking: Two Main Culinary Tribes of the Internet Era

During the last two decades the Internet has become an important medium of communication in almost every field of human life in many parts of the world. It has provided people with a speedy form of communication, it has enabled them to share content of various kinds, and to participate in online communities; and these are only a few examples of the advantages of this kind of communication medium. The twenty-first is proving to be a time for reflection in the field of food culture as it is witnessing the return to popularity of traditional cuisines, the growth of consumer awareness concerning food production, food safety and so on, and the creation of new means of expression based on the culinary art. The global economic crisis dating from 2007 has also served to increase interest in cooking as a means of rationalising household costs.

Moreover, during recent decades, the preparation of food somehow ceased to be regarded as a rather mundane task and became instead an almost egalitarian, or even an élite, hobby. On the crest of the wave of the renewed popularity of home cooking, culinary websites, blogs and focus groups, which served to connect people interested in the culinary art with each other, began to appear. T.V. culinary shows increased in number and their hosts became celebrities comparable to movie stars. People not only started to enjoy cooking but they also felt the need to share their experiences with the world. Websites appeared which made this possible, and the presenting of opinions about, for example, a restaurant, or a food co-operative, or even about so-called "food porn", became a part of life for many people in different regions of the world.

It is my contention that, as a result of the culinary boom in both the public and private spheres, two main culinary tribes of the Internet era have developed, whose representatives I have named *Homo gourmand* and *Homo cooking*. For both of these tribes, the Internet acts as an excellent means of communication with other people devoted to cooking and eating. But how do we define *Homo gourmand* and *Homo cooking*, respectively, and what are the main differences discernible between them? These and other questions are the subject matter of this paper. All of the examples of Internet magazines, programmes, websites and so on, mentioned in this paper, are representative of the Polish situation, but a similar scenario exists in many other countries also.

The term *Homo gourmand* was created from the Latin word "homo" – referring to the genus of hominids, and "gourmand", a word derived from the French word "gourmet", meaning a person who can distinguish and appreciate good wine and food (www.larousse.fr/dictionnaires/francais/gourmand/37654, retrieved 10.6.2014), and a person who eats too much (the word was also synonymous with glutton) (Féraud 1787, pp. 345-346). The enjoyment and the appreciation of food and drink is not a newly-developed or a recently-discovered skill, as it was a part of life for noble and affluent people since ancient times – in Greek, Roman, Chinese, and Japanese society, and in other societies also. One of the best-known epicures was Jean Anthelme Brillat-Savarin (1755-1826), a French lawyer, who gained fame as a gastronome and as the author of *Physiologie du goût* ("The Physiology of Taste") (Brillat-Savarin 1825). But what makes *Homo gourmand* different from all other food lovers from ancient times? The answer lies in the Internet and in the use made of new technologies in everyday life – technologies, including the Internet, which can assist a person like *Homo gourmand* to develop his culinary hobby and associated lifestyle.

Homo gourmand is a person who appreciates good food and beverages; he is a connoisseur who is searching for new tastes and dining experiences, someone who is knowledgeable about cuisine in general and also about subjects related to it. The possession of cooking skills is optional, because *Homo gourmand* is focused on tasting and feasting, rather than on the art of cooking. Such a person likes going to restaurants and tasting parties; he also likes discovering new alimentary products and extraordinary food combinations.

Homo gourmand reads books and printed magazines such as *Magazyn Kuchnia* ("Cuisine Magazine" 1995 –),[1] *Smak* ("Taste" 2012) or *Kukbuk* ("Cookbook" 2012), but he also has access to Internet magazines, portals and blogs, dealing with culinary matters.

Because *Homo gourmand* wants, first and foremost, to explore new tastes, such a person searches for restaurants, cafés, bakery shops, butcher shops, delis, or culinary festivals, to enable him to do this, and the Internet serves as a very useful and convenient tool for organising this kind of activity.

In 2007, a Polish portal entitled Gastronauci.pl was founded (www. gastronauci.pl, retrieved 3 July 2014). It is an online service that gathers information about restaurants from all over Poland and gives logged-in users the opportunity to share their reviews of food establishments, and to rate restaurants under the fol-

---

1   This magazine has been on the market since 1995. It was first published by Prószyński i S-ka, and, since 2002, by Agora S.A., Poland.

lowing four headings: food quality, design, service, and price versus food-quality ratio. The website also provides information about special offers, seasonal menus, new culinary books, and culinary festivals. Gastronauci.pl, which is developing rapidly, is the most popular portal of its kind in Poland.

Information about ordering food for home delivery from certain restaurants and bars is also available online, but this service refers mainly to fast food types of establishments, such as kebab shops, pizza restaurants, Chinese take-aways, and bottom of the range sushi-bars. Some of the best-known websites in Poland dealing with the home delivery of food are: Pyszne.pl (owned by the company "yd. your delivery"; in Poland since 2009) and Pizzaportal.pl (owned by the company "Delivery Hero"; operating in Poland since 2010).

Homo gourmand also gets useful information from foreign web pages and applications – from TripAdvisor (the world's largest travel site: TripAdvisor, retrieved 10.6.2014, from http://www.tripadvisor.co.uk/PressCenter-c6-About_Us.html), for example, where tips about, and ratings for hotels, sight-seeing locations, gastronomic occasions, and so on, are available.[2] He also avails of Foursquare (launched in Poland in 2008), an application for "checking in" one's current location, thus enabling a person to keep in touch with friends while participating in city life. Instagram (2010) (an online service which describes itself as: "a fast, beautiful and fun way to share your life with friends and family") is also of use to *Homo gourmand*. These are only some of Internet services and applications which help *Homo gourmand* to explore and experience the culinary world.

Two types of attitudes are discernible in *Homo gourmand*. First there is *Homo gourmand* with a passive attitude, which is someone who uses all available new technologies to expand his hobby, by finding restaurants, food-related activities and so on, in which to engage, but who keeps all of his experiences to himself (or shares them only with close relatives and friends).

The second type is *Homo gourmand* with an active attitude, that is someone who not only eats and cherishes the moment of tasting food, but also wants to share his experiences and points of view with others. An active *Homo gourmand* writes reviews, for example, of restaurants, culinary festivals, food products, and alcoholic beverages. An active *Homo gourmand* who is a culinary critic or a well-known blogger can become an opinion leader, one whose reviews are often taken into consideration by other people when choosing a place to eat (especially

---

2   The TripAdvisor organisation on was founded in 2000. Its Polish edition (Tripadvisor Polska) is available at www.tripadvisor.pl/, retrieved 3.7.2014.

an expensive one), for example. *Homo gourmand* also likes to make photos of food – an activity often referred to as "food porn".

One of the first scholars to discuss what was later termed "food porn" was the French literary theorist, philosopher and critic, Roland Barthes. In an essay in *Mythologies* (1957),[3] he touched on the theme of cookery columns in *Elle*, a worldwide women's lifestyle magazine which originated in France in 1945,[4] and in *L'Express*, a weekly French news magazine founded in 1953 (www.lexpress.fr/, retrieved 6.7.2014).[5] The recipes presented in *Elle* were simple in content, but their visual presentation was very sophisticated, much more so than what was envisaged by the original recipe. The authors of the cookery columns in *Elle* stressed that the serving of dishes in an eye-catching way made the meal more successful as an event (Mennell 1996, p. 253). The *L'Express* food column was completely different from that in *Elle*, as it consisted of simple and short instructions about the preparation and the serving of the dishes, and no photos were included. The readership of the two magazines was also completely dissimilar (Mennell 1996, p. 254). For many readers, the food presented in *Elle* was not affordable; for them it was just fantasy, a feast for the eyes only (McBride 2010, p. 38).

The term "food porn" appeared in the *Oxford English Dictionary* in 1991, but the variant "gastro-porn" was in use from 1977 (Rousseau 2012, p. 74). In 1979, Michael Jacobson from the Center of Science in the Public Interest (CSPI), Washington D.C. (www.cspinet.org/, retrieved 3.7. 2014), presented two types of food – healthy and unhealthy food – in the Center's newsletter. Good food was regarded as the "Right Stuff" and bad food was called "Food Porn" (McBride 2010, p. 38).

But "food porn" can also refer to professional food photography carried out by advertising agencies or magazines. The aim of these photos is to present food in appetising, stylish, and glamorous ways. Consumer watchdogs and others have noted that this kind of food photography can function as a form of manipulation of consumer behaviour conducted by food marketing agencies (Just 2011, p. 110). "Food porn" has flourished on a large scale thanks to the expansion of digital photography (helped by affordable digital cameras), cell phones with photo cameras, and social media.

---

3   Between 1954 and 1956 Ronald Barthes wrote short essays, which were compiled under the title *Mythologies* (Mennell 1996, p. 250).

4   Nowadays *Elle* has 45 editions (www.ellearoundtheworld.com/, retrieved 3.7.2014), including a Polish edition.

5   For further information on *L'Express*, see: "L'Express - Actualités Politique, Monde, Economie et Culture", retrieved 6.7.2014 from http://www.lexpress.fr/.

But what other kinds of consequences can flow from "food porn" activity? According to the feminist critic Rosalind Coward, a tendency towards "food porn" is apparently especially strong among some women, representing their desire to achieve perfection, while devaluing themselves in the process (Coward 1985, p. 28). On the other hand, calorie-rich food causes people to put on weight, so that they have to choose between "good" and "bad" food (Campos 2004, p. 75). Such a simultaneous conflict between true desires (eating tasty, mouth-watering food) and meeting the expectations of the modern world (slender figure) may be frustrating for many women. Furthermore, when watching beautiful photos of dishes, or when making such photos oneself becomes more important than the act of eating, different pathological situations may develop. People who suffer from anorexia nervosa or bulimia, for example, apparently often watch culinary programmes, collect cookbooks, or even post and share "food porn" on the Internet (O'Doherty 2009, p. 92).

For *Homo gourmand* himself, "food porn" is a very individual issue. He may simply treat it as an informative way of sharing food experiences with both known and unknown readers. There is a group of professional or semi-professional people who post food photos as part of their everyday work. But, of course, there are other motivations involved also, which give rise to the drive to publish photos in social media and blogs, one of them being a desire to show material status.

Another way in which an active *Homo gourmand* can gain experiences, which he can share with his online readers, is by taking part in food events and product tastings. Many companies organise special meetings for the press, critics, and culinary bloggers. The opportunity to participate in some events can also be the result of a prize won in a contest. Afterwards, *Homo gourmand* can share his impressions, about, for example, new products, a new menu, a new product offer, rebranding, and so on, with others.

As stated above, *Homo gourmand* represents a tribe which is focused more on eating and on experience than on cooking, but there are also people who cherish cooking more than the consumption of food. In this paper, I have named the representative of this tribe *Homo cooking*.

The term *Homo cooking* was created from the Latin word "homo" and "cooking" – the latter being the present participle of the verb "to cook" (prepare food, a dish, or a meal) by mixing, combining and heating the ingredients (see: www. oxforddictionaries.com/definition/english/cook, retrieved 10.6.2014). The act of preparing food, inventing new dishes, feeding other people, or creating a new style of plate arrangement or of serving food, often plays a bigger role for *Homo cooking* than the process of eating itself – something that was also mentioned in interviews by a number of culinary bloggers (see: "To ona ma szansę powtórzyć sukces Gessler!"[6] / "She has a chance to repeat Gessler's success!") (ksiazki.onet. pl/, retrieved 3.7.2014). This, however, does not exclude the possibility that one and the same person can be representative of both *Homo gourmand* and *Homo cooking* at the same time, and this dual attitude may even evolve during a person's lifetime.

Like *Homo gourmand*, *Homo cooking* can have either passive or active attitudes to culinary matters. A passive *Homo cooking* cooks at home, attends cooking classes, reads books and magazines about cooking, and takes culinary photography. This he does for his own benefit and enjoyment and that of his close friends. On the other hand, an active *Homo cooking*, in addition to the above activities, also writes culinary blogs, takes part in cooking competitions, does catering or organises private dining events, or even starts his own restaurant.

In general, cooking as an activity is becoming more and more popular worldwide and Poland is no exception to this trend. Some people, including *Homo cooking*, create their own recipes, but most people look for them in cookery books, and on the Internet. According to research carried out by Listonic (a company which launched a shopping list application accessible through the Internet and mobile phones, in 2009), eleven million Poles searched for recipes on culinary blogs in 2012, and 3.5 million of these did so on a regular basis. But, where can people find recipes on the Internet? When looking for a specific recipe – for "French onion soup", for example – people generally use a search engine (such as Google, Bing etc.), but if one does not have a precise idea about what to cook, or if one is just looking for some inspiration, the culinary blog aggregator is probably be the best place to start one's search. Blog aggregators are websites which provide recipe indexes from enrolled blogs, among the most popular of which in Poland are the following: Durszlak.pl (2008, sharing recipes from 4819 blogs; see: www. durszlak.pl, retrieved 22.6.2014) and Mikser Kulinarny (2009, with 4423 enrolled blogs; see: www. zmiksowani.pl/, retrieved 22.6.2014).

Culinary blogging is a relatively new online trend in Poland. Some of the oldest and most popular blogs are: White Plate (2006), Moje Wypieki ("My Baking") (2006), and Kwestia Smaku ("A Matter of Taste"), the latter being the 2007 leader in culinary blogs and the first Polish blog to have amassed more than one million real users by October 2013.[7] A *Homo cooking* with an active attitude, may run a blog containing text only, or with text and photos of a meal (showing a pre-

---

6   Magdalena Gessler is a well-known Polish restaurateur and TV personality.

7   Wirtualne Media: "*Kwestia Smaku pierwszym polskim blogiem z milionem użytkowników, TOP blogów kulinarnych*")" ("Matter of Taste. First Polish blog with a milion unique users [TOP Culinary Blogs]), retrieved 22.6.2014, from http://www.

pared meal or the various steps involved in the preparation of a dish), or a video blog. The recognition and maintenance of the difference between a cookbook and a blog is essential. In general, blogs are not meant to function as a one-way form of communication. They enable (and encourage) dialogue to take place between the creator and the users of a recipe. Users can share their emotions and opinions about whether they like or dislike the dish which has been prepared according to the recipe provided, or they can ask questions connected with cooking.

For some bloggers, the writing of a blog is the first step in the process of changing their hobby into a part-time or a regular job connected with their interest. Some take it even further and make blogging and cooking their main source of revenue. Some well-known, popular, or very representative bloggers, also co-operate with food companies and advertising agencies, and this activity becomes a source of revenue for them as well. They become ambassadors for products, get their own column in magazines, or take parts in morning radio or TV shows, and they often publish their own cookbooks. But it is noteworthy that even the most popular food bloggers in Poland do not become celebrities and do not have the level of influence that fashion bloggers, for example, have.

Another way of being an active *Homo cooking* is to take part in contests organised by food companies, restaurants, or TV corporations. All that is required for participation in many of these competitions is just the submission of a recipe with a photo. But *Homo cooking* may also participate in competitions which are more demanding and challenging than the former, like taking part in "Ugotowani" (literally "Cooked", a Polish version of the British reality show "Come Dine with Me", a TV show launched in 2010, where each evening one participant has to prepare dinner for the other contestants who become jurors for that occasion; the host of the best evening gets the money prize), MasterChef (a world-famous show for amateur cooks who want to become professionals, the first Polish edition of which was launched in 2012), or Hell's Kitchen (a show where the winner gets prize money and an internship in a well-known restaurant, the first Polish edition of which was launched in 2014). Another interesting event targeting culinary bloggers in Poland is BlogerChef (a contest for bloggers only, the first edition of which was launched in 2012/2013). While this event does not have the high profile that most culinary TV shows have, it is still a way of activating the Polish culinary blogosphere.

wirtualnemedia.pl/artykul/kwestia-smaku-pierwszym-polskim-blogiem-z-milionem-uzytkownikow-top-blogow-kulinarnych/page:2.

Homo gourmand and *Homo cooking* are deeply engaged with Internet structures. For Internet purposes, it does not matter whether they have passive or active attitudes to culinary matters because the Internet makes their life easier and more exciting. When difficulties arise during cooking, it is easy to "google" the solution or to ask a friend via social media for advice. The same information can also be found in printed books or magazines, but when it comes to time, the Internet is often the fastest way to get an answer to a query. Social media are also very useful when one is looking for a group of people with a common interest in food. There are discussion alliances, culinary networks, and mailing groups that bring together people interested in culinary subjects. The Internet has virtually no communication boundaries. By means of the different ways in which it is possible to communicate via this electronic medium, one can quite easily and quickly exchange cooking experiences with people all over the world. Even food companies, restaurants, and culinary event organisers now also use websites such as Facebook fanpages, Google+, or mobile applications, as a means by which to communicate with clients. It should also be stated, that when it comes to participating in many culinary activities, virtual contacts and virtual reality do not displace real offline life, but rather that these create a new kind of reality embodying the symbiotic co-existence of the culinary art and technological development.

List of References

Printed

Brillat-Savarin, A.: *Physiologie du goût, ou Méditations de gastronomie transcendante ; ouvrage théorique, historique et à l'ordre du jour, dédié aux Gastronomes parisiens, par un Professeur, membre de plusieurs sociétés littéraires et savantes. Le texte est re-publié aux éditions Charpentier en 1838.* Original edition. Sautelet, A.: 1825, 2 vols, [eBooks@Adelaide].

Coward, Rosalind: "Female Desire and Sexual Identity". In: Díaz-Diocaretz, Myriam / Zavala, Iris M. (eds.): *Women, Feminist Identity and Society in the 1980s: Selected Papers.* Vol. 1. John Benjamins Publishing: Amsterdam 1985.

Campos, Paul F.: *The Obesity Myth: Why America's Obsession with Weight is Hazardous to Your Health.* Penguin: New York 2004.

Féraud, Jean-François: *Dictionnaire critique de la langue française.* Jean Mossy: Marseille 1787, pp. 345-346.

Just, David J.: "Behavioral Economics and the Food Consumer". In: Roosen, Jetta / Lusk, Jayson L. / Shogren, Jason F. (eds.): *The Oxford Handbook of the Economics of Food Consumption and Policy*. Oxford University Press: Oxford 2011.

Mennell, Stephen: *All Manners of Food: Eating and Taste in England and France from the Middle Ages to the Present*. University of Illinois Press: Urbana 1996.

McBride, Anne E.: "Food Porn". In: *Gastronomica. The Journal of Critical Food Studies* 10(1), 2010, pp. 34-48.

O'Doherty Susan: "The Twin Paradox". In: Brown, Harriet (ed.): *Feed Me!: Writers Dish about Food, Eating, Weight, and Body Image*. Ballastine: New York 2009, p. 89-102.

Rousseau, Signe (ed.): *Food Media: Celebrity Chefs and the Politics of Everyday Interference*. Berg: Oxford 2012.

Internet

Durszlak.pl, retrieved 22.6.2014, from http://durszlak.pl/.

"*Elle* International", retrieved 10.6.2014, from http://www.elle.fr/pages/ELLE-International.

Gastronauci.pl, retrieved 10.6.2014, from http://www.gastronauci.pl/pl/artykuly/69-o-nas.

"Instagram": retrieved 10.6.2014, from: http://instagram.com.

Larousse: "Dictionnaires de francais Larousse", retrieved 4.7.2014, from http://www.larousse.fr/dictionnaires/francais/gourmand/37654.

"L'Express - Actualités Politique, Monde, Economie et Culture", retrieved 6.7.20142014 from http://www.lexpress.fr/.

"Listonic": "Blogi Kulinarne zyskują na popularności!" ("Culinary Bogs are Getting More Popular"), retrieved 14.6.2014, from http://blog.listonic.pl/2013/02/blogi-kulinarne-zyskuja-na-popularnosci/.

"Mikser Kulinarny": ("Culinary Blender"), retrieved 22.6.2014, from http://zmiksowani.pl/jak-dziala-mikser.html.

Onet.pl.: "To ona ma szansę powtórzyć sukces Gessler!", ("She has a Chance to Repeat Gessler's Success!") retrieved 14.06.2014, from http://ksiazki.onet.pl/wiadomosci/to-ona-ma-szanse-powtorzyc-sukces-gessler/y63kx.

"Oxford Dictionaries": retrieved 1.6.2014, from http://www.oxforddictionaries.com/definition/english/cook.

"TripAdvisor": retrieved 10.6.2014, from http://www.tripadvisor.co.uk/Press-Center-c6-About_Us.html.

"Tripadvisor Polska": retrieved 3.7.2014, from http: //www.tripadvisor.pl.

"Wirtualne Media": "Kwestia Smaku pierwszym polskim blogiem z milionem użytkowników (TOP blogów kulinarnych)" "A Matter of Taste. First Polish blog with a milion unique users [TOP Culinary Blogs]), retrieved 22.6.2014, from http://www.wirtualnemedia.pl/artykul/kwestia-smaku-pierwszym-polskim-blogiem-z-milionem-uzytkownikow-top-blogow-kulinarnych/page:2.

PART V:
Food Blogging as a New Genre

Anikó Báti

Cooking Know-How:
Virtual and Personal Transmission of Skills.
A Hungarian Example[1]

The blog[2] is one of the most versatile communication genres of the digital age.[3] Because the writing of a blog requires only basic IT skills, it is within the reach of many people who have access to a computer/smart phone and an Internet[4] connection. (It follows, therefore, that the absence of these facilities excludes many people from digital communication.[5]) Many blogs are built around a clearly definable theme and one of the most popular topics is cooking and nutrition. There are now several hundred Hungarian-language gastro-blogs.[6] Consequently, it is almost impossible for a researcher to examine and analyse systematically this vast and constantly-changing mass of data. For this paper,

1   This study was sponsored by the Bolyai János Grant of the Hungarian Academy of Sciences. The author works for the Hungarian Academy of Sciences, Research Centre for the Humanities, Institute of Ethnology.
2   While writing this paper, Klára Kuti's article (Kuti 2014. pp. 51-68) on the same topic was published, but I have not yet had the opportunity to consider it in my work.
3   On the linguistical aspect of blogging, see: http://e-nyelvmagazin.hu/2010/09/10/a-blogok-nyelveszeti-aspektusai/, retrieved 29.5.2014. See further: http://e-nyelvmagazin.hu/lapszam/?sz=blogok-es-bloggerek, retrieved 29.5.2014); Also Balázs / Bódi 2004, pp. 67-84.
4   For further information on this, see: http://www.netkutatasok.hu/2013/09/ksh-szeles-savu-internet-haztartasok-68.html, retrieved 30.5.2014.
5   For the spread of the PC, laptop and the Internet in Hungary form 2005 to 2013, see http://www.ksh.hu/docs/hun/xstadat_eves_/i_oni006.html, retrieved 2.6. 2014.

Access in households (%)	2005	2006	2007	2008	2009	2010	2011	2012	2013
Cellular phone	79,9	84,4	86,4	88,0	90,4	93,2	94,7	95,4	96,0
PC	40,7	47,1	50,6	54,6	56,8	58,6	59,5	59,1	58,3
Laptop	6,3	9,3	11,4	15,7	21,0	26,0	31,0	35,1	41,6
Internet connection	22,1	32,3	38,4	48,4	55,1	60,5	65,2	68,6	71,5
Broadband internet	10,9	22,0	33,0	42,3	50,9	52,2	60,8	68,0	71,0

6   For the content and variety of the Hungarian-language gastro-blogs, see: http://www.gasztroblogok.hu/, retrieved 1.5.2014.

therefore, I have chosen a single blog[7] and its author to present as an example. The case study shows the role that blogs play today in the context of changing food culture and in the life of a blogger. The blog I have chosen is very popular in Hungary. Its main topic is home bread baking ("Limara's Bakery blog") – as the symbol of traditional Hungarian cuisine in today's food culture[8] – and the reason why it came to my attention. I shall begin by dealing first of all with the genre forerunners of the gastro-blog, the way the blog functions, and the role it plays in the process of transmitting cooking skills. In the second part, I shall focus on the blogger, with particular emphasis being placed on her motivations for writing the blog, the steps that she has taken in this context, and the difficulties that she has encountered along the way. In the third part I shall detail her "offline" transmission of the skills of traditional bread baking as I witnessed them in action in her own home.

Literacy became general in Hungary, in all social strata, and among both sexes, in the course of the second half of the nineteenth century and in the early part of the twentieth century. At the same time, women's manuscript notebooks, containing mainly recipes, began to appear in the villages (Keszeg 2008, pp. 356-358). Although they were not written for the public, these handwritten recipe books and diaries can be regarded as the traditional forerunners of today's gastro-blogs. It is, therefore, worthwhile to briefly consider and to compare these two written forms of recipe and culinary knowledge transmission. The handwritten notebooks usually have the name of the author and, in some instances also, the year of their composition, on the cover, thus giving them an individual character. Girls generally began to write these handwritten notebooks before marriage. The notebook reflected the author's taste, her own selection of recipes copied from her mother's collection, or from colleagues, or from the press. Over time, the stock of recipes in such notebooks steadily increased. The progress of technology can also be followed in the handwritten notebooks, because, besides handwritten recipes, typewritten examples appear from the 1960s, although they did not entirely replace the handwritten ones. From the 1990s, the written and printed texts were photocopied for further transmission. Nowadays, growing use is being made of the computer and the Internet, in ever-increasing social circles, for the storage and distribution of recipes.[9] The diary entries, posts, and photos appearing on the

---

7   For the "Limara's Bakery blog", see: http://www.limarapeksege.hu/, retrieved 12.5. 2013.
8   On bread comsumptoin today in Hungary, see Báti 2012, pp. 253-261. On the renaissance of home bread-baking, see Báti 2013. pp. 118-127.
9   On usage of the IT skills in Hungary see: http://www.tarki.hu/adatbank-h/kutjel/pdf/a825.pdf, retrieved 30.5.2014.

Internet give an individualistic touch to blogs intended for a wider public. Like the notebooks, the stock of recipes in the gastro-blog reflects the blogger's taste, but the readers also shape the site with their comments, questions and answers. The handwritten booklets and their counterparts today – the digital documents – serve the same purpose, that is, to stand in for memory (so that their users do not have to keep so much data in mind) (Keszeg, 2008, p. 85). With their help, the method of preparing a dish can be recalled, in unchanged form, at any time. The physical state of the handwritten notebooks is testimony to how often they, and particular recipes, were used. They may contain corrections by a particular individual, the pages may even be stained or torn, and they may even fall open automatically at the most-frequently used recipes, while it is evident that other recipes in the notebooks, often in the majority, have rarely or never been used. In the case of information stored on a computer, on the other hand, it is possible only to follow the time of saving or of making changes to it, rather than having data on its use, and this information is less helpful in judging the author's preferences in relation to recipe use.

The handwritten notebooks were used mainly to record recipes used on festive occasions. This is why they include a large number of recipes for cakes and meat dishes. The recipes for these have shown the greatest variation over the past fifty to sixty years in Hungary. The duplication of the recipes in the ways already mentioned also played a considerable role in their spread.

Considerable differences between the generations, relating to the process of learning to cook, can be observed in the use of the handwritten notebooks. In this short paper, however, I can only touch on this question briefly. In earlier times women did not use recipe books or notebooks to prepare everyday dishes, as up to the mid twentieth century, girls acquired this basic level of cooking skills, including bread baking, by watching their grandmothers and mothers cooking in the home. It was only after their marriage that young women acquired a higher level of cooking skills, generally from their mothers-in-law. Today's oldest generation only needs to consult written recipes for very few dishes as most of their culinary knowledge is stored in their memory. From the second half of the twentieth century, however, the two-earner family model became the norm in both towns and villages, as many women continued with their studies and entered employment. The effects of this on learning how to cook was that the traditional methods of handing down culinary knowledge, based on oral information and imitation in the family kitchen, were no longer being practised. People began to rely more and more on the foods available in shops, and to eat in canteens, with fewer people cooking at home during the week. Nowadays young women increasingly depend on their peers, or on the print and electronic media, to learn how to prepare different kinds of dishes. Today's middle and young generations have large collections of recipes that they add to continually, and this is not limited to foods for special occasions. A recent development of relevance to our topic is that the digital recipe text is now often favoured over the handwritten one. In appearance, the recipe stored on a computer looks very like a cookery book, as even photographs can be added to it. Furthermore, it can be printed at any time in any number of copies, and it can also be shared via the Internet. At the same time, however, there has also been an increase in the demand for printed recipe books. Such books now represent a substantial share of the Hungarian book-publishing business. Most households use several recipe books. Instead of the kitchen of the family home being the place where new recipes are learned, television programmes now play a large role in cookery teaching, and, together with the many gastro-blogs on the Internet, these broadcasts are also a source of new recipes,

One of the reasons for the interest shown in the gastro-blogs is that people try to solve the problem of compiling the weekly household menu by using the Internet. They look at the gastro-blogs for answers to the important question: "What should I cook?" There is a substantial demand from the young generation for variety and novelty in food consumption as well as in other aspects of life. Through food commercials and tourism people have come into contact with the cuisines of other countries, and with the help of the Internet it is relatively easy to find recipes for new dishes. At the same time, the renewed level of interest in foods prepared at home in the traditional way, is significant, as it functions as a form of resistance to globalisation and to food industry products which contain additives. The interest now being shown in home-made bread is one example of this. Because of the fact that even the oldest generation no longer remembers the precise details of the bread-making process, the Internet has become an important source of information, on the best ingredients and traditional recipes to use in this context, and on the actual baking process itself.

The blog I have chosen as an example of this situation has recipes for many different dishes, but its main interest concerns homemade bread and baking with yeast. I visited the blogger (the author of the Liamara Bakery blog) who lives in a small town in Southern Hungary, in her home, where I interviewed her and took photographs as she demonstrated how to make bread. As I am very fond of baking myself, we made bread together, and so I had the opportunity to see her bred-making techniques in action.

Fig 1. The blogger shows the right methods and phases in bread making. (Photo: Anikó Báti, Makó, 2014.)

Fig. 2. Four loaves of hand-made bread. (Photo: Anikó, Báti, Makó, 2014.)

The author of the Limara's Bakery blog says that her passion for making bread began when she acquired a bread-baking machine. She was given one nine years ago and began collecting recipes for it from the Internet. This enabled her to develop her basic bread-making skills and it is the source of many of her ideas in this regard. She became a corresponding member of a blog devoted mainly to breads, which offered a large number of recipes and also much experience in bread making. She decided to begin her own blog in 2008. She created the name of her blog, "Limara", by jumbling the letters of her own name to express her own individuality and uniqueness. Her main motivation for writing the blog was to collect her own recipes into one place, to share her knowledge in this regard with others, and to build up a virtual network interested in baking, independent of locality. The blog now has 20,000 registered followers, the Facebook page has 13,000, and many people with questions about baking write to her on her two electronic mailing lists. Her popularity basically grew from her blog-writing, but her recipes, which were also published in the print press, have led in recent years to interviews and TV programmes, thus also greatly contributing to her success.

This blogger never learnt bread-making at home and she was not a baker by occupation. In fact, she learnt every step of the bread-making process herself by trial and error. This is why the explanations she gives about cooking and baking procedures are so useful and practical to others. The most important source of her knowledge is the Internet. She regularly reads Hungarian gastro-blogs, as well as international ones with the help of translation programmes, and she has a large number of cookery books. She looks for ideas on quantities and methods, and at times she even develops a new recipe from a food photo. Her ideas now appear, not only in her own blog, but also in the print press. Both the popularity of the blog and its name give credibility to her recipes published elsewhere, thus making them her own intellectual creations. AS a result of the blog, she has been approached with many proposals that far exceed the dreams of most gastro-bloggers. For example, on Hungarian national day, the Feast of the New Bread (20th August), she was invited to demonstrate her bread-baking skills in Budapest, together with professional bakers. She has received a number of offers – from Hungary and even from abroad – to become a partner in planned new bakeries! Thanks to the popularity of her blog, she found it easy to get help when she had a problem – when her gas-cooker broke down, she shared this bad news with readers of her Facebook page. Then a leading manufacturer of household appliances gave her a new electric one, their latest top model, and all they asked in return was that she would display their logo on her site for a year! But there are also jealous and ill-intentioned people among the anonymous Internet commentators on her blog – one such commentator even accused the blogger of wanting to force women back into the home and back into the role of housewives. Actually, the values represented by the blog are representative of women's position in traditional family life. However, many of the readers agree and identify with this, as they like to offer their families freshly-baked bread they have made themselves, which, in their opinion, symbolises love and care. And, for them, this is not in conflict with the modern ideal of the woman.

The breads the blogger makes are unique, when compared to those available in shops and bakeries, in that they do not contain additives, and almost every loaf is different in form. She did not learn how to bake bread from her grandparents because they no longer made bread at home during her youth, but she began to learn to cook as a child from the age of eight because of her mother's illness. Today, she bakes bread only for her own family; it is not sold commercially. She speaks with great feeling about kneading the dough, and also about the freshly baked bread:

> "When I begin to knead, I feel the aroma of the dough and it fills me with calm. I knead with the same regular movements and I feel the bread coming to life … you can feel that it has been touched by human hands and made with love" (*Nők Lapja* 2013, p. 33).

The recipes she provides on her blog are detailed and precise – giving particulars of the ingredients, preparation time, oven temperature, and so on – so that readers are able to use them successfully. This is one of the secrets of the site's success. When the blogger makes bread or another dish, details of which are to be included in the blog, she has to measure every step precisely. For this reason, cooking and baking intended for the blog do not resemble everyday practice because they require deliberate, precise planning and execution. She writes her recipes with today's gas and electric cookers – rather than the old-style ovens – in mind, and she uses modern kitchen appliances, such as a kneading machine and a microwave oven. A photo of the dish is an essential part of the blog. She, herself, takes the photos, mainly of the finished dish – rather than showing all the phases involved – with her own camera. She says that it does not take her long to write the recipe for the blog, but that the diary-like stories using a personal tone that she posts together with the recipe, require much more time to compose. These entries reveal many personal details of her everyday life and the values she represents. Firstly, her cooking knowledge and skills represent those that were a part of living practice in every peasant household three generations ago. Secondly, she further expanded her knowledge with the help of the Internet, by collecting all the variants of bread and yeast-based goods that she could find, from different regions of Hungary, and from many other countries worldwide. Among professional bakers, however, she is regarded only as an "amateur" baker, and occasionally they make her aware of this – for example, when they judge her work.

In contrast to the majority of blogs, personal contact, in addition to the virtual connection, in the transmission of bread-baking skills, has become very important for the blogger and her readers. Through the blog, she has found friends in neighbouring areas and they regularly come together in a convenient venue to taste each other's dishes and cakes. For the past three years, she has also been organising bread-baking courses for her readers. Every month, guests come from all over the country to learn bread-making from her, personally. I, too, visited her on one such occasion, and I interviewed her and her guests, while the bread was baking in one of the town's small restaurants where the course was held. The blog readers who participate in these courses, are mainly people who already have a certain level of baking expertise, as they are able to bake with yeast on their own from recipes, but who would like, nevertheless, to add to and to improve their skills. Bread-baking is a difficult and complex process, and it is not always possible to pass on clearly the various elements involved, even when recipes, precise measurements, phase photos, and videos, are included in the blog. This level of know-how that can only be reached with a great deal of practice, is difficult to achieve using those virtual means only. In the past, women learnt these skills in the family, from their grandmothers. Today, the blogger has become the model, revitalising traditional practice. The quality of the flour, the state of the dough, the hand movements involved in the kneading and the shaping of the dough, and the time needed for the dough to rise, are all important steps in the successful process of bread-baking. The blogger makes the bread together with her guests, she observes and corrects their movements and, in the meantime, for hours on end, she tirelessly and enthusiastically explains all the secrets of making bread at home, drawing on her own experience.

Writing the blog, inventing recipes, writing to the commentators, and accepting invitations, now take up most of her time in what has become an almost full-time occupation. In fulfilling her own dreams and the requests of her readers, she has had the opportunity to share the best of her knowledge with a large audience by publishing her recipes in a printed book. Even with the vast amount of information offered on the Internet, there is still a demand for real, paper cookery books, as evidenced by other gastro-bloggers who also have compiled and published cookery books. At the time of the interview, the blogger dealt with in this paper, had been baking several kinds of bread every day for a week, and with the help of a professional photographer and a food stylist, these breads were photographed for the planned book. The blog and the blogger's life are a special mixture of the old and the new, the virtual and the real. The cookery book and the bread-baking course represent older forms of transmitting know-how, as they signify a kind of permanency in a constantly changing virtual world. But it was through regular, careful, reliable blog-writing that the blogger achieved self-fulfilment and recognition.

List of the References

Printed

Báti, Anikó: "The Role of Bread in Hungarian Diet Today". *Acta Ethnographica Hungarica* 57(2), 2012, pp. 253-261.

Báti, Anikó: "The return of the wood-fired baking oven in hungary". in: Partricia Lysaght (ed.): *The Return of Traditional Food*. Lund Studies in Arts and Cultural Sciences 1: Lund University, Sweden, 2013, pp. 118-127.

Balázs, Géza / Bódi, Zoltán (eds.): *Az internetkorszak kommunikációja* ("Communication of the Internet Age"). Budapest: Gondolat-INFONIA. 2005.

Keszeg, Vilmos: *Alfabetizáció, írásszokások, populáris írásbeliség* ("Literacy, Writing Habits and Folk Documents"). Kolozsvár: KJNT-BBTE Magyar Néprajz és Antropológia Tanszék 2008.

Kuti, Klara: "Verzehren oder Zerreden. Alltagswissen in den virtuellen. Tischgesellschaften der Gastroblogsphäre." In: Csáky, Moritz / Lack, Georg Christian (eds.): *Kulinarik und Kultur. Speisen als Kulturelle Codes in Zentraleuropa*. Böhlau Verlag: Wiene-Köln-Weimar. 2014, pp. 51-68.

Molnár, Szilárd: "Sociability and the Internet." *Review of Sociology* 10(2), 2004, pp. 67-84.

Nők Lapja ("Women's Magazine") 33, 13 August 2013, pp. 22-23.

Internet

"A blogok nyelvészeti aspektusai" ("Linguistic Aspect of Blogging"), retrieved 29.5.2014, from http://e-nyelvmagazin.hu/2010/09/10/a-blogok-nyelveszeti-aspektusai/.

"Blogok és bloggerek" ("Blogs and Bloggers"), retrieved 29.5.2014, from http://e-nyelvmagazin.hu/lapszam/?sz=blogok-es-bloggerek.

"Háztartások internethozzáférése" ("Access to the Internet in Households in Hungary"), retrieved 30.5.2014, from http://www.netkutatasok.hu/2013/09/ksh-szelessavu-internet-haztartasok-68.html.

"Háztartások info-kommunikációs eszközellátottsága 2005-2013". ("Hungarian Households Fitted with Means of Mass Communication from 2005 to 2013"), retrieved 2.6. 2014, from http://www.ksh.hu/docs/hun/xstadat/xstadat_eves/i_oni006.html.

"Gasztroblogok" ("Gastro-blogs"), retrieved 1.5.2014, from http://www.gasztroblogok.hu/.

"Limara Péksége" ("Limara Bakery"), retrieved 12.5. 2013, from http://www.limarapeksege.hu/.

"Digitális írástudás" ("Usage of IT skills in Hungary"), retrieved 30. 05. 2014, from http://www.tarki.hu/adatbank-h/kutjel/pdf/a825.pdf.

Katarzyna Orszulak-Dudkowska

Food Blogs in Relation to Culinary Tradition.
A Polish Example

The provision, preparation and consumption of food have always been everyday cultural practices which have determined the traditional patterns of behaviour of various social groups. In former times detailed knowledge of culinary culture was a secret, known only to selected masters of the culinary arts or to talented housekeepers. This knowledge was stored in memory and passed on verbally to people considered to be "initiated" in these arts. The appearance of various collections of recipes could be considered to serve only as a support for the verbal tradition of passing on recipes, and as a means of confirming the importance of the culinary art in culture (cf. Orszulak-Dudkowska 2010). Public culinary discourse began to develop universally in France at the turn of eighteenth and nineteenth centuries (cf. Brillat-Severin 1949), when gastronomy started to establish itself as a theoretical code of culinary practice. Never before had food been so widely discussed. Nowadays, eating habits as well as foodstuffs, food shopping techniques, the methods of preparing dishes, and the final taste of the prepared meals, are the subject matter of various kinds of debates. In present-day society, speaking and writing about food has spread to various social spheres. Cooking has become a topic of popular publications, while culinary T.V. programmes enjoy great popularity. The so-called healthy cuisine forms the basis for new lifestyles and social movements such as Slow Food, and the popularity of culinary blogs shows that the average Internet user has a huge interest in cooking.

Culinary blogs belong to the field of Internet culture, a subject which constitutes quite an obvious topic of interest among contemporary researchers of social life and folklore (cf. Krawczyk-Wasilewska / Meder / Ross 2012). Virtual reality is no longer treated as a separate, not-entirely-real and insignificant space of interpersonal relationships. Those who carry out research on the cultural virtualisation process remark, that the relationship between reality and virtual life should not be seen in terms of a division into two separate social environments, but rather that it should be viewed as a matter of the co-existence and merging of these two worlds – "real" reality and the world created on the Internet. Thus, virtual reality is, to some extent, a reflection of real events, and, at the same time, there is an assumption that a separate social space, where social life goes on and various signs of everyday human activity are carried out, exists. Thus, culinary blogs occupy a special place among those Internet websites which illustrate current cultural trends.

Culinary blogs appearing in the Polish language are the subject of my study. As a cultural researcher, I have treated them as a novel feature of the communications genre, but at the same time I have looked for their relationship to Polish culinary tradition. When trying to present a general characterisation of culinary blogs, it should be noted that they mainly constitute a large collection of recipes which have been tried and tested, and which, for one reason or another, are recommended for use by the authors of the websites. The creators of the blogs, which I have reviewed, try to present themselves as experts in, and enthusiasts of, the art of cooking. They exhibit invention by creating titles for, and descriptions of, recipes presented by them, and by supplementing them with colourful photographs of ready-made dishes. The main motivation for writing blogs would seem to be the possibility it affords the bloggers to exchange the culinary knowledge and experience they have gained in this field with other bloggers, as well as a wish to create their own lifestyles, in accordance with current cultural conditions.

When a recipe for a particular dish is presented in a blog, it is usually preceded by a short introduction written by the author concerning the taste of the dish, its basic ingredients and the amounts required, and the circumstances in which it might be served. In addition, the author sometimes adds some advice and suggestions concerning small modifications which could be made to a given recipe, based on personal experience. The authors of blogs try to present their own knowledge about a certain dish as well as their attitude towards the culinary tradition itself, or towards the ingredients customarily used in making the dish in question. At the end of the blog, every recipe is complemented by a selection of comments by readers about the author's introduction to the dish, and about their own personal experience connected with it.

It becomes evident on reading the food blogs that a certain culinary tradition – in this case, Polish tradition – forms an important basis for the individual practice of many bloggers. The names of the blogs themselves play an important role, as they often refer to a family tradition of good cooking, associated with home, or with mum's or grandma's cooking, such as *Nie ma jak u mamy* ("There's nowhere as good as at your mum's") (retrieved 16.6.2014 from http://dobrakuchniamamy.blogspot.com), *Domowa cukierenka* ("Home Patisserie") (retrieved 16.6.2014 from http://cukierenkaklementynki.blogspot.com), or *Mój blog pachnący domem* ("My blog which smells of home") (retrieved 16.6. 2014 from http://pachnacydomem.blogspot.com). Furthermore, recipes for most of Poland's traditional culinary specialties are to be found among the wealth of recipes posted on Polish language blogs. These usually appear with the inclusion of only slight modifications which reflect the signature of a certain culinary enthusiast. Thus, recipes for *pierogi* (dumplings), pork chops, traditional *Mazurek* (shortcrust tart baked at Easter), broth, *bigos* (a stewed dish made of sauerkraut, meat and mushrooms) or lard, with an individual signature, are to be found, as follows: "Ruthenian (Russian) Dumplings Baked with Nutty Pesto." Let us quote:

> "Everyone knows what Russian dumplings are like – quite bland, and they need some distinctive addition. I usually serve them with fried onion or with pork fat cut into small cubes. This time, I decided to add some spiciness with nutty *pesto*" (*Przy stole* ["At the table"]) retrieved 10.10.2013, from http://przystole.blox.pl/2012/10/Pierogi-ruskie-za-piekane-z-orzechowym-pesto.html przystole.blox.pl/html). (All blogs included in this paper have been translated by the author.)

"Pork Chop and the Secret of a Good Coating":

> "I know that there's nothing complicated about making a pork chop. Of course. But making a pork chop, the coating of which doesn't fall off during frying, is no mean feat. My Beloved Husband, when he wasn't My Husband yet, used to ask me again and again how I made the coating stick so nicely. (Then, my patent on the coating was still in the process of patenting.) Today, I think I've reached perfection in preparing the pork chop, just like a Mum of a Small Guy and A Wife Of A Big Man should;) [...]" (*Z zapachem wanilii we włosach... czyli kulinarne rewolucje młodej mamy* ("With Vanilla Fragrance in her Hair... or the Culinary Revolution of a Young Mum") retrieved 10.6.2014, from http://waniliowysmoczek.blogspot.com/2012/10/schabowy-i-sekret-udanej-panierki.html).

Furthermore, the preparation of traditional Polish dishes is, according to bloggers, connected with the necessity of having a thorough knowledge of the art of cooking, as these dishes are not the easiest to prepare, and their desired taste and quality are, in the bloggers' opinion, difficult to achieve. The majority of blogs contain descriptions of emotions and memories connected with the tradition of home cooking, of, for example, a Polish dish such as broth, which is prepared from different kinds of meat (poultry and beef) and vegetables, traditionally served with hand-made noodles. Here are some examples.

"Broth – A Recipe for a Traditional Polish Soup":

> "A lot of people remember the taste of the broth cooked by their grandmother very well... as I guess only grandmothers have time to prepare real broth.:) I, from time to time, usually in autumn and winter, on my free Saturday, get round to preparing the queen of Polish soups".(Zajadam.pl retrieved 10.6.2014, from http://www.zajadam.pl/przepisy-zupy/rosol-domowy).

> "The classic of Polish cuisine, the queen of soups, the symbol of Sunday, a hangover tamer and a wondrous healer: all in one. The broth wasn't on my list of favourite soups

for a long time, because it's greasy, those noodles and everything.:) Fortunately our tastes mature [for] that hot extract of vegetables and chicken, thin noodles, and vigo-
rously-chopped parsley. There are moments when there's nothing better than a warming
stock, which magically heals not only your body but your soul as well. What is its secret?
You have to cook it with patience. It has to bubble, finish off slowly, almost lazily. It's
going to pay [you] back with a deep, strong taste, for that time. And you mustn't forget
about a grain of love. Broth, like every soup, won't turn out well without it. Really, really"
("Gry kuchenne. Blog bardzo kucharski", ("Kitchen Games. Very Cookery Blog") retrieved 10.6.2014, from http://grykuchenne.pl/rosol-domowy).

It is noticeable that culinary recipes posted on blogs have their fixed specificity of genre. Thus, they have a title which is both the headline and the name
of the dish concerned (e.g. "Ruthenian [Russian] Dumplings Baked with Nutty
Pesto"), then they present the ingredients needed to prepare the given dish, together with the proportions required and, as the third element, a description of
the method of preparation of the dish (Orszulak-Dudkowska 2010, pp. 83-85).
The creator of the blog, as a matter-of-fact "master of the kitchen", who usually
hides under a mysterious pseudonym, acts as the "author" of the presented recipes, and adds his/her own remarks and comments. When the manner in which
the culinary recipes function is taken into consideration, it can be assumed that
their "authorship" is of a fictional and collective nature. The recipes belong to
collective forms, deriving from a certain group tradition (national, local, family), and confirmed by collective memory, but at the same time dependent on
the specificity of the contributing culture. Recipes, like texts of folklore, are
variable by nature, and are characterised by topicality and their relationship to
contemporary social life. They are, therefore, affected by various cultural influences and are competently adjusted to meet new social needs and tendencies.
The fact that a specific person signs a particular collection of recipes does not
cast him/her in the role of an absolute authority or source, but rather as an ad-
vocate (carrier) of a certain kind of knowledge connected with cookery practice.
The entries presented on blogs are dialogic in nature and resemble a record of
a verbal exchange between people who are having a chit-chat about cooking.
The following example is illustrative of this:

"Marshmallow Ice Cream Cones – The Taste of Childhood:)":

"In principle, I should have written "the nightmare of childhood" as I could never finish
my portion. Terrible sweetness:))) They contain a huge amount of sugar. There are people who gorge on them. Even at home I have enthusiasts for such sweets. And this recipe
is especially for such sugar devourers. For me, that is an insurmountable sweetness:)"

[Comments]:

"It's also too sweet for me, but my dad and husband love it too, so I'm definitely going to make it for them:) [Madleine]"
"I'm also not going to change my mind – it's too sweet, and nauseating, even – but my Man has fond memories of warm ice cream, so maybe I'll serve it to him some day:) [Maggie]"
"It looks great and doesn't seem too difficult:) [Gosia]"
"Beautiful Anne!"
"It really is the taste of childhood. The best marshmallow ice cream cones in my neighbourhood could be found in a small cake shop called Murzynek in Gdańsk.:) I also wasn't able to eat the whole portion, though, hehe:D"
"Cheers:) [Majana]"
"I've sent my mum the link with a note "mum, make me some": D [biedrona]" ("Na Miotle" ["On the Broom"] retrieved 5.10.2013, from http://namiotle.pl/3953/cieple-lo-dy-smak-dziecinstwa).

Longer forms of blog expressions resemble a deep-rooted culinary tale, usually given during feasts among people who are close to each other or who are relatives. A tale, as a folk genre, is usually connected with customs and is characterised by the freedom of choice with regard to the threads used, by referring to details from the speaker's experience, and by numerous references to the listeners, all of which underlines its relevance to the dialogue. The narration of a tale is based on spinning a story about seemingly real events, as they were heard from one of the participants; it is direct in nature, filled with warmth and memories, and presents a kind of reality which is accessible to the senses of the observer (Krzyżanowski 1965, p. 119; Sławiński 1989, p. 163). In longer blog entries, one can also notice that the author's narration is often vivid, detailed, and informal in structure, that it is dominated by sensuously-depicted food threads and by numerous vague references to the author's life experiences, and that there is also a clear focus on the recipient.

The textual form of communication characteristic of a blog enables it to keep its deeply oral character, but its illustrative aspect is also an equally important element of a blog (cf. Mórawska 2012). The dishes presented in written form on blogs can also be seen, thanks to the inclusion of photographs.. Thus, the visual element, which is so typical of popular culture, complements the written form and situates the blog in the real, everyday-life circumstances of a folklore performance.

The culinary recipes presented on blogs are usually reflective of the seasonal foodstuffs available at the time, or of upcoming celebrations, for example. Thus, prior to Christmas, the creators of blogs try to outdo each another in presenting recipes typical of that particular festival, such as recipes for fish dishes, dumplings with sauerkraut and mushrooms, and mushroom soup or red *borscht*, while at Easter one can find recipes for traditional *Mazurek*, cheesecakes, white *borscht*, stuffed eggs, or pâté. In summer, recipes for dishes involving strawberries dominate, while in September one will find recipes for dishes with mushrooms, peppers, tomatoes, and plum or apple preserves.

Most blog authors include recipes handed down in their own family, recipes found in culinary columns in newspapers or in native cookery books, or even recipes found on other websites about cooking, in their own culinary blogs. The recipes presented on blogs are in social circulation in many different ways – some appear in only some websites, for example, and their conventional content is complemented by a layer of colouring in the form of remarks, author's contextual descriptions, and readers' opinions. Thus, we are dealing with a form of transmission appropriate to present-day culture, and characteristic of folklore content. As emphasised by folklore researchers, "the present situations, in which folklore forms function, are different from those traditional ones only in the fact that specificity is outlined by the electronic media. Not only do they influence the creation of new interactions connecting people with the media, they also orient interactions between people" (Hajduk-Nijakowska/ Smolińska 2012, p. 161).

In the collection of recipes presented on blogs, one can find references to different cultural traditions, Polish tradition being just one of them. A wide range of gastronomic solutions are dealt with, and, in this way, Internet users can find what is to their taste in the gastronomic context. The recipes presented on blogs help people to develop a passion for cooking, something which is common in today's culture, but, in a more general sense, they also encourage discourse about cuisine, thereby leading to an increase in culinary knowledge. They are, therefore, aptly set in the context of popular cultural trends which includes discussion of culinary issues. In addition, it would also appear that the aforementioned blogs provide one of the few remaining opportunities available today for telling others about specific culinary customs, which show identity with, and attachment to, a certain cultural content. Thus, the recipes which are presented on blogs are reflective of the specificity of given family ties, of Polish tradition and cultural space, and of references to various contexts of Polish personal life.

Culinary blogs are a product of pop culture itself, which at the same time is, to a great extent, an area of the folklorisation of ancient cultural content. Cultural researchers emphasise that present popular behaviour, which results from the process of the globalisation of culture, appears strangely tinted because it is viewed through a local-world context (cf. Kuligowski 2005). Popular culture, as Waldemar Kuligowski has noted, is not identical in all parts of the globe. The reality is quite the opposite, in fact, because it encompasses different meanings and has a multidimensional nature, and also because it refers to different individual and joint needs and outlooks (Kuligowski 2012, p. 154). Traditional values, which are so vital in folk culture, lose their privileged status when viewed from the point of view of the logic of popular culture. Kuligowski has also noted that, in the context of popular culture, the role assigned to tradition is that of an element that can be used in various ways to mix and join together different kinds of cultural content (Kuligowski 2012, p.150). The recipes presented on blogs do not necessarily represent individual ideas; rather they come from a very complex reservoir of contemporary culture, in which traditional content is mixed and co-exists with cultural innovations. And we, the users of popular culture, are given the right, through blogs, to make free choices in seeking recipes which we, for different reasons, need.

Therefore, people who write blogs and who use modern technology to transmit this information, do so in the shadow of tradition, and use well-known forms of interpersonal communication techniques in the process. Using the Internet to share information is not the beginning of a completely new social reality, but it does create new communication possibilities, and allows people to present narrations of a personal nature in a public and unrestricted forum on a global scale. Culinary blogs can, therefore, be seen as providing evidence of the unusual elevation that culinary culture has achieved in the today's world, and they also strongly illustrate the complex relationship that exists between the current, almost domineering attitudes towards food, and the type of culture that contributes to it.

List of References

Printed

Brillat-Severin, Jean Anthelme. Translated by Fisher, Mary F.K: *The Physiology of Taste or Meditations on Transcendental Gastronomy*. The Heritage Press: New York 1949.

Głowiński, Michał: "Gawęda". ("Long Tale"). In: Sławiński, Janusz (ed.): Słownik terminów literackich ("The Dictionary of Literary Terms"). Ossolineum: Wrocław 1989, p. 163.

Hajduk-Nijakowska, Janina / Smolińska, Teresa: "Obecność kultury typu ludowego we współczesnej kulturze masowej" ("The Presence of Folk Culture in Popular Culture"). In: Smolińska, Teresa (ed.): *Między kulturą ludową a masową. Historia, teraźniejszość i perspektywy badań*. ("Between Folk and Popular Culture.

History, Presence and Perspectives of Study"). Scriptum: Kraków-Opole 2012, pp. 159-185.

Kuligowski, Waldemar: "Ludowa – masowa – popularna". ("Folk – Mass – Popular"). In: Smolińska, Teresa (ed.): *Między kulturą ludową a masową. Historia, teraźniejszość i perspektywy badań.* ("Between Folk and Popular Culture. History, Presence and Perspectives of Study"). Scriptum: Kraków-Opole 2012, pp. 139-158.

Kuligowski, Waldemar: "Fast Food, Slow Food, smalec babuni" ("Fast Food, Slow Food, Grandma's Lard"). In: Burszta, Wojciech J. / Kuligowski, Waldemar (eds.): *Sequel. Dalsze przygody kultury w globalnym świecie* ("Sequel. The Further Adventures of Culture in the Global World"). Warszawskie Wydawnictwo Literackie Muza SA: Warszawa 2005, pp. 88-123.

Krawczyk-Wasilewska, Violetta / Meder, Theo / Ross, Andy (eds.): *Shaping Virtual Lives. Online Identities, Representations, and Conducts.* Wydawnictwo Uniwersytetu Łódzkiego: Łódź 2012.

Krzyżanowski, Julian: "Gawęda". ("Long Tale"). In: Krzyżanowski, Julian (ed.): Słownik folkloru polskiego. ("The Dictionary of Polish Folklore"). Wiedza Powszechna: Warszawa 1965, p. 119.

Mórawska, Eliza: *White Plate. Słodkie* ("White Plate. Sweet"). Wydawnictwo Dwie Siostry: Warszawa 2012.

Orszulak-Dudkowska, Katarzyna: "Co kryją w sobie przepisy kulinarne? Od folklorystyki do antropologii zmysłów" ("What is Hidden in Culinary Recipes? From Folklore Studies to Anthropology of the Senses"). *Literatura Ludowa* 4-5, 2010, pp. 79-89.

Internet

"Nie ma jak u mamy" ("There's Nowhere as Good as at Your Mum's"), retrieved 16.6.2014, from http://dobrakuchniamamy.blogspot.com.

"Domowa cukierenka" ("Home Patisserie"), retrieved 16.6.2014, from http://cukierenkaklementynki.blogspot.com.

"Mój blog pachnący domem" ("My Blog which Smells of Home"), retrieved 16.6.2014, from http://pachnacydomem.blogspot.com.

"Przy stole" ("At the Table"), retrieved 10.10.2013, from http://przystole.blox.pl/html.

"Z zapachem wanilii we włosach… czyli kulinarne rewolucje młodej mamy" ("With Vanilla Smell in her Hair… or the Culinary Revolution of a Young Mum"), retrieved 10.6.2014, from http://waniliowysmoczek.blogspot.com.

"Cook and Celebrate Blog", retrieved 10.06.2014, from http://www.cookandce-lebrate.com/.

Zajadam.pl, retrieved 10.6.2014, from http://www.zajadam.pl.

"Gry kuchenne. Blog bardzo kucharski" ("Kitchen Games. Very Cookery Blog"), retrieved 10.6.2014, from http://grykuchenne.pl.

"Na Miotle" ("On the Broom"), retrieved 5.10.2013, from http://namiotle.pl.

"Strawberries from Poland", retrieved 8.10.2013, from http://strawberriesfrom-poland.blogspot.com.

Klaudyna Hebda

Food – Blogging – Identity: Free Expression or Lifetime Project?

Blogging about Food – Does Only Food Matter?

Food blogging is one of the first things which come to mind when thinking about food and the Internet. Food bloggers not only share recipes, they can also inspire fashions, create devoted communities, and become celebrities. The question is – is food blogging only about tried and trusted recipes from grandma's notebook, or is it also about mouth-watering food porn photography,[1] about a cherished hobby and a passion for cooking, about discovering new tastes, creating (or following) cooking trends, and about being a part of a foodies community? As I am also a food blogger I often feel that there is much more than just the recipes themselves involved, and, as a researcher, I have found a gap in the descriptions of blogging phenomena. For this reason I have decided to conduct text analysis of specific Polish food blogs in order to show the motivations, lifestyle nuances, and personal narrations hidden behind stories, recipes and pictures. It is almost impossible to distinguish between two activities of food bloggers – cooking and publishing posts on the Internet. Thus, in this paper, both actions will be discussed. I argue that food blogging goes far beyond cooking and writing about food as it can be much more than a hobby or about creating a community with aesthetics and dreams (Bauman 2008, p. 89). It can also be a powerful tool for forming ongoing personal narratives and one's own identity. Food blogging can affect friendships, everyday choices, future plans, and the image of self. In this paper, I shall try to show that writing about food can contribute to the creation and the re-creation of self, based on Anthony Giddens's theory of identity. The topic will be explored by using examples of Polish food blogs which have a special place in the Polish blogosphere.

Polish Food Blogs – Characteristics

Food blogs are among the largest and most influential blogs sector in Poland and they seem to be undergoing continued expansion. When talking about food blogs in Poland it is important to point out that they are part of a bigger phenomenon,

---

1   I understand food porn photography to consist of food photos which make you instantly hungry. The term is used freely by foodies, in social media, for example.

that is, blogging itself. The blogosphere – understood as referring to blogs and interconnections that exist between communities of bloggers – is becoming a more and more influential part of the Polish Internet scenario, and food bloggers constitute a huge and well-recognised part of this community. Food blogs are one of the oldest and the fastest-growing thematic blogs in blogosphere, having evolved from cooking forums or from small personal sites hosted by Polish companies (mostly by Onet.pl). At the present time, they are mainly to be found on Blogspot (Google owned) or Wordpress (wordpress.org or self-hosted wordpress.com), and, as they are often visually stunning, they are gathering large numbers of devoted followers. There are several studies, conducted mainly in 2012/2013, which confirm the importance of food blogs. These studies were undertaken mainly from a marketing perspective and, despite some methodological problems, they show that food blogs constitute a mainstream element of the blogosphere.

Listonic research claims that half of Polish Internet users read food blogs on a regular basis (http://socialpress.pl/2013/02/co-drugi-internauta-odwiedza-blogi-kulinarne, retrieved 2.7.2013). Research based on Megapanel PBI/G methodology (http://www.gemius.pl/pl/badania_audience_metodologia, retrieved 1.2.2013) has shown that the most popular (understood as the most visited) blogs in Poland are the food blogs, with Kwestia Smaku ("A Matter of Taste") (kwestiasmaku.com) with around 700,000 real users per month, and Kotlet.tv ("Escalope. tv") with 430,000 real users per month, being the largest ones (http://www.wirtualnemedia.pl/artykul/kwestia-smaku-i-kotlet-tv-najpopularniejszymi-polskimi-blogami, retrieved 1.2.2013). There is also a report about the various activities of food bloggers, such as the publishing of books, working as food photographers, and so on, based on data delivered by fellow bloggers, and published online by food blogger Smile (Smile 2012: retrieved 1.2.2013, from www.olgasmile.com/raport-blogi-kulinarne-2012.html). The report has proved that food bloggers are very active outside of their sites as many of them also publish articles and cookbooks, or work as food photographers, or engage in professional marketing activities in co-operation with various companies. Another report dealing with blogs in general from a marketing point of view shows that food blogs feature among the best and most recognisable blogs on the Internet (Hatalska 2012, retrieved 1.4.2014, from http://hatalska.com/blogosfera-2012-pierwsze-badanie-polskiej-blogosfery-z-perspektywy-reklamodawcow/).

It is important to note, however, that the above-mentioned studies are not overly reliable as the gathering of the data necessary for the analysis can be problematic. The evaluations rely solely on data delivered by bloggers. Some research based on Megapanel PBI/Geminus methodology (ibid.) tried to use its own analytic tools, but this failed as only a few bloggers agreed to install it. Hence, it is important to remember that the data used in the studies might be inconsistent or incomplete. Nevertheless, despite these drawbacks, the studies show that food blogs are easily recognisable, that they are frequently visited, and that some of them are the most substantial blogs on the Internet in Poland.[2]

Methods

This study is a part of a larger project in which food blogs and travel blogs were compared. I have chosen the extended text analysis method in this article because it allows me to analyse multimedia content and to observe changes in time in this context (Mayntz 1985). Text analysis is also useful for gathering information about everyday life (Rapley 2010, p. 23) and daily life is mostly what food blogs are about. Some might argue that the use of structured interviews could be another analytical option, but in this study I decided to use text analysis in order to cause as little interference as possible with the subject matter (Babbie 2006, p. 352).

Ten food blogs were chosen using the following criteria: each blog had to be written on an ongoing basis (at least three blog posts per month) for more than two years; each had to be active at the time when the research was being conducted (2013); each blog had also to be interactive, that is, that the commenting function had to be active and each blogger had to be engaged in discussion with his/her readers. When choosing food blogs I also considered so-called "trendy blogs", and those which were easily recognisable in the blogosphere. These criteria were based on my long-term personal experience as a food blogger.

The text analysis of food blog content, created between January 2011 and January 2013, was carried out using MAXQDA software. Included in the analysis were blog posts, comments (both by visitors and bloggers), and also pictures if they were available in the blog content. Furthermore, personal pages (like "about me" or similar pages created by the blogger) were also included. Food blogs were then tagged with the letter "K"[3] and an additional number.[4] The analysis was made using three main categories connected with Giddens's theory of self-identity (Giddens 2001, 74). I thus distinguished the main areas of blogging which are parallel to Giddens's theory. These are as follows: 1. Self-consciousness, reflexivity and motivations, that is, being aware of what one does and why (ibid.). 2.

---

2   It should also be pointed out that, as far as most food blogs are concerned, Christmas or Easter are the times of the year when they are most visited. Sometimes the number of visitors doubles or triples at those times.

3   "K": "kulinarne" – culinary / food blogs.

4   See Appendix.

Self-observation, understood as observation of one's behaviour and conferring meaning on it. 3. Life-style, understood (after Giddens, ibid.) as consisting of everyday choices which give material shape to one's creativity.

Passion for Cooking and Eating

According to Giddens, reflexivity is connected with the post-modern world and is directly involved with the continuous generation of self-knowledge (Giddens 2008, p. 87). Using Giddens's terminology, motivations should be understood as basic feelings of self, which are connected with reflective behavioural management, something which is a common feature of people's lives (ibid. p. 29).

Food bloggers declare that the writing of a food blog is derived from their love of food and cooking. For them, the creation of a dish might lead to the re-creation of memories and the sharing of them with a boarder audience. The acts of cooking and blogging about food are perceived as being experiences which engage all of the senses and which have the power to bring back the past, especially with reference to childhood:

> "One day while lying in bed I remembered that, as a child, I would eat warm brioche. As with many tastes from my childhood, this one is very vivid and clear in my "taste memory". I remembered how this buttery, warm brioche crumbled in my mouth. I could see myself sitting somewhere near a warm stove, eating it [...] and I craved to eat it right then. Immediately (K 14)"

The blogger's favourite brioche recipes follow this memory, so the readers might consume a part of it. It is not only explicit consumption that is involved here, but also metaphoric consumption, something which Krzysztof Podemski might call the sensual absorption of impression (Podemski 2004, p. 8).

Self-observation: Who Am I?

Food bloggers in Poland are very well aware of their "blogging identity". Food bloggers also publish their own online magazines, such as, *Apetyt* ("Appetite") (http://magazynapetyt.pl/, retrieved 6.7.2014) – a magazine of Food Bloggers from Małopolska (a region in south Poland), or *Cool Mag* (http://www.coolmag. pl/, retrieved 6.7.2014) from Opole, also in southern Poland. Food bloggers even invented a word – "kulinarka"[5] – to describe themselves. They feel that they are

---

5 This term is difficult to translate into English. One of the food bloggers (K16) derived it from the world "szafiarka" which literally means "a girl who has a wardrobe", meaning a girl with a fashion blog. "Kulinarka" can be translated as "a girl who has a kitchen".

somehow different from other bloggers and they are afraid that they might be viewed and judged just as "girls who cook and do this stuff" (it is highly feminised niche). They often emphasise that they are much more than just "recipe girls" (K14). Of course, these bloggers identify themselves as food lovers but this can also be a complicated situation. When you say that you love eating you should bear in mind that this might be bad for your figure. Some bloggers solve the problem by promoting diet indulgence recipes, but others have decided to accept their fate:

> "I never understood [before] that our bodies are always with us and that we experience the best things in our lives with them. How could one not like one's own body? (K12)"

These kinds of arguments are important in the context of identity-creation processes as they show that people want to take control over their own bodies (accept them or change them). Giddens calls them "identity regimens" and points out that they are of central importance in the context of self-identity, because they connect with visual aspects of the body and take control of and manage them (Giddens 2008, p. 92). Moreover there is a common consensus among food bloggers than homemade food is generally "healthier" (even when it is made only from sugar) than a store bought version; thus they can be food lovers and responsible eaters at the same time.

Being a "true and credible blogger" is extremely important to them – in fact, it might be so important to their sense of integrity that in extreme cases they might forego engaging in any form of advertising whatsoever (K16).

To sum up, food bloggers describe themselves as food lovers, as being passionate, credible, and trustworthy people, who are helpful to other cooks, and who are always ready to share their knowledge with them. When dieting the food bloggers claim to be "reasonable" (K17) and moderate, and sometimes even willing to sacrifice their progress for the sensual pleasure of food.

Food Blogging and Lifestyle

Food bloggers use their blogs to communicate their particular lifestyle forms to others. Giddens understands lifestyle as consisting of everyday, individuals choices which people make, not because they are necessarily useful, but because they shape their personal narration (Giddens 2001, p. 113). For bloggers, the lifestyle element might include the choosing of healthy food, good quality dairy products, and free-range eggs, and encouraging readers to do the same. Considering lifestyle as involving everyday choices (including shopping options) bloggers often collect some special items, such as dishes and plates used solely for food photography – which they sometimes show on blog posts). Some of them feel that they are overwhelmed by objects and need to stop collecting them (K13), but others, despite knowing that they buy too many things, cannot help that (K12).

There are also some things that bloggers really aspire to – a food frame DRSL camera with macro lenses is often mentioned as dream-gear, alongside the famous Kitchen Aid Mixer, in this context. These are universal dreams and some bloggers are willing to put a lot of their savings and effort into fulfilling them (K16). Blogs are platforms where lifestyle matters are continuously being created and re-created.

Summary

Blogs might be seen and analysed with reference to bloggers' personal space and their "lifetime programme" when they can fulfil their wishes, satisfy needs, and share their thoughts with others. Bloggers might plan their life as a reflexive project, involving the sum of their personal choices, which are thoroughly considered and evaluated. When considering Anthony Giddens's theory of post-modern identity as being a continuously-created narration (based on the constant re-definition and re-justification of one's choices), we can look on blogs as being an instrument for the creation and the re-creation of bloggers' personal stories.

Future Research Possibilities

Blogging, as an activity, is becoming more and more popular (there are also professional bloggers), so there is surely a need for ongoing research in order to describe the phenomenon more closely.

The term cybersociology (Kubczak 2002, p. 154) might not be an accurate term when talking about carrying out research on blogs, as a lot of activities have moved from the online arena into the real world. Thus, as Dominik Batorski and Marta Ocloń-Kubicka have shown, an analysis of food blogs might be a good starting point for carrying out research on phenomena which occur beyond the border of Internet sphere (Batorski / Ocloń-Kubicka, 2006, p. 100). The use of visual sociological methods (Sztompka 2005) might also be beneficial, since food blogs in particular are famous for their appealing visual content. Food bloggers give much attention to the aesthetics of their work – pictures and other visual elements (e.g. photo-collages) might be considered as being a part of the personal narration as well (Banks 2009, p. 23). Furthermore, some theories seem to be particularly suitable for describing food blogs. Their content might be analysed from the perspective of a risk society (Beck 2004), or of creating new Internet communities, which extend far below the Internet itself (Castells 2003).

List of References

Printed

Banks, Markus: *Materiały wizualne w badaniach jakościowych* ("Visual Materials in Qualitative Research"). Państwowe Wydawnictwo Naukowe: Warszawa 2009.

Batorski, Dominik / Ocloń-Kubicka, Marta: „Prowadzenie badań przez Internet, podstawowe zagadnienia metodologiczne" („Conducting Research on the Internet: Basic Methodological Issues"). *Studia Socjologiczne* 182, 2006, pp. 99-132.

Bauman, Zygmunt: *Konsumowanie życia* („Consuming Life"). Wydawnictwo Uniwersytetu Jagiellońskiego: Kraków 2009.

Bauman, Zygmunt: *Zindywidualizowane społeczeństwo* ("Individualised Society"). Gdańskie Wydawnictwo Psychologiczne: Gdańsk 2008.

Beck, Ulrich: *Społeczeństwo ryzyka: w drodze do innej nowoczesności* ("Risk Society. Towards a New Modernity"). Wydawnictwo Naukowe Scholar: Warszawa 2004.

Castells, Manuel: *Galaktyka Internetu. Refleksje nad Internetem, biznesem i społeczeństwem* ("The Internet *Galaxy*: Reflections on the Internet, Business, and Society"). Dom Wydawniczy Rebis: Poznań 2003.

Giddens, Anthony: *Konsekwencje Nowoczesności* ("The Consequences of Modernity"). Wydawnictwo Uniwersytetu Jagiellońskiego: Kraków 2008.

Giddens, Anthony: *Nowoczesność i tożsamość. "Ja" i społeczeństwo w epoce późnej nowoczesności* ("Modernity and Self-identity: Self and Society in the Late Modern Age"). Państwowe Wydawnictwo Naukowe: Warszawa 2001.

Kubczak, Anna: "Cybersocjologia. Internet jako przedmiot zainteresowania socjologów" ("Cybersociology. The Internet as an Object of Interest to Sociologists"). In: Haber, Henryk (ed.): *Polskie doświadczenia w kształtowaniu społeczeństwa informacyjnego: dylematy cywilizacyjno-kulturowe* ("Polish Experiences in the Development of the Information Society: The Civilisational and Cultural Dilemmas"). Wydział Nauk Społecznych Stosowanych. Akademia Górniczo-Hutnicza: Kraków 2002.

Podemski, Krzysztof: *Socjologia podróży* ("Sociology of Travelling"). Wydawnictwo Naukowe UAM: Poznań 2004.

Rapley, Tim: *Analiza konwersacji, dyskursu i dokumentów* ("Doing Conversation, Discourse and Document Analysis"). Państwowe Wydawnictwo Naukowe: Warszawa 2010.

Szpunar, Magdalena: "Internet jako pole poszukiwania i konstruowania własnej tożsamości" ("Internet as a Field Exploration and Construction of Self-identity"). In: Hałas, Elżbieta / Konecki, Krzysztof (eds.), *Konstruowanie jaźni i społeczeństw. Europejskie warianty interakcjonizmu symbolicznego* ("Constructing the Self and Society. European Variants of Symbolic Interactionism"). Wydawnictwo Scholar: Warszawa 2005.

Sztompka, Piotr: *Socjologia Wizualna* ("Visual Sociology"). Państwowe Wydawnictwo Naukowe: Warszawa 2005.

Tomczyk, Tomasz: *Blog. Pisz. Kreuj, Zarabiaj* ("Blog. Write. Create. Earn"). Zielona Sowa: Warszawa 2013.

Tomczyk, Tomasz: *Bloger. Poradnik dla blogerów* ("Blogger. A Handbook for Bloggers"). Wydaje.pl: Katowice 2012.

Internet

"Cool Mag Magazine", retrieved 6.7.2014, from http://www.coolmag.pl/.

Geminus.pl: "Metoda badania Megapanel PBI/Geminus", retrieved 1.2.2013, from http://www.gemius.pl/pl/badania_audience_metodologia.

Hatalska, Natalia: "Blogosfera 2012. Badanie opinii marketerów na temat wizerunków blogerów, reklamy na blogach i przyszłości badań marketingowych w blogosferze", retrieved 1.4.2014, from http://hatalska.com/blogosfera-2012-pierwsze-badanie-polskiej-blogosfery-z-perspektywy-reklamodawcow/.

"Magazyn Apetyt", retrieved 6.7.2014, from http://magazynapetyt.pl/.

Miłkowski, Grzegorz: "Co drugi internauta odwiedza blogi kulinarne", retrieved 2.7.2013, from http://socialpress.pl/2013/02/co-drugi-internauta-odwiedza-blogi-kulinarne.

Smile, Olga: "Raport Polskie blogi kulinarne 2012", retrieved 1.2.2013, from www.olgasmile.com/raport-blogi-kulinarne-2012.html.

Wojtas, Tomasz: "Kwestia Smaku i Kotlet.tv najpopularniejszymi polskimi blogami", retrieved 1.2.2013, from: http://www.wirtualnemedia.pl/artykul/kwestia-smaku-i-kotlet-tv-najpopularniejszymi-polskimi-blogami.

Appendix

Analysed Food Blogs

K11: http://mmintafood.wordpress.com/, retrieved, 4.5.2014.

K12: http://wbrzuchu.blogspot.com/, retrieved, 4.5.2014.

K13: http://strawberriesfrompoland.blogspot.com/, retrieved, 4.5.2014.

K14: http://whiteplate.blogspot.com/, retrieved, 4.5.2014.

K15: http://kucharnia.blogspot.com/, retrieved, 4.5.2014.

K16: http://table-table.blogspot.com/, retrieved, 4.5.2014.

K17: http://dietetyczniesiostro.blogspot.com/, retrieved, 4.5.2014.

K18: http://www.jedzonkomalucha.pl/, retrieved, 4.5.2014.

K19: http://www.justmydelicious.com/, retrieved, 4.5.2014.

K20: http://truffle-in-a-rum-chocolate.blogspot.com, retrieved, 4.5.2014.

PART VI:
Food: Ancient and Medieval
in the Light of Internet Source

Zofia Rzeźnicka

Ancient and Byzantine Food and the Internet

Today, in the age of the Internet, it is possible to find hundreds of well-tested recipes for national as well foreign dishes without much difficulty. With the help of various websites and blogs, American pancakes or Japanese sushi can be prepared in any kitchen, and the recipes used can be posted online for friends. The use of the global net to ensure that traditional cuisine does not fade into oblivion, and to facilitate the distribution of people's favourite recipes, has become as common as the use of cookbooks for these purposes.[1] The worldwide network is also used to popularise historical cuisine. By surfing the Internet it is possible to find many websites which provide general information about food in Antiquity (e.g. from www.en.wikipedia.org/wiki/Ancient_Greek_cuisine, retrieved 1.6.2014), or which give modern versions of ancient recipes, (e.g. Evans, Dyfed L.: www.celtnet.org.uk/recipes/roman-recipes.php, retrieved 1.6.2014), or which include short films to demonstrate how old-time food is prepared. The online project entitled "Archaeology Gastronomy: Feasting Throughout History", organised in connection with the Olympic Games held in the United Kingdom in 2012 (www.youtube.com/watch?v=JcY-p4CNJzM, retrieved 1.6.2014) was a good example of this kind of undertaking. As part of this project authors posted a series of educational presentations online related to eating in ancient Greece. Each of these presentations contained a video showing how meals could be made according to ancient recipes. Nowadays, however, old-time cuisine is promoted, not only by food lovers who like to spend their free time in cooking, but also by scholars, such as Sally Grainger, Mark Grant, Patrick Faas, or Andrew Dalby – the latter has also put links concerning the history of gastronomy on his website (Dalby, Andrew: //dalby.pagesperso-orange.fr/links.html, retrieved 1.6.2014). These authors have published their own versions of ancient Greek and Latin recipes in cookbooks aimed at contemporary readers, which can be bought (online or in a bookstore), or the recipes themselves can be accessed on the Internet (e.g. www.press.uchicago.edu/Misc/Chicago/233472.html, retrieved 1.6.2014). However, for historians working on food history, a dish, which has been successfully made, is

---

1 Sometimes recipes that were first posted on blogs are subsequently published in books – cf. Wnuk, Paulina: http://www.frommovietothekitchen.pl/, retrieved 10.6.2014. Cf. id. 2013.

but the last step in their research. The first, and most important one, is the studying of sources devoted to this question, and for that purpose, the global net is an essential research tool nowadays, as it provides access to professional digital libraries such as, Perseus (Crane, Gregory R. (ed.): www.perseus.tufts.edu/hopper/collections retrieved 1.6.2014), The Latin Library (www.thelatinlibrary.com, retrieved 1.6.2014), or Corpus Medicorum Graecorum / Latinum (www.ancientworldonline.blogspot.com/2010/04/open-access-corpus-medicorum-graecorum. html#uds-search-results, retrieved 1.6.2014), in which collections of original ancient Greek and Latin texts concerning alimentation can be found. All of this has made the Internet a vital source of culinary and historical knowledge, especially for generations familiar with the social network. Thus, whether searching for culinary inspiration or for material for a research paper, the Internet, as a central research tool of the twenty-first century, is almost invariably used. But, is all of this as original as it would seem at first glance?

The desire to post recipes online, so that others can read, use, or comment on them, springs, perhaps, from the same wish that ancient authors apparently had when they wrote about food. When reading ancient and Byzantine literature, it is evident that people living thousands of years ago also wished to share their culinary knowledge and experience with others. The homeland of the European cookbook is ancient Greece where the first gastronomy poems came into existence, in which their authors elevated the preparation of meals into an art form. One of the most important *opera* in this connection is *Deipnon* ("Dinner") written before 391 B.C. by Philoxenus of Cythera. Here can be found not only an exquisite description of meals that were served during a banquet (Dalby 2003, p. 258), but also Greek dining customs. A specific category of written works concerning aspects of ancient gastronomy is medical treatises composed over the ages by Galen (2nd/3rd century A.D.) and his Byzantine followers, one of whom was Oribasius (4th century A.D.). According to the medical doctrine of those times, food was treated as medicine, hence these authors wrote not only about how it should be prepared, but they also provided its dietetic profile. For a food historian, however, the most important source is a compilation of recipes entitled *De re coquinaria* ("On the Art of Cooking"), attributed to a Roman gourmet, Apicius, who lived in the 1st century A.D., although the collection is usually thought by scholars to date to the 4th or early 5th century A.D. This *opusculum* is unique for a number of reasons. First of all, it is the only remaining ancient cookbook. Next, arising from the various recipes to be found in this *opusculum,* the most popular culinary trends and techniques, as well as the most-frequently used kitchen tools and ingredients of the time, can be determined. Furthermore, on the basis of *De re coquinaria*, the influence of ancient culinary tradition on dishes, which, today, are regarded as belonging to *haute cuisine*, can also be observed.

A good example of the latter is *foie gras* – the famous pâté made from the liver of ducks or geese that were specially fattened for this purpose. Although this delicacy is particularly associated with France, the liver of fowl was a much sought-after product in Antiquity. According to Galen, Hellenic people fed dried figs (Greek: *sykai*) to pigs in order to obtain sweet-flavoured liver called *sykoton* from them (André 1961, pp. 132-133). And, according to Pliny the Elder's *Natural History*, the same method was practised in Rome, where it was promulgated by Apicius, who gave this sort of food both to pigs and geese, and where the result-ing liver was called, in Latin, *ficatum* (Pliny 1940, VIII, LXXVII, 209). The prac-tice of feeding animals with figs was still known in Byzantine times, something which is attested in medical (Oribasius 1928-1933, II, 44, 2, 1-2) and agricultural (*Geoponica* 1895, XIV, 22, 1-16) sources of that period. But this was not the only practice concerning goose liver that was known in the Mediterranean Basin. In medical treatises by Galen (1923, 704, 4-7) and Oribasius (e.g. 1928-1933, II, 44, 2, 2-3), for example, mention is made of the use of whey to enrich food given to fowl in order to obtain a product analogous to *sykoton*. According to available sources, there appears to have been no strict norms regulating the types of food that should be given to livestock, since, as mentioned above, figs were given to pigs as well as to geese. And, as is evident in an anonymous *opusculum* entitled *De cibis* (1963, 6, 8-9) there were also no objections to the adding of some whey to food given to geese. In addition, medical sources provide a dietetic profile of *sykoton*, and, thanks to them, we learn that it was highly valued, not only for its unique taste (e.g. Galen 1923, 679, 7-8; Oribasius 1928-1933, II, 39, 2, 1-2), but also because of the influence which it was said to have on the human body. Galen (1923, 704, 3-6) and Oribasius (1928-1933, II, 44, 2, 1-4) regarded it as a food that was nutritious and as one that produced good juices (Galen 1923, 704, 3-6; Oribasius 1928-1933, II, 44, 2, 1-4). They also claimed that it passed easily through the digestive system (Galen 1923, 704, 3-7; Oribasius 1928-1933, II, 44, 2, 1-3, 1). The same authorities recommended the use of livers obtained from geese that had been fed with whey, because they believed that such livers were not only a tasty, but also a rich, delicacy (Galen 1923, 704, 4-6; Oribasius 1928-1933, II, 44, 2, 2-3). Furthermore, just like *sykoton*, such liver caused the beneficial humours to be produced (Galen 1923, 704, 4-6; Oribasius 1928-1933, II, 44, 2, 2-4), it passed easily through the digestive system (Galen 1923, 704, 4-7; Oribasius 1928-1933, II, 44, 2, 2-3, 1), which made it (Galen 1923, 704, 3-7; Oribasius 1928-1933, II, 44, 2, 2-3, 1) easy to digest (Oribasius 1928-1933, III, 17, 1, 1-11, 1).

Some data about using *ficatum* in the culinary art also exists. According to Pliny the Elder (1940, X, XXVII, 52), it was beneficial to drown goose liver in a mixture of milk and honeyed wine (*mulsum*) because by doing so the liver would increase in size. Another way to make it grow was, according to *Geoponica* (1895, XIV, 22, 15), to put it into a pot filled with fresh, clean water, which should be changed two or three times a day. These were probably the first steps in the gastronomic preparation of fig-fattened liver. More details on this subject can be found in *De re coquinaria*. According to one of the recipes for *ficatum* in this work, the incised liver should be covered with ingredients such as fish sauce (*liquamen*), pepper, lovage and some laurel berries. Next, in order to make it juicy, it should be wrapped in caul fat and grilled (Apicius 2006, VII, 3, 2). The dish could be served with a spicy sauce made of *liquamen*, olive oil, wine, pepper, thyme and lovage (Apicius 2006, VII, 3, 1).

As can be seen, the methods of preparing dishes did not change much until the twenty-first century. Hundreds of years ago, just like what happens today, those who could afford it, took pains not only to get food that came from well-fattened animals, but also to transform it into tasty and healthy dishes. The methods presented above provide insight into a piece of ancient *ars coquinaria*, thanks to which, a step-by-step reconstruction of particular courses of action in the preparation of certain dishes can be provided.

Before being treated with heat, the liver might be incised and dipped into marinade so that it soaked up its flavour. The marinade proposed in *De re coquinaria* was made with the addition of a fish sauce, which was used instead of salt at that time, and which was one of its most important ingredients. This sauce was well known in Greece in the 5th century B.C., where it was called *garos*, and it was also known in Rome where the terms *garum* or *liquamen* were used interchangeably for it (cf. Kokoszko 2006, pp. 289-298). Apart from the use of *liquamen*, the compiler of *De re coquinaria* calls also for the inclusion of some spices (e.g. pepper, thyme, lovage, bay berries) and (in the case of the sauce) other liquids (e.g. wine, oil), in food preparation. According to the ancient gastronomy rules, all of these ingredients should first of all be pounded and then mixed together in a mortar with the help of a pestle (Solomon 1999, pp. 116, 119). The author also stated that the liver should not be allowed to become too dry during grilling and that is why he suggested that it should be covered with caul fat before being put on a heated gridiron.

For those interested in cooking, most of the information given so far would seem to be obvious. But, for a present-day cook, the above-mentioned recipes are unclear since they tend to lack details about the quantities and types of ingredients to be used, as well as about the preparation time and methods involved. This is the basic difference between ancient recipes and those to be found in culinary blogs and modern cookbooks today. Why, it might be asked, is this important information missing from these ancient recipes? The answer is that it was not necessary to include it as gastronomic literature was addressed to professional cooks, who were familiar with the ingredients concerned and the quantities to be used in particular dishes. They also knew whether the spices to be used should be fresh or dry, and for how long the food should be cooked. Thus, those who would like to prepare some "ancient" food, nowadays, would have to struggle with a serious problem concerning the types and quantities of ingredients to be used, if this obstacle had not been overcome by the above-mentioned scholars with a culinary passion, who, in their kitchens, set out to discover how to prepare old-time food and then to share their knowledge with other Internet users and readers. Much practical and helpful data are also included in recent scholarly works on food studies, where information about spices and other ingredients characteristic of ancient times, is given, as well as suggestions about products by which they can be replaced today – e.g. using readily available South East Asian fish sauce instead of making *garum* (Grainger 2006, pp. 27-29). Another piece of data provided in a recent scholarly work concerns the use of lovage. In *De re coquinaria* it is not clear whether fresh leaves or other parts of this spice should be used. According to Sally Grainger, however, the author of the recipe had seeds in mind (Grainger 2006, p. 24), since lovage was placed at the beginning of the list, next to pepper, and never between other herbs.

Let us now analyse a recipe from *De re coquinaria*, according to the instructions given by contemporary cooks, starting with Sally Grainger (2006, p. 47), who claims that marinated liver is an ideal *hors-d'œuvre* that can be served at parties. Instead of using a fig-fed liver, however, she recommends that 220 g. of lamb's or calf's liver be used instead. After skinning the liver and removing the sinews, it should be cut up into 5 cm pieces and left to rest for a short while. In the meantime, a marinade made of ½ teaspoon of dry-roasted lovage seeds and 2 bay berries (or a broken bay leaf), pounded in a mortar, should be prepared, and mixed with 2 tablespoons of fish sauce. All of this should be added to the liver and left aside for a few hours. Next, each piece of liver should be wrapped in (probably pork) caul fat cut into somewhat larger pieces than the liver. Grainger warns against the addition of too much caul fat. The liver should then be grilled (or baked in the oven) until it is crispy on the outside and well baked on the inside. The dish, spiced generously with freshly-ground pepper, can be served speared on cocktail sticks, and dipped in sauce (Grainger 2006, p. 33) consisting of a mixture of 1 part of fish sauce, 1 part of medium white wine, 1 part of sweet heavy wine e.g. Malaga (a modern alternative for Roman raisin wine called *passum*[2]), 1 part of oil, and freshly ground pepper. Another recipe, developed by Patrick Faas (2005, p. 258), suggests that about 1 kg. of incised and cleaned calf's liver should to be covered with a mixture of ground lovage seed, crushed pepper, *garum*, and 2 bay berries. Then the liver should be left aside for a few hours, after which it was wiped clean, sprinkled with salt and pepper, and wrapped in a pork caul. Liver prepared like this should be roasted on a barbecue for 10 minutes on each side, and, when firm, it should be removed from the heat for another 10 minutes. The author suggests that it be cut into pieces and served with modern versions of sauces (Faas 2005, pp. 258-259) proposed for this purpose in *De re coquinaria*. The sauce combination consists of 100 ml. of the best fish sauce, 100 ml. of sweet white wine, and 100 ml. of olive oil. When all the liquids are mixed together they should be spiced with pepper, a teaspoon of fresh thyme, and a tablespoon of ground lovage seeds.

And, finally, let us look at the recipe available from TaccuiniStorici.it ("Historical Notes"), the official website of Accademia Italiana di Gastronomia Storica (Italian Academy of Historical Gastronomy), which is a non-profit organisation bringing together, for example, oenologists, chefs, journalists, researchers and dieticians. On the aforementioned Internet site, apart from information about traditional Italian cuisine, local food-feasts or culinary traditions from all over the world, links concerning food in Antiquity (various curiosities, literature on food, videos, etc.) can also be found. A link to ancient recipes, where guidelines for the preparation of *ficatum* are to be found, is also included (www.taccuinistorici.it/ita/ricette/antica/celebrita'/Ficatum-di-Apicio-Archeologia-gastronomica.html, retrieved 1.6.2014.). According to these recipes, pig's liver, cut up into little pieces, should be marinated in a combination of vinegar, ground pepper, chopped celery and bay berries. After removing it from the marinade, the liver should be sprinkled with salt and pepper and stuffed into a pig's small intestine, which afterwards should be well-tied and grilled. This type of cuisine is attractive because it is not complicated, it is based on natural ingredients, and the way in which these ingredients are combined guarantees new taste sensations. It is thus evident that a recipe which was written centuries ago has become an inspiration for contemporary chefs, and each of them has created his own way of preparing *ficatum*, while trying, more or less, to keep as close to the original recipe as possible. By comparing modern recipes with the ancient ones, differences in how the quantities of ingredients are stated can be observed. As mentioned above, *De re coquinaria*

---

2   For more information on the production of sweet heavy wine – *defrutum or sapa* cf. Grainger 2006, p. 32.

was dedicated to professional cooks, who, due to their expertise and knowledge, did not need exact data, so they probably treated the recipes presented there just as *sui generis* a collection of tips, and every one of them went on to prepare the same meal in his own way. Contemporary scholars, who, thanks to their experience and knowledge, have transformed an inaccurate Latin text into an authoritative recipe, used an identical method. The recipes given by Faas, for example, and posted on TaccuiniStorici, do not provide much information about the amounts of particular ingredients to be used, so if we wish to prepare food according to them, we must trust our skills as well as our taste. At first glance, all recipes require the same basic preparation and technology: first of all, the liver should be cleaned, then marinated for a few hours, then covered with a pork caul and barbecued. But the recipes differ in details, with some sources suggesting that the offal should be cut up (*De re coquinaria*; Faas), or cut into small pieces (Grainger; TaccuiniStorici). While the ingredients of the mixture given by Grainger and Faas correspond with those found in the ancient *opusculum* (as an alternative for bay berries both suggest the use of bay leaf), the anonymous author of the Italian version replaced fish sauce with vinegar and salt, and instead of using lovage seeds, he advised that chopped celery should be used.[3] Although there is no mention in the Latin text of removing the marinade combination before putting the liver into the intestine, Faas claims that this is the way that it should be done. Furthermore, Grainger and Faas, using data from *De re coquinaria*, propose that the dish be served with the addition of sauce. Although Grainger offers us her own version of *oenogarum*[4] (Kokoszko 2006, pp. 294-295) it is still based on "ancient" ingredients, while, by contrast, Faas in his recipe follows Apicius exactly.

To sum up, the global net has become a very important source of information for the historian, because by means of it access can be gained to texts that are often unavailable, or not easily accessible in library collections. In addition, for people working on food history, the Internet is an ideal tool for searching for modern versions of recipes based on old-time formulas. The examples presented above prove that this topic is becoming more and more popular not only in academia, but also among those who follow online instructions about how to prepare something different from the food which is served by fast food chains. But, by and large, people are unaware that meals, which nowadays seem to be so common (e.g. cereals, pancakes), exquisite (*foie gras*), or exotic (fish sauce), often have their roots in Antiquity, and the Internet is a great tool for bringing this situation to the attention of a wider audience.

---

3   We do not know why lovage is not used, but celery seems to be a good alternative, because it is of similar flavour, cf. Grainger 2006, p. 24.

4   Fish sauce mixed with wine.

List of References

Printed

André, Jacques: *L'alimentatione et la cuisine à Rome*. C. Klincksieck: Paris 1961.

Apicius, *De re coquinaria*. In: Grocock, Christopher / Grainger, Sally (eds.): *Apicius. A Critical Edition with an Introduction and an English Translation of the Latin Recipe Text "Apicius"*. Prospect Books: Totnes, UK, 2006.

Athenaeus of Naucratis, *Deipnosophistae: Athenaei Naucratitae dipnosophistarum libri XV*, ed. Kaibel, Georg, vols. 1-3. Teubner: Lipsiae – Berolini 1887-1890.

Dalby, Andrew: *Food in the Ancient World from A to Z*. Routledge: London / New York 2003.

De cibis. In: Ermerins, Franz Z. (ed.): *Anecdota medica Graeca*. Luchtmans: Leiden 1963.

Faas, Patrick: *Around the Roman Table*, trans. S. Whiteside. The University of Chicago Press: Chicago / London 2005.

Galen, *De alimentorum facultatibus libri III*. In: Helmreich, Georg (ed.): *Corpus medicorum graecorum*, vol. 4, 2. Teubner: Leipzig 1923.

Geoponica: Geoponica sive Cassiani Bassi Scholastici de re rustica eclogue, ed. Beckh, Henricus, Teubner: Lipsiae 1895.

Grainger, Sally: *Cooking Apicius. Roman Recipes for Today*. Prospect Books: Totnes, Devon 2006.

Kokoszko, Maciej: "Sosy w kuchni greckiej. Garum (ΓΑΡΟΣ) i pochodne" ("Sauces in Greek Cuisine. Garum and Garum-Based Sauces"). *Vox Patrum* 26, 2006, pp. 289-298.

Oribasius, *Collectiones medicae: Oribasii collectionum medicarum reliquiae*, vols. 1-4, ed. Raeder, Johannes, Teubner: Lipsiae – Berolini 1928-1933.

Pliny, *Natural History*, trans. H. Rackham, vol. 3. William Heinemann: London / Harvard University Press: Cambridge, Massachusetts 1940.

Solomon, Jon: *The Apician Sauce. Ius Apicianum*. In: Wilkins, John / Harvey, David / Dobson, Mike (eds.): *Food in Antiquity*. University of Exeter Press: Exeter 1999, pp. 115-131.

Wnuk, Paulina: *Kuchnia filmowa*. ("The Film Kitchen") Wydawnictwo Otwarte: Kraków 2013.

Internet

"Ancient Greek Cuisine" retrieved 1.6.2014 from http://www.en.wikipedia.org/wiki/Ancient_Greek_cuisine).

"Archaeology Gastronomy: Ancient Greece: Honey Glazed Prawns", retrieved 1.6.2014, from http://www.youtube.com/watch?v=JcY-p4CNJzM.

Dalby, Andrew: "A Food World Site = Des Mets et des mots", retrieved 1.6.2014, from http://dalby.pagesperso-orange.fr/links.html.

Evans, Dyfed L.: "Celtnet Ancient Roman Recipes and Cookery", retrieved 1.6.2014, from http://www.celtnet.org.uk/recipes/roman-recipes.php).

Fass, Patrick: "Eight Ancient Roman Recipes from Around the Roman Table: Food and Feasting in Ancient Rome", retrieved 1.6.2014, from www.press.uchicago.edu/Misc/Chicago/233472.html.

"Perseus Collections/Texts – Perseus Digital Library", Crane, Gregory (ed.), retrieved 1.6.2014, from http://www.perseus.tufts.edu/hopper/collections.

TacciuniStorici.it, retrieved 1.6.2014, from http:// www.taccuinistorici.it/ita/page/Taccuini-Storici-chi-siamo.html.

TacciuniStorici.it: "Ficatum di Apico – archeologia gastronomica", retrieved 1.6.2014, from http://www.taccuinistorici.it/ita/ricette/antica/celebrita'/Ficatum-di-Apicio-Archeologia-gastronomica.html.

"The Latin Library", retrieved 1.6.2014, from http://www.thelatinlibrary.com.

"The Ancient World Online: Corpus Medicorum Graecorum/Latinum", retrieved 1.6.2014, from http://www.ancientworldonline.blogspot.com/2010/04/open-access-corpus-medicorum-graecorum.html#uds-search-results.

Wnuk, Paulina: http://www.frommovietothekitchen.pl/, retrieved 10.6.2014. Cf. Id. 2013.

Johanna Maria van Winter

A Database of Medieval Plant Names

In Graz, Austria, an online database of medieval plant names has been established and made available to scholars as a tool for interdisciplinary research for a large range of sciences. It is called "Portal der Pflanzen des Mittelalters" (PPM) or "Medieval Plant Survey" (MPS) and it can be reached under http://medieval-plants. org (retrieved 1.6.2012). Although the field is restricted to medieval studies, the number of disciplines which are involved is rather large. As summed up in their introductory article about the database by Helmut W. Klug and Roman Weinberger in 2012, the disciplines concerned (arranged alphabetically) are: "archaeology, art history, botany, classical philology, folklore studies, history, linguistics, literary studies, medical and pharmaceutical history, pharmacy, and theology" (Klug / Weinberger 2012, p. 335). Ethnology and food history should also ideally have been included.

This database has been designed by Helmut W. Klug, an Austrian medievalist and researcher of Germanic philology, who is especially interested in medieval cookery recipes. Philology uses several kinds of sources, such as literary works, colloquial speech, proverbs, political propaganda, songs and so on, and, from the nineteenth century onwards, it has also occupied itself with cookery recipe collections. These texts have been studied mainly for their dialectical peculiarities, because they originated from different regions, each with its own non-standardised common language. The culinary content of these texts was of less importance to philology than the linguistic aspects, although strange ingredients had to be explained. Happily this situation has changed in the last decennia, and now the culinary elements of these recipes are also studied by philologists.

It must have been due to this insight into the multifaceted character of their sources, and with the hope of profiting from the scientific expertise of others, that the wish to share their material with colleagues from other disciplines was born. The interpretation of the ingredients, and of the ways of processing medieval cookery recipes, sometimes requires the help of experts from other disciplines. Furthermore, medieval cookery turns out to be connected with the medieval world view about food and health and thus with the health rules of those days. A certain level of medical knowledge is required in order to understand these rules correctly. Food research is thus pre-eminently an interdisciplinary field of study.

However, in Graz it is not only food in the Middle Ages that is of interest, but also associated folkloric and ethnological connotations. An existing German website www.klostermedizin.de (retrieved 1.6.2014), has raised the question of whether the herbs that had been traditionally used in the medical practice of the medieval monasteries, really had the effects that they were believed to have, or whether this was a matter of folk belief only and based on superstition. In order to investigate this subject, the website has connections with a German pharmaceutical firm called "Abtei" that investigates the chemical workings of plants. The research group "Klostermedizin" ("Monastic Medicine") is part of the Institut für Geschichte der Medizin ("Institute for the History of Medicine") of the University of Würzburg, Germany, whereas Abtei is a pharmaceutical business that "combines traditional natural healing knowledge with modern pharmaceutical technology", and also sells products based on that expertise. The question is whether age-old medicines are still useful for present-day purposes (www.abtei. de, retrieved 1 June 2014).

These questions, however, are not matters of concern for the Graz database, which asks rather how, and for what purposes, the different plants were used, named, and surrounded with legends and other curious beliefs in the Middle Ages. The inducement for Klug and Weinberger to build their database arose from their cultural historical research of the plant called mandrake (*Mandragora*), which, from Greek and Hebrew antiquity onwards, was known by over twenty different names in many vernaculars. Because the root of this plant looked more or less like a man with a head, arms and legs, stories were told about the deadly cry emitted by the plant, as soon as it was exposed to the air, as it struggled against being dug up from the earth. This should not have been done by a human being but by a dog, which was then sacrificed for the act. It is not quite clear, why it was considered worthwhile to cause this animal sacrifice to be made because, although the plant was thought to produce the love apples from the biblical Song of Songs, these could only refer to the fruits and not to the root. Because of its human-like shape, however, the root was thought to have magical powers (Klug / Weinberger, pp. 347-349).

Anyhow, it would be of interest from a linguistic point of view, to map as many as possible of the names of this plant that are to be found in medieval manuscripts, and to compare them with each other. Because this would be a laborious enterprise, and since medieval manuscripts collected in libraries all over the world are not easily accessible for a single researcher, the idea was born to gather these data together, and to publish them online with their exact catalogue and folio numbers, and also including the name of the library in which they are held, in order to make them available for the serious worker. It was decided that it was not only the plant names that should be mentioned but also the context in which they appear, so that these data could be cited in the footnotes of books and articles. If the whole sentence, or even the entire paragraph in which the plant is named, were to be transcribed, then the plant might be of interest to scholars from other disciplines as well. Ideally, of course, this approach should not be limited to this one plant (the mandrake) but should apply to as many plants as possible. In this way, portraits of such plants could be sketched with reference to all of the languages in which they are described. Moreover, in order to be as complete as possible, pictures from medieval manuscripts should be collected to illustrate the plants in question. In this way, the database might also be of interest to art historians. Now, mandrake is not a plant for the kitchen, but because the team in Graz includes culinary-text experts, plant names from cookery books have been chosen as the basis for the database. German and Austrian libraries possess quite a number of medieval manuscripts which include recipe collections, both culinary and medical. As most of them have not been edited and published, they are difficult to access for research. For the database team, the emphasis is on the Middle High German language area from the late Middle Ages, that is, from the thirteenth to the fifteenth centuries. The ambition of the team, however, is to process as many manuscripts as possible from the "Repertory of Medieval Manuscripts with Culinary Recipes". This Repertory lists medieval manuscripts from all over Europe, with recipes in many medieval languages, which are held in libraries all over the world (Hieatt et al. 1992, pp. 315-379).

Medieval cookery recipes, do not, of course, contain just plant names as they also refer to ingredients like meat, fish and poultry, as well as to dairy produce and eggs. However, plants form an important part of these recipes, and they include reference to not only green herbs but also to oriental spices like cinnamon, ginger and pepper, and dried fruits like figs, dates, raisins and currants. It is not always easy to decide whether a recipe is meant especially for the kitchen or whether it was intended for medical use, because food and health were inseparable in the medieval world view. To be well equipped for its ambition of bringing together plant names from as many different sources as possible, the Graz database contains not only cookbook recipes but also health rules, "Regimina Sanitatis". Here follows a short explanation of the medieval theories in that field, to make clear how this database could be of use to researchers from a broad range of disciplines, among them food historians (Weiss Adamson, "Introduction", pp. 9-24).

During the Middle Ages, the theories of the Greek physicians Hippocrates of Kos (fifth century B.C) and Galen of Pergamon (second century A.D.) were in general use. These physicians had developed a system of quartets in which man as a micro cosmos stood in the middle of the macro cosmos. It was assumed that four dominant corporeal humours existed: blood, yellow bile, black bile and phlegm, which created four temperaments: the sanguine, the choleric, the melancholic and the phlegmatic. Four qualities were also postulated: warm and cold, humid and dry, of which each temperament was regarded as having two: thus the sanguine temperament with blood was humid and warm like spring, the choleric temperament with yellow bile was warm and dry like summer, the melancholic temperament with black bile was dry and cold like autumn, and the phlegmatic temperament with phlegm was cold and humid like winter. It was claimed that not only the four seasons, but also the life periods of man were influenced by these quartets: thus youth was "designed" by spring, adolescence by summer, adulthood by autumn and old age by winter. Of course, each person's temperament was thought to have remained the same but to have undergone the effects of these influences.

It was presumed that each person had been created well and healthy and that illness was caused by the disruption of the balance between all of these influences. Food, as well as medicaments, had, thus, the task of keeping the right balance between them in order to prevent illness, or in the case of illness, to repair it by food therapy. In this way, dietary theory was a culinary as well as a medical concern and so cookbooks had both of these functions. Sometimes, it is difficult to decide if certain recipes found in cookery books would not have been more suitable for a medical book. Examples of this are the comfits, such as quince jelly and mulberry jelly, which originated in the Greek apothecary as a means for healing pain in the stomach, but which, in the course of time, gained their place among culinary sweets (Plouvier 1988, pp. 28-47; van Winter 2007a, pp. 341-354; van Winter 2007b, 355-360).

To fulfil their medical task, plants had to meet the same qualifications of warm and cold, humid and dry, as the seasons and the human temperaments. The physician, Galen of Pergamon, in the second century A.D., had already recorded hundreds of plants and had listed their qualities in rather refined detail. From the eighth century onwards, this system, sometimes enlarged by their own insights, was translated from the Greek by Syrian and Arabic scientists, both Christians and Muslims. Then, through the Syrian and Arabic languages, the system passed into Latin, and, in this way, it reached the world of Western Europe. Here it was translated anew into vernaculars, often in rhyming verses to facilitate memorisation. The centres from which this diffusion took place were Salerno in the South of Italy and Toledo in Spain (Weiss Adamson 1995, pp. 50-56, 97-102; Glaze 2012, pp. 63-83).

Another transfer route for Greek medical knowledge was probably a direct one from Byzantium to Ravenna in Northern Italy – which thus bypassed the

Syrian and Arabic connections – through translations from the Greek into Latin, and thence from Italy to Switzerland and South Germany (Groenke 1986). This Greek medical knowledge was based on the lists of Galen of Pergamon, just like the seasonal system was, but it did not give health rules by season, but rather by month. Perhaps (according to my hypothesis), the origins of the health rules by month are to be sought in the early Christian church of the East-Roman Empire with its capital Byzantium, where their purpose might have been to enable the priests and other clergymen of the cathedrals to achieve eucharistic purity They were required to attain a state of mental purity before performing their priestly duties in the cathedrals, through first cleansing their bowels by drinking either potions of laxative or astringent herbs on empty stomachs.

In this way, two kinds of medical-culinary texts came into existence: the *Regimen Sanitatis Salernitanum* ("Regiment of Health from Salerno") with health rules for the seasons, and the *Regimen duodecim mensium* ("Regiment for the Twelve Months") with health rules for each of the twelve months of the year. Nowadays, these two kinds of texts, in which each season can be divided into three parts, are regarded as one by most researchers, which they call "Monks Medicine" or "Monastic Medicine" – the name of the Würzburg website www.klostermedizin.de. In my opinion, however, neither the name "Monastic Medicine", nor the conflation of the two kinds of medical-culinary texts, is appropriate, because these texts reached Western Europe through different channels and in different ages and, besides, they were not meant for monks in the first place. Whereas the rules by season were diffused from Salerno and Toledo from the twelfth century onwards, the rules by months probably came directly from Greece and Byzantium through Ravenna in Northern Italy and were already known in the Frankish Empire in the eighth and ninth centuries. However, the vernacular versions of both systems date only from the thirteenth century onwards and have a tendency to merge with each other. So it is necessary to commence research on these two sets of health rules before the late Middle Ages in order to correctly register the differences between them.

Generally, it can be said that the rules by season have a culinary character, in order to compensate for the heat or coldness of the season by using viands with a contrary quality. The rules by month on the other hand contain herbs with, first and foremost, cleansing properties. Every month has its own herbs that have to be soaked in wine overnight and drunk on an empty stomach in the morning. Since the herbs that are recommended for use for this purpose are, according to the lists of Galen of Pergamon, just laxative, constipative, or diuretic in character, they are thus less appropriate for use in the kitchen. Having conducted my research as I have outlined above, I found mention of the herb absinth in wine as the potion for the month of May, in Latin texts from the eighth century onwards, and subsequently in quite a number of West-European vernaculars from the thirteenth century and later periods. Surprisingly, I could follow this use of the herb absinth in texts until well into the sixteenth century (van Winter, 2010 p. 107).

In the extensive appendices of an article in Dutch from my hand, published in December 2012, and based on a lecture which I gave in Brussels in 2004 (van Winter 2012), many examples of both kinds of health rules from West- and Central-Europe had been collected. As the publication of my article was considerably delayed, and as I wished that the medieval texts which I had included in this work to be of some use, I sent my material to Helmut W. Klug in Graz as soon as I heard about the "Medieval Plant Survey" that he was leading. As it happened, some months afterwards my article finally appeared and was published in Dutch. For the international researcher, however, Klug's database is more accessible than my article, although at the moment it is necessary to know the German name of the plant one is looking for in order to search the database; e.g. Absinth is Wermut in German. The texts can be accessed either sorted by Regimen or by month. At any rate, as a result of the inclusion of my material in the database, it now contains plant names from medieval High German cookery recipes as well as from medieval Low Dutch and West-European health rules. Both kinds of plant names are now at the disposal of the researcher from all sorts of disciplines, among them ethnological food research.

List of References

Printed

Glaze, Florence Eliza: "Speaking in Tongues: Medical Wisdom and Glossing Practices in and around Salerno, c. 1040–1200". In: Arsdall, Anne van, and Graham, Timothy (eds.): *Herbs and Healers from the Ancient Mediterranean through the Medieval West. Essays in Honor of John M. Riddle* (Medicine in the Medieval Mediterranean). Ashgate: Farnham, UK, et al. 2012, pp. 63-83.

Groenke, Franz-Dieter: Die frühmittelalterlichen lateinischen Monatskalendarien. Text – Übersetzung – Kommentar. Dissertation zur Erlangung der zahnmedizinischen Doktorwürde am Fachbereich Zahn-Mund- und Kieferheilkunde der Freien Universität Berlin, 1986. Typescript.

Hieatt, Constance B. / Lambert, Carole / Laurioux, Bruno / Prentki, Alix: "Répertoire des Manuscrits Médiévaux contenant des Recettes Culinaires". In: Lambert, Carole (ed.), *Du Manuscrit à la Table, Essays sur la Cuisine au Moyen Age et Répertoire des Manuscrits Médiévaux contenant des Recettes Culinaires.* Les Presses de l'Université de Montréal: Montréal 1992 / Champion-Slatkine: Paris 1992, pp. 315-379.

Klug, Helmut W. /Weinberger, Roman: "Modding Medievalists: Designing a Web-based Portal for the Medieval Plant Survey/Portal der Pflanzen des Mitelalters (MPS/PPM)". In Arsdall, Anne van / Graham, Timothy (eds.): *Herbs and Healers from the Ancient Mediterranean through the Medieval West. Essays in Honor of John M. Riddle. Riddle* (Medicine in the Medieval Mediterranean). Ashgate: Farnham, UK et al. 2012, pp. 329-358.

Plouvier, Liliane: "La confiserie européenne au Moyen Age". In: *Medium Aevum Quotidianum, Newsletter* 13. Institut für Mittelalterliche Realienkunde Österreichs: Krems an der Donau 1988, pp. 28-47;

Weiss Adamson, Melitta: *Medieval Dietetics, Food and Drink in Regimen Sanitatis Literature from 800 to 1400.* (German Studies in Canada, 5.) Peter Lang: Frankfurt am Main et al. 1995.

Van Winter, Johanna Maria: "Sind die *Regimina duodecim mensium* als 'Mönchmedizin' zu betrachten?". In: Hofmeister-Winter, Andrea / Klug, Helmut W. / Kranich, Karin: *"Der Koch ist der bessere Arzt". Zum Verhältnis von Diätetik und Kulinarik im Mittelalter und in der Frühen Neuzeit.* Fachtagung im Rahmen des Tages der Geisteswissenschaften 2013 an der Karl-Franzens-Universität Graz, 20.6.–22.6.2013. Peter Lang Verlag: Frankfurt am Main 2014 (Reihe Mediävistik zwischen Forschung, Lehre und Öffentlichkeit 8), pp. 151-159.

Van Winter, Johanna Maria: "Middelnederlandse voedings- en gezondheidsregels per maand en per seizoen: geleerde raadgevingen voor een ongeleerd publiek". In: *Geneeskunde in Nederlandstalige teksten tot 1600.* Handelingen van het zesde symposium "Geschiedenis der geneeskundige wetenschappen", ingericht door de Koninklijke Academie voor Geneeskunde van België op 20 maart 2004 (Academia Regia Belgica Medicinae – Dissertationes Series Historica nr.12). Koninklijke Academie voor Geneeskunde van België: Brussel 2012, pp. 169-218.

Van Winter, Johanna Maria: "*Regimina Sanitatis* by Month and by Season". In: Lysaght, Patricia (ed.), *Food and Meals at Cultural Crossroads. Proceedings of the 17th Conference of the International Commission for Ethnological Food Research, Oslo, Norway, September 15 – 19, 2008.* Novus Press: Oslo 2010, pp. 98-109

Van Winter, Johanna Maria: *Spices and Comfits, Collected Papers on Medieval Food.* Prospect Book: Totnes UK 2007.

Van Winter, Johanna Maria: "Cookbooks, Medicinal or Culinary?" In: Winter, Johanna Maria, van, *Spices and Comfits, Collected Papers on Medieval Food.* Prospect Book: Totnes, UK 2007(a), pp. 341-354.

Van Winter, Johanna Maria: "Medieval Recipes for Invalid Food". In: van Winter, Johanna Maria, *Spices and Comfits,* Prospect Book: Totnes, UK 2007(b), pp. 355-360.

Internet

www.abtei.de, retrieved 1 June 2014.

www.klostermedizin.de, retrieved 1 June 2014.

http://medieval-plants.org, retrieved 1 June 2014.

List of Contributors

Arpasanu, Rodica is an M.A. student in Applied Cultural Analysis at Lund University, Sweden. Her research interests include sociology, cultural and food narratives, and consumer behaviour in the food sector (rarpas@afs.edu.gr).

D'Auria, Déirdre completed her Ph.D. on the influence of Italian food on Irish foodways in the twentieth century, at University College Dublin, in 2013. She is Assistant Editor on the Historical Dictionary of Modern Irish, *Foclóir na Nua-Ghaeilge*, in the Royal Irish Academy, Dublin, Ireland (deirdre.dauria@gmail.com).

Bartsch, Silke is a Professor for nutrition and home economics and specialised didactic at the University of Education at Karlsruhe (PH Karlsruhe, Bismarckstr. 10, D- 76133 Karlsruhe, Germany), where she has worked since 2010 (bartsch@ph-karlsruhe.de).

Baschali, Aristea is a Ph.D. candidate at Harokopio University, Athens. She works as a dietician in the General District Hospital "The Eyaggelismos" in Athens, Greece (abaschali@gmail.com).

Báti, Aniko, Ph.D., is a senior research fellow at the Institute of Ethnology of the Hungarian Academy of Sciences, Budapest, since 2009. Her current fields of interest include questions concerning foodways, lifestyle, and the eating habits of children in Budapest (bati. aniko@gmail.com).

Boulianne, Manon is a Professor at the Department of Anthropology at Université Laval, Quebec, Canada. Her recent research is devoted to urban agriculture, the social production and construction of fine cheese, and "local food" initiatives in Quebec (Manon.Boulianne@ant.ulaval.ca).

Brombach, Christine is a Professor for nutrition and consumer sciences at the Institute of Food and Beverage Innovation, University of Applied Sciences at Wädenswil, Switzerland, where she has worked since 2008 (christine.brombach@zhaw.ch).

Carson Williams, Fionnuala, is a graduate of the UCD Delargy Centre for Irish Folklore. In 2012 she was awarded a D. Litt. from the National University of Ireland, in recognition of the contribution on an international level to the study of proverbs over a sustained period, which she has made. From her earliest writing she has noted the connection of proverbial material and food (fionnualawilliams@hotmail.co.uk).

Dimitrievski, Ivanche, M.A. is a lecturer at Perrotis College – American Farm School, Thessaloniki, Greece. His field of expertise includes ethnographic methodology and socio-cultural theories, as well as their application in the business context. His publications deal with organisational culture, moral vegetarianism and food. He is a Ph.D. candidate at the Department of Thematic Studies (TEMA), Linköping University (LiU), Sweden (ivanched@yahoo.com).

Dutra Campos de Almeida, Rogéria is Professor of Anthropology at the Federal University of Juiz de Fora, Brazil, and carries out research on food and culture. She graduated in the Social Sciences at the Federal University of Juiz de Fora, and she also has a Master's degree and a Ph.D. in Anthropology from the Federal University of Rio de Janeiro, Brazil (rcadutra@uol.com.br).

Godina Golija, Maja, Ph.D., Associate Professor of ethnology, has a BA in ethnology and philosophy. Since 1996, she has been employed with the Section for Material Culture of the Institute of Slovene Ethnology, SRC, SASA, Ljubljana, where she carries out research on food, economy, and urban life in Slovenia. She has written four monographs and more than 90 scientific articles and papers, for publishers, including Berg Publishers, Oxford; Charles Scribner's Sons, New York; Ashgate, Burlington; Greenwood, Santa Barbara, The Finish Literary Society… (maja.godina@zrc-sazu.si).

Hebda, Klaudyna received her M.A. degree in the Faculty of Comparative Studies of Civilizations (Jagiellonian University, Poland), in 2011. In 2013, she obtained an M.A. in Sociology from Jagiellonian University, and she also completed postgraduate herbal studies at the University of Agriculture in Kraków, Poland. She is interested in food studies, the sociology of knowledge, and also in ethnobiology. She is also a food blogger and a photographer (klaudyna.hebda@gmail.com).

Kopczyńska, Ewa, Ph.D., is an Assistant Professor in the Institute of Sociology, Jagiellonian University, Poland. Since 2010 she has taught the anthropology of food. In 2008-2011 she carried out research on wine making in Western Poland. The results are published in a number of articles and in a chapter in *Wine and Culture. Vineyard to Glass* (ed. R. Black, R. C. Ulin, 2013). She is currently investigating short food chains in Poland (ewa.kopczynska@uj.edu.pl).

Krawczyk-Wasilewska, Violetta, Ph.D., Professor in the Humanities since 2002, Head of the Folklore Department at the University of Łódź, Poland, from 1991 to 2013. Her articles and books deal with the anthropology of culture and folklore. She is the editor of the international proceedings on *Ecology and Folklore* (1992–1998, in addition to her 2012 co-edited work (with Theo Meder and Andy Ross): *Shaping Virtual Lives. Online Identities, Representations, and Conducts.* Her published works (in Polish with English summaries) include *Contemporary Studies on Folklore* (1986), *AIDS: An Anthropological Study*

(2000), and she has co-edited *Culture as a Factor of Town Development. On the Example of Łódź* (2012) (wasil@uni.lodz.pl).

Krupa-Ławrynowicz, Aleksandra, Ph.D., is an ethnologist and cultural anthropologist at the Institute of Ethnology and Cultural Anthropology, University of Łódź. She is the author of fifteen articles and one book (Ph.D. thesis) written in Polish (*Bałuckie chronotopy. Opowieść o łódzkiej dzielnicy*, Łódź 2013) with an English summary. Her major research interests focus on urban anthropology and the anthropology of the senses (aklawrynowicz@uni.lodz.pl).

Laviolette, Claudia is a Ph.D. candidate in Anthropology at Université Laval, Quebec, Canada. She works with Professor Boulianne, and studies the transformation of food-provisioning practices in urban Australia (Claudia.laviolette.1@ulaval.ca).

Lindqvist, Yrsa, Fil.lic., is a senior archivist at the Archives of Folk Culture in Helsinki. Her fields of interest include food and ethics, and ecology and lifestyle, in private life and in marketing. She specialises in examining the historical dimensions of foodways as expressed in archive collections in relation to foodways in contemporary society (yrsa.lindqvist@sls.fin).

Lysaght, Patricia, Ph.D., Professor *em.* of Irish Folklore, (University College Dublin, Ireland), is the President of the SIEF Food Working Group. She organised the 9th International Ethnological Food Research Conference in Ireland in 1992. She has edited the proceedings of most of the international ethnological food research conferences since 1994. She is the author of monographs, numerous research articles in international journals, and other publications (patricia.lysaght@ucd.ie).

Matalas, Antonia, Ph.D. Ass. Professor, teaches nutrition at the department of Nutrition and Dietetics at Harokopio University, Athens, Greece. She holds a B. Sc. in Chemistry, and a Ph.D. in Nutrition from the University of California, Davis (amatala@hua.gr).

Medina, Xavier F., Ph.D. is Professor and Academic Programmes Director of the Department of Food Systems, Culture and Society, School of Health Sciences, Universitat Oberta de Catalunya (Open University of Catalonia) (UOC), Barcelona, Spain. He is also Director of the UNESCO Chair on Food, Culture and Development, President of the European section of the International Commission on the Anthropology of Food and Nutrition (ICAF Europe), and author of several books and articles, mainly in the field of the anthropology of food (fxmedina@uoc.edu).

Minami, Naoto is Professor of History at Kyoto Tachibana University, Japan, since 2005 (minami@tachibana-u.ac.jp).

Mlekodaj, Anna, Ph.D. is a graduate of the Polish Philology Department at Jagiellonian University of Kraków. Her studies deal with the literary aspects of the folklore of the mountain region called Podhale in southern Poland. She is a lecturer at the Institute of Humanities, The Podhale State Higher Vocational School in Nowy Targ, Poland (qaz10@poczta.onet.pl).

Orszulak-Dudkowska, Katarzyna, Ph.D. in ethnology, has been working as a lecturer in the Ethnology and Folklore Department, University of Łódź, since 2001. Her fields of interest include everyday life and popular culture. She has published (in Polish) *Lonely Hearts' Advertisements. Studies Bordering Folklore and Cultural Anthropology* (2008), and over 20 scientific papers (k.dudkowska@uni.lodz.pl).

Papadopoulos, Philippos, Ph.D. (London School of Economics, 1989), is Acting Academic Dean at Perrotis College – American Farm School, Thessaloniki, Greece. His research interests include entrepreneurship and innovation, organisational and national culture, product development and consumer behaviour in the food sector (fpapad@afs.edu.gr).

Pilarek, Rafał is a postgraduate student at the Institute of Ethnology and Cultural Anthropology, University of Łódź, Poland. His main line of research is ethnography represented in geographical and travel magazines. He is also interested in non-European ethnology and ethnic minorities. He studied ethnic stereotypes among schoolchildren in Poland, Canada, and Belarus. He is the author of a number of articles (r.k.pilarek@wp.pl).

Robertson, Una is a freelance historian who focuses on Scottish social and domestic life. For many years she lectured at Edinburgh University's Office of Lifelong Learning but also talked to other organisations, cooked dinners to 18th century recipes and helped set up a Butler's Pantry as a Visitor Attraction at nearby Hopetoun House. She has written two books, several pamphlets and innumerable articles (una.robertson@btinternet.com).

Rzeźnicka, Zofia, has an M.A. in history from the University of Łódź since 2010. She achieved a B.A. in Classics from the University of Łódź in 2011and she is currently a Ph.D. at that University. The title of her doctoral thesis is, "Meat in Ancient and Byzantine Diet According to Selected Medical Sources". Her scientific interests include the history of food and medicine (zosia_pwp.historyk@wp.pl).

Solanilla Demestre, Laura, Ph.D., is an Associate Professor, Arts & Humanities Department, Open University of Catalonia (UOC), Spain, with an interest in Cultural Heritage and ICT (Information and Communications Technology), especially intangible cultural heritage aspects. Her current focus is on identity, food and new media in a Catalonian context (lsolanilla@uoc.edu).

Spalvēna, Astra, is a doctoral student at the Latvian Academy of Culture. She is writing a thesis entitled "Food in Latvian Culture (1990–2013)". Her research interests include food semiotics, and food in the arts and the media. She lectures at the Riga International School of Economics and Business Administration (astra.spalvena@gmail.com).

Tomaszewska-Bolałek, Magdalena, Ph.D. is a Japanese culture expert and an independent Food Studies scholar. She obtained an M.A. and a Ph.D. from the Department of Japanese Studies, Warsaw University. Her new book, *Japanese Sweet,* has been nominated in *Gourmand World Cookbook Awards 2013* in three categories (m.tomaszewska@hanami.pl).

van Winter, Johanna Maria, is Professor emerita of Medieval History at Utrecht University. She has published mainly about Knighthood and Nobility in Western Europe, including *The Order of St John in the Netherlands, Local History of the Low Countries,* and *Food and Nourishment in Medieval Europe* (j.m.vanwinter@uu.nl).

Winkler, Gertrud is a fulltime Professor at the Albstadt-Sigmaringen University. Her main topics are nutrition and food sciences. She is engaged in the German Nutrition Society and other relevant institutions. Her current research focuses on the nutritional situation of various groups of the population (children, the elderly), and on food service/catering with an emphasis on nutrition at schools and workplace health management (winkler@hs-albsig.de).